# Economics and its Stories

T0358552

# Economics and its Stories

## Amal Sanyal

Routledge
Taylor & Francis Group

LONDON AND NEW YORK

First published 2018
by Routledge
4 Park Square, Milton Park, Abingdon, Oxon OX14 4RN
605 Third Avenue, New York, NY 10017

First issued in paperback 2023

*Routledge is an imprint of the Taylor & Francis Group, an
informa business*

© 2018 Amal Sanyal and Social Science Press

*British Library Cataloguing in Publication Data*
A catalogue record for this book is available from the British
Library

*Library of Congress Cataloging in Publication Data*
A catalog record for this book has been requested

ISBN-13: 978-1-138-09960-9 (hbk)
ISBN-13: 978-1-03-265280-1 (pbk)
ISBN-13: 978-1-315-09896-8 (ebk)

DOI: 10.4324/9781315098968

Typeset in Plantin 10/13
by Eleven Arts, Delhi 110 035

SOCIAL
SCIENCE
PRESS

I dedicate this book to Dr Sukhamoy Ganguli,
who showed me by his example how to think about the economy

# Contents

*Acknowledgements*                                        ix

1. Introduction                                            1

2. Markets, Efficiency, and Adam Smith                    23

3. Many Forms of Market: Sellers Big and Small            53

4. Markets Often Fail and So Do Governments               90

5. Unemployment and J.M. Keynes                          116

6. After Keynes                                          148

7. Money, Banks, and Finance                             175

8. Trade, Foreign Investment and Migration               217

9. Economic Growth and Development                       262

10. Conclusion                                           316

*Index*                                                  323

# Acknowledgements

The inspiration for writing this book came from my mother Kalpana Sanyal and my cousin and friend, Subas Maitra. The book would have been abandoned unfinished without their constant prodding.

A number of people have read parts of the earlier drafts of the book and helped me improve it by their suggestions and criticism. I acknowledge their help gratefully. They are Chandan Sanyal, Ramzi Addison, Pradipta Chaudhury, Rajiv Jha, Sagar Sanyal, and Greg Liyanarachchi. I am also grateful to my wife Ratna Sanyal for her constant support over the long period I spent writing the book.

# 1 Introduction

## 1.1 About This Book

'An economist is an expert who will know tomorrow why the things he predicted yesterday didn't happen today.' This is from Laurence Peter, a twentieth century US author. Although many people share Peter's view, there is nevertheless an amazingly widespread interest in economics. The economy touches the lives of all, the tycoon as well as the pauper. A sign on US President Bill Clinton's desk used to remind, 'It is the economy, stupid!' My excuse for writing this book comes from this widespread interest in economics and its relevance in our times.

This book will introduce the basic ideas of economics along with how the subject has grown and acquired the shape it has today. The growth of economics as a subject is fascinating because it is mixed up with the development of capitalism, modern government, world wars, the rise and fall of the Soviet Union, and much of today's philosophy and art—in short, with life as we know it and live today. Two clarifications are in order at the start. First, the book is more about economic ideas and issues than the history of economics. So it does not follow a historical sequence. It follows issues and ideas as they relate to one another and moves back and forth in time with clippings of history. Quite often the historical episodes and personalities appear in special boxes rather than in the text. Second, it is not a scholarly book. It picks up only major viewpoints for discussion and avoids the finer points. There are footnotes but they do not necessarily follow scholarly norms and etiquettes; they are meant to clarify and arouse curiosity.

## 1.2 The Birth of Economics

Ancient discourses on the economy and public administration date back to at least three thousand years. Some of them are stunningly relevant even today.[1] However, economics, with a well-defined borderline separating it from subjects like politics, ethics, law, and administration,[2] is a relatively new academic field. What we now call 'economics' began tentatively in the 16th century.

A new science can be born only out of new questions in some areas of life. Questions about trade and wealth and how they work started appearing with increasing urgency as the sixteenth century dawned on Europe. Closely preceding that century, Bartholomeu Diaz had sailed round the Cape of Good Hope (1487), Columbus had 'discovered' America (1492), and Vasco da Gama had landed in India (1498). In the aftermath, gold from America and exotica from other continents started flooding Europe. As merchants and monarchs got busy with the new realms of gold and wealth, of export and import, of lending and borrowing, new questions started rising in the mind of Europe. It was these questions that sowed the seeds of the new discipline, economics. Chasing gold across the seas and amassing it in Europe had brought about a radical change in some sections of the European society. Christopher Columbus wrote about it in these telling words, 'One who has gold does as he wills in the world and it even sends souls to Paradise'.[3] Gold, as referred to by Columbus, and wealth in general were as enticing as they were enigmatic. Hence, the search for laws to govern them started in earnest.

The subject of economics developed over the next few hundred years. Philosophers and scholars played a role in the development

---

[1]Many Indian, Middle Eastern, and Chinese documents fit this description.

[2]Some economists have questioned if there should be such a sharply defined discipline boundary at all. We will see that economics is replete with controversies. Quite fittingly then, controversy surrounds the scope and definition of the subject itself!

[3]From *The Log of Christopher Columbus' First Voyage to America the Year 1492*, quoted in Edwardo Galeano, *Open Veins of Latin America*, New York, Monthly Review Press, 1973.

as we would surely expect. But there were also serious contributions from people in the administration, professions, and various trades. The rising power of Europe's parliaments meant a lot of political debate around the issues of the day. Hence public-spirited persons happened to contribute to the fledgling subject. Questions that appeared first, and theories and conjectures that answered them were more about the bigger questions of the time. Typical questions would be about where society was heading, towards progress or chaos? Hence, early ideas were rich in moral philosophy, political theory, and sociology. The discussion, of course, evolved and soon interest began to be focussed on more down-to-earth issues of business, government, and household purchases. Through all these quests and debates, and no less with the growth of new types of vested interest, economics grew its characteristic methods and concerns. Before long, economics would be clearly distinguishable from related social disciplines.

Thus economics was born in a very special period of our history. The sixteenth and seventeenth centuries saw big social and political changes in Europe. Following on from there, the next two centuries led to spectacular development of technology, business, public administration, and standards of living. Boxes 1.1 and 1.2 reveal the stunning breadth of the changes. They give some idea about the new things and firsts that began appearing every so often. Institutions that were born with them touched every bit of life and changed European society beyond recognition. The period of most intense change, a hundred years ending roughly around the third quarter of the nineteenth century, is called the *Industrial Revolution*.[4]

These changes brought about a fundamental shift in the way Europeans perceived life, society, and human endeavour. Life shifted out from idyllic villages: from farms and pastures to factories, ports, and market towns. The power of the church and the nobility was on the wane and that of parliaments on the rise. The number of things that farmers, traders, and the ordinary people could do without seeking anyone else's permission increased spectacularly. This environment of political freedom was boosted by an increased

---

[4]This is the period that most historians associate with the *Industrial Revolution*.

economic freedom as well. Markets sprang up for food and everyday things. They were the most outrageously modern places where anyone could buy and sell as equals, no matter what their status.

But there were dark clouds as well. For many people the traditional source of income disappeared with no alternative in sight. Age-old skills suddenly became useless, attracting no takers. New skills and trades seemed alien and difficult. Villagers, swept out of their traditional ways of life, thronged the cities. However, they generally found nothing other than starvation and squalor, and crime increased at an alarming rate. Thus, the period was characterised by serious dualism. Charles Dickens would later describe this dualism in these words:

It was the best of times, it was the worst of times, it was the age of wisdom, it was the age of foolishness, it was the epoch of belief, it was the epoch of incredulity, it was the season of light, it was the season of darkness, it was the spring of hope, it was the winter of despair....[5]

Germs of economic ideas had been developing since the sixteenth century but they remained nebulous until they had to face sterner questions raised by the Industrial Revolution. The revolution that appeared so scaringly contradictory, challenged thinkers to the limit. Out of this challenge came up the most important building blocks of economics.

## 1.3 The Industrial Revolution: Order or Chaos?

Among the myriads of smaller concerns, two very big questions loomed in the minds of that era. The first was that with the diminished power of lords, churches, and tradition, no one was left to take basic economic decisions. No one was there to order what to produce and how much, and what resources to use for them. Nor was there any guidance as to who would get how much of the produce. These are the three central questions of an economic system. Determining the mix of things produced is called the *production* decision. How much

[5]*A Tale of Two Cities*, published in 1859.

of various resources are used to produce the mix is called *allocation* of resource. And, who gets how much of the product or income is the decision about income *distribution*. After the breakdown of feudal authority, it appeared that there was no one in charge of these decisions. They were being addressed by uncoordinated actions of the crowd of buyers and sellers. How would these actions come together to produce some sort of consistency? Wouldn't all that lead to either over-production or short supply of most goods? There would also be misallocation of inputs, that is, things not going to their best uses; and unfair distribution of income, that is, people not getting according to their contribution. In short, the new system might have been the start of a perennial chaos in the garb of political and economic freedom; the beginning of the end.

---

**Box 1.1: 'Firsts' and new things were coming thick and fast. The momentum increased with time. Here are some 16th century oddments.**

- English Parliament declares the Pope's authority void in England
- Regular mail between Vienna and Brussels started
- London's waterworks founded
- London Exchange established
- First scientific society founded in Naples
- The first life insurance on the life of William Gibbons
- A marine insurance policy issued at Florence
- Royal College of physicians of London empowered to dissect humans
- Attempt to restrict medicine practice to qualified doctors
- Public lottery held in London to repair the port
- Slave trade begins

*Scientific breakthrough*:
- Tycho Brahe finds a new star in the Milky Way
- da Vinci designs a water turbine
- Copernicus states that the earth and other planets move around the sun
- Frisius suggests that longitude can be calculated from time difference

---

*(contd...)*

*Box 1.1 continued.*

- Francois Viete introduces decimal fractions
- Galileo discovers the property of pendulums
- Telesio's *De Rerum Natura* foreshadows empirical methods of science
- Varolio studies anatomy of human brain
- Galileo's experiments on falling bodies
- Mercator's maps

*Discoveries and inventions:* pulmonary circulation of blood; magnetic dip; variation and movement of a magnetic needle; anatomy of the teeth; earth's magnetic pole; thermometer; 'Nuremberg Egg', the first watch; glasses for the short sighted; the spinning wheel; the knitting machine.

*Firsts*: bladder and cataract operations; caesarean delivery by a living woman; first botanical garden; use of letters for algebraic quantities; trigonometric tables; silk manufacture in France; a lunatic asylum; ether produced from alcohol; workman's bench; newspaper; travelling and standing clocks; coffee and chocolate come to Europe; bottled beer; black-lead pencil.

*Books*: 35,000 books with approximately 10 million copies were printed during 1445–1500. In the century 1501–1600, first treatises were published on: mineralogy; agriculture; animal husbandry, herbs; epidemiology and infectious diseases; paints and inks; flowers of Spain and Portugal; *Historia anemalium*; *Tabulae Anatomica*; optics and binocular vision; veterinary science; ornithology; pharmacopoeia.

*Universities and colleges* founded: Universities of Konigsberg, Granada, Frankfurt (Oder), Wittenberg, Lima, Pisa, Jena, Geneva, Berlin, Leiden, Warsaw, Messina, and Edinburgh. Royal College of Physicians, London; Christ's College, Magdalen College, and Emmanuel College, Cambridge; Trinity College and Jesus College, Oxford.

## 1.4 The Industrial Revolution: The Question of Poverty

The second question that arose amidst the confusion of the Industrial Revolution was about poverty. Earlier, landowning noblemen had no interest in the output from their land. With the growth of commerce they started getting interested in it. They converted the land in their fiefs for commercial cropping. The permission to enclose land by the nobility for private use had been in force for several centuries. However, land enclosure and displacement of commoners became pronounced by the end of the seventeenth century. This displaced poor people who earlier relied on subsistence farming and cattle grazing on common land. Displacement of the commoners—generally forceful and ruthless—was an event of immense consequence for England and Western Europe. Watched helplessly, it was recorded in the folk memory for posterity:

The law locks up the man or woman
Who steals the goose from off the common
But leaves the greater villain loose
Who steals the common from off the goose (anonymous)

Displacement over many decades created a mass of destitute people who migrated to the emerging industrial towns in search of a living. Life was not very kind in those towns either. Poverty and filth in the workers' neighbourhoods in boomtowns were pathetic. The situation disturbed many contemporary thinkers profoundly. They asked if the prevalent poverty and destitution were only a passing phase or permanent features of the new order. Thus, income distribution of the emerging social order became a vital question of the time.

Debate around the above two questions characterised the intellectual and political scene of the period. It was joined by not only scholars and philosophers, but also people from other walks of life. Politicians—both statesmen of stature as well as the small-time rabble-rousers—made their contribution. Many contributed with serious thought, vision, and philosophy. Some tried to construct methods of analysis barely realising that they were laying the foundations for a new subject. And, of course, many others chipped in with opinions and rhetoric. From all this were born not only alternative viewpoints but also useful theory and methods. They will make up the subject of the following chapters.

From these two questions grew two extremely influential traditions of economics in the eighteenth and nineteenth centuries. They have provided the background for a major part of the development of economics since then. I will try to present the big picture here before explaining the details in later chapters.

## 1.5 The Free Market Tradition is Born

One of these two traditions addresses the first question. Recall that the question was whether the uncoordinated action of buyers and sellers, based on their personal interests, would lead the system into chaos. The answer by this tradition is, no, it would not. When producers guide production according to their profit and buyers buy where they get the best deal, it is order rather than chaos that gets created. Buyers' efforts to get things at the least price and sellers' competition to attract them get the society those products at the least cost. As a result, the system has a tendency to use the least possible amount of resources for producing a unit of any product. This means that with its given resources the economy would produce the maximum amount possible when things are decided by the marketplace! I am sure that the readers would recognise this as the so-called 'free market idea' about which there is so much debate today.

The idea was not stated so explicitly at that time nor did any single scholar develop it completely. Many contributed, stating it more fully and with more logical rigour over a period of time. To formulate these questions in a way suitable for analysis was an achievement of the early days. The basic arguments of this viewpoint gave rise to a line of research that has continued to our time. It analyses the action of buyers and sellers in the market place closely. It examines its own claims with more rigour, develops acceptable generalisations, analyses their implications for resource use, general welfare, and the growth of the economy. It also explores the issue of why the order-generating property of markets happens to fail in many cases. What difficulties arise when markets 'misbehave' in this sense? A closely related line of research is to produce corrective policies for intervening in these situations. Research into these features has continued from the eighteenth century to modern times. The most elegant and authoritative statements of this line of enquiry appeared as recently as in Debreu (1959)[6] and Arrow and Hahn(1971).[7]

---

### Box 1.2: The Seventeenth Century

- The last recorded burning of a heretic in England, 1612
- English replaces Latin as the language of official documents in England
- Amsterdam Exchange built
- Public advertising and advertisements in newspapers begin
- Parcel post begins
- Patents law in England
- Manufacture of cotton goods starts in Manchester
- Income and property tax in England
- Modern trade fair held in Holland
- English property insurance company founded
- Chamber of commerce founded in Marseilles

*Firsts*: copper coins come into use; harbour with sluices in France; a periodical published from London; fire engines; hackney coaches and speed limit on coaches in England; plate glass casting; street lights in London.

*Inventions and discoveries*: telescope; clinical thermometer; micrometer; quinine; barometer; air pump; anatomy of glands; fountain pens; stenography; coke made from coal; balance spring for watches; manometer; microscope; midwifery forceps; flexible hose; pump with piston and raised by steam; ammonium chloride; magic lantern; cut-glass.

---

*(contd...)*

[6]Debreu, G., *Theory of Value*, New York: Wiley, 1959. Gerard Debreu won the Nobel Prize for economics in 1983.

[7]Arrow, K., and F. Hahn, *General Competitive Analysis*. San Francisco: Holden-Day, 1971. Arrow won the Nobel Prize in 1972. His contribution to economic theory is both profound and diverse. He is also counted as a prominent political thinker for his beautiful mathematical theorem establishing that there cannot be any consistent decision rule 'democratically' based on the preferences of individuals. The word 'democratic' here refers to decision rules with features that are generally supposed to be associated with democracy.

*Box 1.2 continued.*

---

*Science and maths*: Differential and integral calculus; the binomial theorem; theory of probability; logarithm; Jupiter's satellites, Orion nebula and sunspots; explanation of rainbows; refraction, diffraction, and polarisation of light; circulation of blood; nature of combustion; explanation of sea tides; a map of the moon made; red blood corpuscles observed; diabetes recognized.

*Publications*: Manuals of surveying, anatomy, bees and beekeeping, glass making; Treatises on metabolism and perspiration, usury, political economy, melancholy and depression, philosophical discourse on death, international law, primary education, flowers, comparative politics, the present state of Ireland, art of rhetoric, witchcraft, dendrology, freedom of the press, political theory of monarchy, separation of church and state, foundations of freedom; Studies of the Plague, absolute monarchy, surgical instruments and procedures, history of philosophy, divorce, American language, the nervous system, earthquakes, trade and the interest on money, silkworms, flora and fauna of England, small pox and measles, geology, freedom of the sea, England's kings; History of Netherlands, France, the Latin American countries, Japan, Great Britain, and the World; Natural history of the Swiss landscape. Dictionary of European languages; Latin–English dictionary; English to other European language dictionaries; Dictionary of law.

*Founded*: The Royal Society of London; *Academie Francaise*; Academy of Sciences, Moscow; Universities of Parma, Rome, Groningen, Strasbourg, Utrecht, Budapest, Palermo, Kiel, Innsbruck, Bologna, and Venice; and Wadham College, Oxford.

---

Adam Smith (1723–1790),[8] a Scottish thinker, is credited as the most influential early proponent of this line of thought. He saw quite clearly that markets are not just places to buy and sell. They connect together the economic decisions of many people. Income earned by workers employed in the production of one good is spent on the products of others. Similarly, revenue from the sale of a good goes to buy inputs for it. These intricate connections between buying and selling of goods, inputs and labour make the economy an inter-

[8]See Box 2.4 Chapter 2 for a short note on Adam Smith.

connected system. Formulating the properties of these relations was a breakthrough in terms of analytical vision and led to clearer understanding of markets, by Smith and others.

Smith tried to lay at rest the worries raised about the outcome of individual actions of many unconnected buyers and sellers. He argued that these unconnected decisions get connected through the market which constrains them so that they become consistent in the end. His classic book *The Wealth of Nations* published in 1776 examines these issues clearly. When seeking income, no matter whether as wage or profit, individuals are motivated by self interest. Producers strive for the maximum possible profit as they buy inputs and sell their products. Likewise, buyers look for the best deal available when buying goods for consumption. Arguing that an economy is but a web woven from individual self-interests, he wrote rhetorically, 'It is not from the benevolence of the butcher, the brewer, or the baker, that we expect our dinner, but from their regard to their own interest'.[9] Self-interest of isolated individuals leads to the provision of goods and services for one another because of the way markets are connected. It is also in the interest of producers to produce with the least possible cost and so resources are used in the best possible manner. Smith saw an 'invisible hand' in competitive markets that reconciles individual interest with overall systemic efficiency.

Though he discussed these themes in many places, Smith did not provide a fully developed analysis of the market system and its various inter-relations.[10] This remained to be clearly formulated, and then refined, by economists of later periods. Leon Walras (1834–1910),[11] a French economist and a professor at the University of Lausanne, set up the analysis of inter-relation of markets using a system of inter-related or simultaneous equations. His work appeared almost a

[9]From his book, *The Wealth of Nations: An Inquiry into the Nature and Causes*, first published in 1776.

[10]Smith and many other authors of the time appear more impressed by another aspect of markets: their ability to create incentive and induce initiative.

[11]*Éléments d'économie politique pure, ou théorie de la richesse sociale* (1874) by Walras, later translated into English as *Elements of Pure Economics*, provides the foundation of modern general equilibrium analysis of markets. Joseph Schumpeter, an acclaimed economist of the twentieth century, described Walras as 'the greatest of all economists' in his encyclopaedic book *History of Economic Analysis* (1954).

hundred years after Adam Smith's *Wealth of Nations*. Those hundred years were a period of intense scholarly activity in Europe around the question of markets. Of course, not all were toeing Adam Smith's line. There were seriously dissenting notes that claimed that markets were a faulty and inconsistent system. We will note some of them below. Walras' mathematical formulation made the interrelation among markets clearer to understand as well as to dispute. Later scholars refined the analysis to shed light on various intricacies of the mechanism. A renowned Italian sociologist and economist Vilfredo Pareto (1848–1923) succeeded Walras to his chair at Lausanne. He produced a full-blown mathematical proof that a system of competitive markets tends to use productive resources optimally in his celebrated book, *Manual of Political Economy*.[12] The theoretical structure and views developed from these authors are collectively referred to as classical and neo-classical theory depending on the vintage. Neo-classicals are of more recent times and use more abstract models. Together they are often labelled as free market theories.

## 1.6 The Socialists

Before taking a closer look at the classical theory, let me outline the second important line of thought that originated during the Industrial Revolution. It is radically different from that of Smith, Walras, and Pareto. Scholars of this line did not find anything drastically new in the proliferation of markets. They observed that markets had been in existence even prior to the middle ages. Markets could not, therefore, characterise the new era and their analysis would not produce any major insight into the emerging system. In their view what was really new was not markets *per se* but the market for labour that came to replace artisan and own-account production. While the market for goods and loans had existed previously, labour markets had not. To buy and sell labour time like any other commodity was the real breakthrough in history. They observed that the emerging factory system relied on the labour market and was very different from earlier

---

[12]Pareto, V., *Manual of Political Economy*, 1906 (in Italian); English translation in 1971 by A.S. Schwier and A.N. Page.

ways of managing production. This school of thought, therefore, focused on the labour market and the factory system.

The general view was that workers were exploited by factory owners in labour markets. This exploitation generated profits for capitalist factory owners. The profit in turn was invested in new factories and machines and thus was the driver of the new industrial system. Hence, exploitation was the hallmark of the new system. For want of a better title, we will refer to the group of people who saw capitalism in this light as socialists. The discussion by socialists went in several directions. Some raised moral questions about exploitation and tried to analyse moral and ethical issues. Others focused on the social effects of the factory system and urban poverty. A beginning was made in what we now term industrial and urban sociology. Some socialists were of the view that industrial exploitation created not just poverty but a number of systemic problems which would render the new economic system untenable in the long run. For instance, it created an imbalance between the increasing output from the growing number of factories and the lagging means of poorly-paid people to buy them. Thus, production for profit created a widening gap between potential supply and actual demand. This would create a growing imbalance of supply and demand rather than harmony and equilibrium as expected by Smith.

The idea that the system was fundamentally exploitative did not remain confined to academic writings. It led to social and political activism as well. Some groups wanted to reverse industrialisation and go back to the good old days while others wanted to establish communities with different production organisation and rules of living. There were also calls to overthrow the capitalist system altogether, with violence if need be, to establish a new form of society.

---

**Box 1.3: Karl Marx**

Karl Marx was born in Trier, Germany in 1818. He received a classical education, studied law for a while in Bonn and went to Berlin for further studies. There he became a part of the Young Hegelian movement, which had attracted official ire by producing a radical critique of Christianity

---

*(contd...)*

*Box 1.3 continued.*

that indirectly implicated the Prussian Government. Predictably, Marx's university career was soon ended by the Prussian Government. He then came to Cologne and turned to journalism—writing editorials for a liberal newspaper. The newspaper was supported by business and industry and could be assumed to be a relatively safe place for a young radical. But the government soon caught up and ordered the paper to close down because of Marx's extremely critical editorials.

Marx then shifted to Paris where he met emigrant German workers and French socialist groups. Here he became seriously involved with politics. The writings for which he is well-known are dated from this time onward. His work around this period focuses on contemporary political events and philosophy and shows the evolution of his thinking and analysis. He was elected to the general council of the First International[13] when it was formed in 1864 and gave a lot of his time for it.

The most important political event in the life of the First International was the Paris Commune of 1871. The people of Paris rose against the government and held up the city for two months. After the violent suppression of the uprising, Marx wrote one of his most famous pamphlets, *The Civil War in France*. It contained a powerful defence of the Commune and a commentary on the tactics of organised uprisings.

Volume I of Marx's most famous book, *Capital* was published in 1867. Volumes II and III were drafted during the 1860s but Marx continued working on them until his death. They were published posthumously by his friend and comrade Frederick Engels. These three volumes provide an account of his theory of the capitalist system and its dynamics.

One group among these dissenting voices would subsequently leave a very significant imprint on the rest of the nineteenth century and the better part of the twentieth. It reasoned that the new system, capitalism, was doomed to break down because of its own contradictory features. It was like a poorly designed mechanism whose inconsistencies unleash mutually opposed forces. The inevitable breakdown should be sped up pro-actively so as to shorten the era of exploitation. The intellectual leader of this group, Karl

[13]It was an international organization of workers and was to function as an overarching structure for communist parties of participating countries.

Marx (1818–1883), was among the most influential thinkers of the nineteenth century. He avoided the stereotypes of moral outrage against capitalism or nostalgia for the good old pre-industrial life by developing a detached scientific analysis of the system. His analysis claimed an inevitable doom of capitalism and the rise of more advanced forms of economic organisation. He laid down the basis of a method for analysing social change which was very different from the majority paradigm of positivism of the time. Marxism has survived to our days both as an intellectual tradition as also a guide to activism.

The two traditions that I have presented here are the extremes of a spectrum. There is a continuum of viewpoints and positions stretching between them. These positions have developed over the last two centuries. Further, there are scholars with sympathy for both traditions. They see a certain amount of rationality in the functioning of markets and yet an overarching unfairness in the social system in which markets are embedded.

## 1.7 The Great Depression and J.M. Keynes

Adam Smith wrote *The Wealth of Nations* in 1776. The first volume of Karl Marx's economic work *Das Kapital* came out in 1867. Thus, two of the defining influences of economics were laid out long before the twentieth century started. By contrast, the third major influence to shape the subject came in the twentieth century. Interestingly, this one too developed in the middle of a traumatic time—a period known as the Great Depression. The tradition started with a British economist, John Maynard Keynes (1883–1946). Like Smith, Keynes believed in the spirit of private initiative and capitalism. But unlike Smith and his followers, he did not believe in the ability of markets to allocate resources rationally or to use them fully. He claimed that markets require serious guidance and intervention. So the Keynesian position stands out as a distinct third tradition. It accepts capitalism like Smithians and unlike socialists; but unlike Smithians and like socialists, it believes that markets are inherently not a good mechanism. It neither accepts that markets are efficient nor does it suggest that capitalism and private property should be replaced by another economic system. Keynes' ideas have cast an overwhelming influence on government policy since the Second World War. Even though many of his arguments have been challenged in the last fifty years, his influence on policy continues. We will discuss his ideas and their implications for economic policy at length later. Here, I outline how he came up with his views when the world was helplessly witnessing the Great Depression.

Economists of the market tradition believe that a market works like an automatic mechanism. The two sides of a market are the buyers who provide demand and the sellers who bring in the supply. Their actions eventually lead to a price at which demand and supply are equalised. The way this is expected to happen is as follows. If supply entering the market exceeds demand, then sellers are forced to reduce the price. This boosts demand and at the same time discourages some supply. The net result is that the amount of excess supply is reduced. If excess supply is not entirely removed, then there would be some further price fall. The process continues until the price is such that supply and demand are just equal. In the opposite case, if demand exceeds supply, then buyers bid up the price as they are anxious that they may fail to procure the good. This induces more supply as well as discourages some of the demand. The process goes on until the price rises to the point where supply and demand are equal. Prices are assumed to be flexible enough for this to happen. The mechanism is expected to work unless non-market forces jam its working. The price at which demand and supply become equal is called the 'equilibrium price' for that market. As long as demand and supply are not equal, the market is said to be in 'disequilibrium'.

Let us now ask how much time a market would take to settle to its equilibrium price, starting from an initial imbalance? The time required would depend on how easy it is to reduce or increase the consumption of the good and its supply; whether or not the good can be stored; what the storage cost is; and so on. Accordingly, the price in some markets would adjust quickly while others would take more time. But overall, the belief is that it should not take too long for market disequilibrium to be corrected.

One of the most distressing issues during the Great Depression was the very high rate of unemployment—nearly 25 per cent in some countries—continuing for a very long period. Unemployment means that the demand for labour is less than its supply. If we accept the theory of markets, we would expect unemployment to be eliminated by the automatic mechanism of the labour market. Because labour supply exceeds demand, the wage rate[14] would start falling. The fall will raise the demand for labour and in a reasonable time the excess supply would disappear. In other words, unemployment should not persist for very long. Economists were familiar with bouts of unemployment and recession from time to time. The phenomenon was called business cycles. Generally these recessions had not lasted too long and unemployment did disappear after a reasonable amount of time. This made sense according to the theory of markets. Hence the consensus was that unemployment is a *disequilibrium* state of the market which is expected to end soon. The market mechanism would soon establish the equilibrium wage rate that would employ all those who seek jobs.

This was one of the central beliefs that had grown from the classical theory of markets following Smith, Walras, and Pareto. This belief was severely jolted by the Great Depression (1929–1939). The Depression began towards the end of October 1929 with a severe crash of the US stock market. On 24 October stock values dropped rapidly, creating panic among stockholders and the financial circle. The day was later named 'Black Thursday'. However, things steadied on Friday and even on Monday the market held itself tenuously. But on 'Black Tuesday' stockholders became nervous and dumped a record number[15] of shares in the market leading to a free fall of share prices. Share owners lost staggeringly large amounts of money and many went bankrupt. A large number of banks failed. Other banks, factories, and stores shut their doors and left millions of Americans jobless.

It was the most spectacular stock market crash until then. Nevertheless, mainstream economists who had grown up with the classical tradition believed that the depression and unemployment would clear away soon enough. Prices would fall to entice customers back to the goods market. And, wages would fall making employers hire those who had lost jobs. But nothing of the sort happened. The

[14]Wage rate is the price for a unit of labour time.
[15]16,410,030 to be precise.

depression persisted, deepened, and spread to all sectors of the US economy and then to other countries. The fall in US demand cut her imports from other countries. So the contagion reached Europe and Japan. At the height of the depression, some countries found a quarter of their working population jobless. The depression showed no sign of lifting and it condemned an entire generation of workers to joblessness and farmers to penury. The desperate tale of American farmers during the period has been told graphically by John Steinbeck in his novel *The Grapes of Wrath* published in 1939. The depression lifted only in 1939 when the Second World War knocked on closed factory gates with its shopping list for the war.

The experience raised serious doubts about the self-correcting nature of markets. Yet, the majority of the economics profession could not think beyond the familiar model. Their reflex was to think that the time needed for restoring equilibrium depended on a list of factors, which might not have been adequately understood. They tried to study the events closely to find factors responsible for the abnormally slow recovery. It is in this context that Keynes presented a radically new paradigm.

In 1936 Keynes published *The General Theory of Employment, Interest and Money*, which is amongst the most important books on economics ever written. He argued that the theory of individual markets cannot be used to explain economy-wide events. A recession affects the whole economy, during which *all* markets face deficient demand. Given the slump in demand, producers would be unable to sell if they were to produce their capacity level output. So they operate at less than capacity and lay off workers. If wages are reduced to make it possible to employ the jobless workers, the total wage income earned by workers is reduced. However, it is wage income that is the source of consumption demand. Hence the wage cut would simply worsen the demand slump.

Hence, in a recession wages may fall here and there but that does not lead the economy out of trouble. If, however, there is a loss of jobs in a single market, wage fall can restore the number of jobs quite promptly. Thus, he claimed, the classical market theory was right when applied to one or a few markets but misleading when used for the economy as a whole.

**Box 1.4: John Maynard Keynes**

J.M. Keynes (1883–1946) was born in England. His father had an administrative position at Cambridge University and his mother was one of the earliest female students to attend Cambridge. Keynes too went to Cambridge for higher education. There he wrote a dissertation on the theory of probability. After passing out he joined the British Civil Service and got a position at the India desk in the ministry of foreign affairs. But it appears that he soon got bored and resigned from the job. He then got a teaching position at Cambridge. At the time Alfred Marshall was the head of economics. Marshall had taught Keynes at Cambridge. Keynes would, however, deviate radically from the economics of Alfred Marshall which was an English variant of the neoclassical theory.

During the First World War, Keynes was offered a job at the British Treasury (that is, the Ministry of Finance). With this began his serious involvement with policy. He took an active part in designing war financing at the treasury. After the war, he participated in the Paris Peace Conference of 1919 as an official member of the British team. Keynes did not approve of the outcome of the Conference as it imposed a deadening burden of reparations on Germany. He resigned his treasury job after coming back and published a critique of the Peace Conference, *The Economic Consequences of the Peace*. He claimed that the crushing reparations that Germany was forced to pay to the victorious allies would disable Germany's economic recovery and eventually force it to default or repudiate. This might lead to a renewal of hostility and rearmament of Europe. Subsequent developments vindicated his view.

*The General Theory* came out in 1936 in the middle of the Great Depression. It opened up a new way of looking at the economy, and became a classic almost as soon as it was published. Apart from its arguments and analysis, a very heartening contribution of the *General Theory* was to restore some common sense into the economic theory of that time. The subject had developed elaborate and intricate analytical structures which could not generally give a straight answer to a straight question. The *General Theory* restored this ability. That is part of the reason that its reasoning was accepted so overwhelmingly. However, one cannot conclude that as a book the *General Theory* is simple and easy to read. It packs enough intricacy for the intellectuals and the scholarly to keep them debating till today.

## 1.8 Calculated Intervention in a Private Economy

The above is an oversimplified outline of Keynes' argument. But it does capture his line of attack on the classical theory. In a nutshell, he argued that markets have no automatic mechanism for curing a recession though an individual market may correct its imbalance soon enough. In that sense, using the classical theory to understand a recession involves a fallacy of aggregation. Hence, there is no reason why a recession would end by itself. A recession and general unemployment could very well be an enduring equilibrium state. He believed that the existing theory was wrong in asserting that unemployment is always a disequilibrium event and would go away by itself.

Keynes, therefore, reasoned that the way out of a recession cannot be to just wait for it to go away. His suggestion was to inject some demand into the economy from outside. Demand from outside, called exogenous or autonomous demand, is demand that does not depend on the present state of the economy, that is, it does not rely on today's income or GDP.[16] Demand from consumers and business firms contracts in a recession and increases with an increase in income. Thus, it cannot be termed 'autonomous demand'. On the other hand, a government can buy things or put up orders no matter if the economy is in a good state or bad. So the demand of the government is autonomous of the income process. Note that autonomous demand means demand created not through the working of markets but from outside. Besides directly buying things, a government has a few other ways of creating autonomous demand. It can cut taxes, provide consumption support such as unemployment benefits or income support for low-income families. These steps boost the demand from consumers and business. The thrust of Keynes' theory is that when the market fumbles, it needs help from outside the market mechanism. This suggestion is radically different from the *Laissez Faire* philosophy based on traditional theory. *Laissez Faire* advocates

[16]GDP or Gross Domestic Product is a measure of the total income of the economy. It is the rupee value of everything produced in a year for final use. Intermediate goods, that is, those to be further processed are not counted. We will discuss GDP fully in a later chapter.

that a government should not intervene in markets because help is already built into its economic mechanism. By contrast, Keynes assigned an activist role to the government.

The 1930s was a period when governments, politicians, and scholars were quite sharply divided on the issue of capitalism *vs* socialism. So a question that interested many at that time was which camp was strengthened by Keynes' arguments. Keynes' criticism of free markets, however, did not mean that he was advocating socialism. He believed in free enterprise and saw calculated intervention in markets simply as a way of helping enterprise. His influence on government policy and economic organisation of life has been immense. It has changed national and international institutions profoundly since the end of war. Further, his method of reasoning about the economy as a whole rather than individual markets established a new branch of economics called *macroeconomics*.

## 1.9 The Book

The rest of the book discusses the major ideas and issues in economics. We will first discuss competitive markets to get a flavour of the so-called free market view (Chapter 2). Then we will survey the working of markets that are not competitive. Non-competitive markets dominate today's world. How do they work and how would free market ideas fare in such markets? (Chapter 3) In Chapter 4 we come across things that create economic benefits or costs without requiring markets to do so. These rather curious animals are called externalities and public goods. They abound in our economies and are a challenge to today's economic management. In the next two chapters, 5 and 6, we get a view of the central problems of economic life, unemployment and inflation. We survey related policies and their shortcomings. In the next chapter we take a look at the world of money and banks which are closely related with inflation (Chapter 7). Thereafter we turn to international issues (Chapter 8) without which a discussion is not complete in today's globalised world. We talk about international trade, migration, and multinational companies. These, as you would recognise, are areas of intense debate right now. Chapter 9 takes us to the question of economic growth. What is the recipe for economic growth? How have European countries and North America sustained centuries of economic growth? These are surely of immense concern today as developing countries grow faster and aspire to join the rank of rich countries. Finally, the last chapter sums up the discussion in the book.

A curious feature that you will come across is that there are multiple views on almost all economic issues. As an example, we will encounter the above three traditions time and again. You may wonder how all of them can survive even though they contradict one another. To be sure, these ideas have been rejected by critics as often as they have been pronounced as the last word by their followers. However, the attacks have failed to eliminate them because each contains some enduring truth. They have come back centre stage again and again as majority opinion in economics has swayed from one tradition to another a number of times.

George Bernard Shaw had written with his characteristic sarcasm, 'If all the economists were laid end to end, they'd never reach a conclusion'. But the multiplicity of ideas and methods is a sign of strength of economics, not weakness. Economic events take shape as we participate in our social life—each with a different interest, motivation, and perception. It would, therefore, be surprising if we all viewed economic events in the same way. The 'truth' is unlikely to be seen by any one scholar viewing the economy from his or her viewing position. It waits to be constructed from many accounts of many viewers; much like an animation studio constructs a complex three-dimensional object from shots taken from different angles. A good way to appreciate economics is to take a look at all the photo shots. We will do that and consider them together with the time and events through which the photographers lived. To help us make sense of the richness of this story our storyline will not proceed chronologically. We will focus on ideas and issues and move back and forth as if in a time machine.

# 2 Markets, Efficiency, and Adam Smith

Of the three traditions discussed in the last chapter, Adam Smith's is the oldest. It has contributed to what is commonly called the free market theory. Marxists and Keynesians contrast their views against those of the free market theory. So it is good to get an idea of the Smithian tradition as a starter. In this chapter I will describe the theory and its claims.

But rather than just describing the claims, I will also present the building blocks of the theory. This will help us delve a bit deeper into various ideas. These building blocks or concepts have developed over many years. They often arose as mere hints or the germ of a concept that can be useful in keeping our thoughts straight. They were made more definitive and precise by later authors and now they are indispensable tools of economic analysis. As I describe them, I will provide some digressions (in text boxes) to alert the reader to their historical connections.

## 2.1 What is Efficiency?

Oscar Wilde had once asked, 'What is a cynic?' and gave a reply himself 'A man who knows the price of everything and the value of nothing'. In his time (1854–1900), it was understood that the price of a good does not have much to do with its intrinsic value. But just a few years before Oscar Wilde was born, European scholars were puzzling over the so-called 'Diamond–Water Paradox'. Why diamonds are so pricey while water is free even though the latter is essential for life and a diamond is a mere trinket? They of course eventually realised that it is not the intrinsic value but the scarcity of a commodity that determines its price.

We are willing to pay for a good only if it is scarce. If things were available in unlimited amounts there would be no *economic*[1] *goods*, that is, things for which we pay. Economics and its cousins such as accounting and marketing would never have been born. Scarcity of goods is a result of the scarcity of resources that are used to produce them. Therefore, the proper use of resources has a central place in economics. I am sure you have come across the catch phrase 'efficiency of resource use' in one context or another. We will start our discussion of markets with this phrase.

We should first clarify what exactly is meant by the efficiency of resource use. This is how economists view the idea: if an economy is using its resources with a hundred per cent efficiency, then it is not possible to increase the output of anything without cutting down that of something else. Suppose at the moment our economy is producing a million different things. You then step in and ask, 'Hey, can I have one more loaf of bread, please?' Suppose we can make an extra loaf for you and to do that we do not have to reduce the output of anything else; that would be possible if some resources were unused earlier, and we use them now to make the extra loaf. In that case the economy was not efficient when you came in. Recall that resources are scarce. So a state in which resources remain idle is a kind of inefficiency.

There is also a second possibility. Maybe all the resources were being used but not in the best possible way. In that case by using them in a better way, we can save some resources and make an additional loaf. Consider an example. Suppose power plants and fast food shops use both coal and gas as fuel. So we can exchange some coal used in power plants for some of the gas used in food shops. Suppose this swap maintains the output of power and food, and yet saves some coal. This is possible if some producers were using the resources callously, and we transferred resources to those who use them better.

---

[1] The word 'economic' is noted to have appeared around 1585–1595. It came from Latin *oeconomicus via* Greek *oikonomikós* which means relating to household management (*oiko(s)* house + *nómos* manager).

Similarly, say, by reallocating the flour used by bakeries among them, we find that some flour can be saved without reducing the bakers' total output. We can then use the saved flour to bake an extra loaf with the saved coal. Cutting down the production of something else will not be required to get you the extra loaf. Note that it means that a loaf is produced without depriving anybody of anything! And, that will mean that the economy was not efficient earlier. In an efficient economy the possibility of making an extra something with idle or callously-used resources is already exhausted. Therefore, when an economy functions at a hundred per cent efficiency, no reallocation of resources can produce an extra bit of anything without cutting the output of some item. Theoretically speaking, the production of even an extra pin would require a sacrifice of something else in an efficient economy. There is no free lunch in an efficient economy.

## 2.2 Marginal Product

I will chase the idea of efficiency a bit further. Are there conditions or signs by which we can tell that an economy is efficient? Let us think of two firms that use both coal and gas. It can be said that they are working efficiently if we cannot raise the output of one firm without affecting the other's by just swapping their coal and gas. Under what condition will that happen? To answer this we need a very widely used concept called *marginal product*. If a firm increases any input by one unit, the resulting extra output is called the marginal product of that input. If by increasing a unit of labour (and nothing else) a firm can raise its output by 4 units, then the marginal product of labour is 4.

We can tell if efficiency is attained by examining marginal products. If the ratio of marginal products of coal and gas is equal in the two firms, then it is impossible to increase one's output without reducing the other's. It is easy see this with an example. However, if you want to accept this at face value and skip the example, you can move to the next section.

Suppose the marginal product of coal is double the marginal product of gas in both firms. This means that a unit of coal produces twice as much extra output as a unit of gas in both firms. Now try to transfer coal from firm 1 to 2 and gas from firm 2 to 1. If you take a unit of coal from 1 and yet want to maintain its output, then you have to give it two units of gas to compensate. To do this, you take two units gas from firm 2. But if you take two units gas from 2 and give it one unit coal that has been taken away from 1, its output remains exactly at the old level. Thus if we swap inputs so that the output of one firm does not fall, then that of the other cannot increase either. This means that if we want to increase either firm's output, then that of the other has to fall. This is what is expected if the economy is efficient. In an efficient state, if any two firms are using a pair of inputs then the ratio of the marginal products of the inputs must be equal for them.

## 2.3 The Law of Diminishing Returns

Marginal product has an intriguing property. When the use of an input is increased without increasing the quantity of other inputs, the marginal product of successive units keeps falling. If a farmer uses more and more fertiliser but does not increase land and other inputs, the gains from successive doses of the fertiliser will fall. At some stage the marginal contribution will even become zero and then get into the negative zone. If inputs did not have this spoil-sport property, we could feed the whole world by growing wheat on a cricket ground just by using more and more fertilisers. This property implies that to increase output we need progressively more and more input. Put differently, each unit of output is costlier than the previous one. This is why the average cost of output generally goes up as we produce more.

The tendency for the marginal product to fall is a nearly universal property. It holds for most production situations. Economists refer to it as the *Law of Diminishing Returns*. You should note that it is really not a law of economics. It results from the laws of nature, that is, from the physical and chemical properties of things that we combine in production and biological properties of things that we grow. This inconvenient property of the physical and biological worlds is at the centre of our economic problem.

---

### Box 2.1: The Law of Diminishing Returns

This is one of the oldest ideas in economics. Its first written discussion is most probably by a French economist called Anne Robert Jacques Turgot (1727–1781). Turgot came from a family that was part of the French high bureaucracy. He himself became France's finance minister. But more than a minister, he was renowned as an intellectual and a prominent 'Physiocrat'. Physiocrats were a group of intellectuals of that time based in France. They became very influential during the days leading up to the French Revolution of 1789. They were profoundly influenced by Isaac Newton's (1642–1727) discoveries and his mechanistic model of the universe. They believed that there must be similar mechanistic explanations of social events too.[2] Because of this they looked for natural laws that govern the economic world and loved the law of diminishing returns when they found it.

Please note that diminishing returns does not contradict the possibility of *economy of scale*. In many industries, by increasing the scale of production, output can be increased by more than the scale-up factor. This is known as the economy of scale. An increase in the scale of production means increasing all inputs in tandem. The law of diminishing returns on the other hand refers to the result of increasing a single input while keeping others unchanged.

---

## 2.4 How Many Workers does a Firm Hire?

Let us now go back to the idea of efficiency. Suppose a firm has to decide if it should hire an extra worker. We assume that the firm is driven by profit alone. So it will hire only if it costs less to hire than what it would get by selling the worker's marginal product. Suppose the marginal product is indeed higher than the wage and the firm hires this worker, and for similar reasons, hires another and another and so on. As more workers are hired in the same workplace, marginal product of the worker last hired will be less than that of the one hired before him. This will happen because of diminishing returns. At some stage the marginal product will become so small that by selling it the firm

---

[2] The word Physiocracy means 'rule by nature' which shows the influence of Newton's vision.

would just recover the wage it pays to this worker. If the firm hires a worker beyond this point, it would be paying the worker more than what the latter would add to the firm's revenue. So it will stop hiring at this point. Thus a firm hires as long as the marginal product of workers exceeds the wage rate, and stops when the two become equal. As the jargon goes, the firm attains equilibrium hiring at this point.

Using the same reasoning we can find out how much of other inputs will be used by a firm. The firm will use an input up to the point where the value of its marginal product becomes equal to its price. This is equally true of labour as well as other material inputs. So we can say that the last rupee spent on an input produces exactly one rupee of extra product for a competitive firm.[3]

The last rupee spent by a firm on every input gets it the same amount of marginal product and that is worth exactly 1 rupee in the market. Therefore, it is easy to see that a firm cannot increase its output by spending its money differently, for example, fewer rupees on labour and that much more on another input. If it spends one rupee less on labour, it will lose a rupee of output. When it uses that saved rupee on any other input, it will get only a rupee of extra output and no more. Hence once in equilibrium, a firm cannot increase output or profit by simply reallocating its outlay on the inputs. Each firm produces the maximum amount possible with its money and uses the least costly input combination for what it produces.

---

### Box 2.2: Physiocrats

Physiocracy as an active intellectual movement lasted just a few decades. Its influence peaked a few years before the French Revolution. It had serious influence on the French Government and economic policy of the time. Physiocrats also made important contributions to the development of economic thought.

---

*(contd...)*

[3]So the firm gets nothing from the *last* unit of an input because what it is paid cancels what it produces. The firm's profit comes from selling the marginal product of all units before the last.

*Box 2.2 continued.*

With increasing prosperity, a question that intrigued Europe's intellectuals of the time was what is it that creates value and wealth. The reigning view before physiocrats was that wealth consists of gold, silver, and precious stones acquired through trade. This idea is known as 'mercantilism'. It advised restriction of imports because imports had to be paid for with gold. On the other hand it championed exports and the acquisition of gold and silver from overseas by any means. In sum, mercantilists held that a country can grow wealthy only at the cost of another because there is only so much gold in the world. Physiocrats challenged this 'zero sum' idea. They reasoned that wealth comes from productive work and hence all countries can grow wealthy at the same time.

However, the Physiocrats' modern outlook had a limitation. They thought that all productive work takes place in agriculture. France was still predominantly agrarian. Tax on agriculture was the main income of the emperor and the nobility. Part of this was just beginning to be invested in commerce and banks and the rest was spent on consumption of manufactured goods. To Physiocrats it appeared that agriculture alone produced a surplus over production cost. This surplus was then spent on manufactures and luxury goods sustaining workers and traders in those areas. Thus wealth was created by agriculture alone and the source of all value was land. In following up how land could be made to yield more wealth they came upon the problem of diminishing returns.

Physiocrats used illustrative arithmetic tables to show the relation among outputs of agriculture and other sectors and worked out conditions of relative balance among them that could maintain a steady proportional growth of all of them together. The most famous of this group of works is *Tableau Économique* (1758) by François Quesnay (1694–1774). Quesnay was the official doctor of the French court and a leader of the physiocrats. Possibly because he was a physician, he visualised the economy like the human body. He looked at the flow of annual production and income from agriculture through other sectors like the circular flow of blood. The *Tableau* is possibly the earliest attempt to study income and spending relations among different sectors and is a forerunner of national accounting and macroeconomics.

## 2.5 What does Free Market Economics Claim?

If you have followed the discussion so far you are ready for the central proposition of free market economics. The proposition says that a perfectly competitive economy, where producers chase profits and consumers shop for best value, will be fully efficient. It means that the resources will find their best possible use if markets work freely and competitively. This proposition is at the heart of free market economics and provides the rationale of all market-oriented policies. It is this idea that is used when advising governments to not interfere in the working of markets unless absolutely necessary. We will consider the logic of the proposition in the next section.

Needless to say, many find this free market proposition hard to accept. A common reaction to it is complete disbelief; that it is patently untrue. This reaction is the source of a good number of business school jokes:

Question: How many free market economists does it take to change a light bulb? Answer: None. If it really needed changing, market forces would have already made it happen.

The following business school joke targets the idea that there is no free lunch or unused opportunity in a market system:

Two economists walk down the street in New Delhi. One sees a thousand rupee note lying on the sidewalk and says so. 'Obviously not,' says the other. 'If it was there, someone would have already picked it up!'

No one can blame you if you buy into these business school jokes, because you will have a lot of company among economists themselves. Though business works with its profit motive, it ends up producing a benign outcome using resources in the best possible manner, was jeered at by J.M. Keynes in these words: 'Capitalism is the astounding belief that the most wickedest of men will do the most wickedest of things for the greatest good of everyone'.

Before we go further I should, however, get a common misunderstanding out of the way. The efficiency proposition is not about all markets. It does not claim that any market economy would use resources efficiently. It is only about *competitive* markets. In a competitive market, buyers and sellers are atomic in size compared to the size of the market. So they cannot influence the going price by altering their purchase or sale quantities. These markets are very different from a monopoly or an oligopoly where only one or a handful of companies dominate the selling side. Efficiency is compromised in all non-competitive markets. We will discuss those markets in the next chapter.

It is also important to place this and other theoretical propositions in a proper perspective. Their purpose is to describe outcomes in ideal conditions knowing fully well that ideal conditions do not prevail in reality. They challenge economists to diagnose why these outcomes are not attained in a given real world situation. The diagnosis can help to devise policy or institutions that could take us closer to the ideal outcomes. This is why we give so much attention to the theory of competitive markets, though most markets we deal with are far from competitive.

## 2.6 Logic of the Free Market Claim

The reasoning behind the claim that competitive markets are fully efficient is actually quite simple. We have seen that in competitive markets what a firm gets from selling an input's marginal product equals the price of that input. So the ratio of the marginal product of any two inputs is also equal to the ratio of their prices. Further, as markets are competitive all firms would buy inputs at the same price. So the ratio of marginal products of any two inputs is the same for all firms. Now recall from Section 2.2 that if this happens then we cannot reallocate inputs across firms and increase one's output without reducing another's; we cannot produce anything without sacrificing some other output. Hence in this situation the economy is one hundred per cent efficient. It is not possible to do better than what competitive firms do with the economy's given resources.

This is the logic of the central proposition of competitive markets. It establishes that competitive markets form a mechanism which leads to efficient resource use. Smith himself did not reason this out in its present form but had discussed the matter sufficiently so that it could be built upon. He had referred to markets' ability to lead to an efficient allocation as an 'invisible hand' working through the system.

The proposition is the culmination of economists' study of market behaviour. From Adam Smith's time and through the nineteenth century a large number of economists have explored how individual business units and consumers act in a market environment. This sort of analysis with its focus on small decision-making units—a firm, a consumer etc.—is called 'microeconomics'. In the rest of this chapter we will explore the microeconomic behaviour of firms. It will give us some more insight into the market system. It will also help appreciate the criticism of free market economics that we will discuss later on.

---

### Box 2.3: The Fascinating Journey of a Physiocrat

Around the time of the French Revolution, there lived in France a person named Pierre Samuel du Pont (1739–1817). He was an influential person, a well-known author, and a Physiocrat by persuasion. He was initially a supporter of the French Revolution and served as the president of the National Constituent Assembly. But it happened that he along with his son Eleuthère Irénée du Pont and a few others saved Emperor Louis XVI and the Empress Marie Antoinette from a mob at the Tuileries Palace during the uprising of 1792. As a result, Pierre attracted the wrath of the revolutionaries. Having survived in spite of being in their bad books for a few years, Pierre finally got sentenced to the guillotine during the Reign of Terror (1793–1794). Fortunately, before he was to be guillotined he was freed from jail when Robespierre fell. But he and his family remained blacklisted and lived under significant uncertainty. In 1797, his house was attacked by a mob and his life was threatened again. This time he managed to flee with his family to the United States.

In the States, Pierre developed good relations with the then President Thomas Jefferson. A few years later during Napoleon's rule in France, Pierre helped the US Government to negotiate territorial matters with France. His advice led the US to buy Louisiana from the French and this prevented a possible battle with the French army in New Orleans.

Pierre remained an influential person, and his family sought to establish itself in the States. His son, Eleuthère Irénée, founded du Pont. It is one of the most successful American corporations and the second largest chemical firm in the world today.

## 2.7 Opportunity Cost

Generally we think of cost as a rupee item. But there is another way of looking at it. We have seen that to get an extra loaf may require us to give up the production of some other output(s). Like the rupees needed to make a loaf, this sacrifice too can be seen as a cost of producing the loaf. Economists call this *opportunity cost*. It is measured by the things that are required to be sacrificed to produce an item. Depending on what is given up to make the loaf, its opportunity cost can be stated in many different ways. It may be half a kilo of sugar or a hundred grams of beef or a litre of milk or a square metre of cloth and so on. And in that case the opportunity costs of all these quantities are equal—they equal a loaf of bread. Rupee price helps us compare different items in terms of rupees. By contrast, opportunity cost helps compare produced items of an economy in physical terms. When an economy has unused resources, it may be possible to produce an item without reducing the output of anything else. In that case the opportunity cost of that item would be zero, though it still costs rupees to produce it!

Like products, we can also talk about the opportunity cost of inputs. If a unit of labour is withdrawn from use, the economy loses its marginal product whatever that product may be. So the opportunity cost of a unit of labour is the marginal product of labour in its present use. Note that there is no opportunity cost of an idle resource because its withdrawal does not reduce the output of the economy. Employing an unemployed worker has no opportunity cost because it does not reduce the output of anything. A country with large unemployment has a resource—labour—that can be used without any sacrifice of output. Note, however, that it does not mean that labour can be therefore employed without paying wages. It has to be paid a wage as everywhere else. But the society would not lose any output when these workers are employed. Though the rupee cost is positive, the opportunity cost is nil. This is one reason why labour-intensive production is recommended for countries with a large unemployed workforce.

Many ex-colonies of Europe gained freedom in the two decades after the Second World War. The new countries, later called developing countries, generally had large rural populations with chronic unemployment. Quite curiously, the unemployment was sometimes 'disguised'. The people did not appear to be idle. They were generally seen to be working on their family land, herding the family cattle, or minding the family orchard. However, not all of those working on a job were necessary for getting it done. For example, all adult members of a family might be working on a small plot of land which could be cultivated by just two persons. So leaving any two of them, the others could be considered unemployed. The output of the plot of land would not be affected if they did not come to work. Using economic jargon we might say that the marginal product of all but two persons is zero. The opportunity cost of labour of these people is also zero. These people could be employed in new industries or in infrastructure projects without reducing the country's agricultural or other rural output. Hence, people who were unemployed either openly or in a disguised manner were a possible source of capital formation in the third world.

---

### Box 2.4: Adam Smith (1723–1790)

Interestingly, Adam Smith's idea of the 'invisible hand' was not so much the result of his thinking about the economy as about moral philosophy. Smith was strongly influenced by a foremost thinker of the time, another Scottish philosopher David Hume (1711–1776). Like Hume, he was convinced of the importance of liberty and free human action. Smith lived in a period when the idea of liberty and freedom had a deep influence on intellectuals. His book *Wealth of Nations* was published in 1776, the year in which America declared freedom from Great Britain. Ideas that were to lead to the French Revolution in the next decade were already in the air. Belief in liberty had taken hold of Europeans in Europe and her colonies.

Some European traditions glorified freedom for its own sake. British philosophy on the other hand looked at freedom and liberty from a utilitarian viewpoint (see box 2.5), that is, as an instrument for attaining coveted things, for example, a better society. Smith's view of liberty was utilitarian in this sense. His economic analysis is an imaginative

*(contd...)*

*Box 2.4 continued.*

extension of the idea of the value of free human action into the sphere of economics. It asserts that free interaction among people in the market place creates the right incentives to produce an efficient and fair social arrangement.

At the time when he was developing these ideas Smith was also fighting the prevalent mercantilist philosophy. It held that a nation gets rich by acquiring gold which it gets through exports and loses through imports. Mercantilism recommended import restrictions, aggressive exports, and acquisition of gold and silver by other means. Import restrictions by one country led to retaliation by others and the philosophy had resulted in a restriction of trade and markets. The title of Smith's book *Wealth of Nations: An Inquiry into the Nature and Causes* shows his intention of breaking fresh ground on the origin of wealth. The point of the book was that wealth is created by production in the first place. His emphasis on markets came as a by-product. Production would increase only if markets are allowed to develop and are not restricted. He argued that productivity grows when producers specialize in products and processes. This can happen only if demand increases sufficiently to require large-scale production. Hence it is necessary to encourage expansion of markets through vigorous internal and external trade.

Smith saw the market as an institution that harnesses free human action to produce social gain. Markets help in efficient use of resources, specialisation, and economic growth. Further, rewards given out by markets according to marginal product create incentive for hard work and creativity.

Though Smith emphasised the useful aspects of markets, he believed that markets would remain under constant threat of subversion by traders themselves. While in competitive markets traders cannot manipulate prices, they have significant control on prices in non-competitive markets. This lets them make more profit than in a competitive environment. But for the economy it leads to misallocation of resources and so a loss for the society as a whole (see Chapter 3). Obviously the non-business public has to bear this loss. Smith noted that traders subvert competition with various forms of collusion and association and winning over the government to their side. However, rather than abandoning the market system because of this, he suggested that we should be vigilant and fight these forces.

*(contd...)*

*Box 2.4 continued.*

Adam Smith is very often considered the spokesman of free market economics and the critique of market economics is directed against his work. There are two strands among the critics. Some believe that markets are unjust by nature. They rob many for the gain of a few. Their criticism is from the angle of justice and fairness. Others believe that the market system is a poor mechanism with major internal problems and contradictions. Their criticism is from the angle of efficiency and mechanism design. Both groups prefer regulation of markets and control over prices and production of important products.

In a competitive equilibrium, the prices of things with equal opportunity costs are expected to be the same. The reason is easy to appreciate. Suppose the opportunity cost of a loaf of bread is a quarter litre of milk. Now if the price of the loaf is greater than that of a quarter litre milk, then milk producers will reduce milk production. Every quarter litre they reduce gives them additional resources to produce a loaf which would fetch a higher price than a quarter litre of milk. So they will produce loaves with the resources saved from cutting milk production. This process will stop only when so much increase of loaf supply has taken place that its price comes down and becomes equal to that of a litre of milk. Thus, in an equilibrium situation, the prices of all items with equal opportunity costs should be equal.

Note that these are the prices that consumers pay. So an important implication of this is that consumers pay for the sacrifice involved in producing a product, no more, no less. This is the reason that the competitive mechanism is considered to be fair to buyers even as it keeps production efficient.

### Box 2.5: Utilitarianism

Utilitarianism is the idea that the value of an action is derived from the utility it contributes. In particular, the moral value of an act is determined only by its contribution to total utility. It is a form of 'consequentialism', meaning that the value of an action depends on its outcome alone. It

*(contd...)*

*Box 2.5 continued.*

claims, indeed emphasises, that there is no *a priori* standard for judging an act and deciding if it is moral or immoral.

Jeremy Bentham (1748–1832), a British thinker and social reformer, was the most influential proponent of utilitarianism. He wanted to provide a 'scientific' principle for all moral, ethical, and legal questions as at that time religious and other tradition-bound answers were not satisfying any more. He argued that actions are morally supportable if they increase utility. Utility in this context is the happiness or pleasure generated by the action summed over all people. Utilitarianism was described as the principle of attempting 'the greatest good for the greatest number of people'. James Mill (1773–1836) was a foremost exponent of Bentham's philosophy. The classical utilitarianism of Bentham and Mill helped in developing a reductionist and quantitative approach to ethics, moral philosophy and, of course, economics.

Utilitarianism, however, has been almost abandoned by today's economic theory. Maximising the sum of everyone's utility, giving equal weight to all, creates a number of unacceptable outcomes. On the face of it, treating everyone equally appears to be a fair principle. But it can be unfair in many situations. For example, if we reckon the utility of the wealthy and the deprived people as equal, decisions would generally fail to redress existing deprivation.[4] Hence utilitarianism is rejected as a basis for social and government decision making.

Second, the quantitative and reductionist method emphasises definiteness and measurability in the analysis of economic phenomena. So, economists found the idea of a vaguely defined concept such as *utility* embarrassing. For an individual person utility cannot be given any meaning other than as a subjective and psychological quantity. It is not possible to measure it nor is it possible to compare one person's utility with another's or to add them together. Hence economics moved away from the use of utility as a basis for both social and individual decision making.

Economists now start with the premise that every person has a preference ordering, that is, he/she can compare all the available alternatives as more preferred or less preferred. Microeconomic

*(contd...)*

[4]Amartya Sen, Nobel laureate, has written extensively on the implications of utilitarian premises for social decision making.

*Box 2.5 continued.*

theory proceeds on the assumption that these preferences have certain rational properties. The word utility is still used, but not to describe any psychological object. It has become a short hand description of preferences. Utility from A is more than that from B if the person prefers A to B. Thus utility does not represent a measurable quantity; it represents a ranking. The distinction is similar to that between giving marks to students and ranking them according to their performance using letter grades.

## 2.8 Marginal Cost, Price and Supply

We should now explore how a competitive producer decides how much to produce. The supply of a competitive market comes from many such producers. Individually each is too small to affect the market price. If one firm raises price, customers will not buy from it. On the other hand, it would be silly to reduce the price when all that the firm can produce can be sold at the higher price that others are selling for. So a competitive firm's decision involves only output or supply, not price. It has to decide the most profitable output at the price it faces.

Let me now introduce a useful measure called *marginal cost*. It is the extra cost of producing an extra unit of a product. More input is needed to produce more output. So, marginal cost must be a positive amount for all kinds of production. Now recall that the marginal product of inputs falls when more input is used. Therefore, when a firm produces more the marginal cost of output cannot stay constant. It has to increase because the firm would need proportionally more inputs for successive units of output.

Now, think of a competitive firm trying to decide its output. If marginal cost for producing a unit of its product is less than its price, the firm will profit by producing the unit. Following this logic, it will continue to increase production as long as marginal cost remains less than the price. But as production increases marginal cost rises too. At some point the marginal cost of producing the good will catch up with its price. The firm should then stop producing any more. That point is the firm's equilibrium production. At that point marginal cost is just equal to price.[5]

So we now know how a competitive firm fixes output when it faces a given price for the product. How will the output be affected if the price of the product increases? Well, if price increases the firm will find that the new price is higher than the marginal cost. This will prompt it to increase production until marginal cost increases and equals the new price. This is why supply positively responds to price, and more supply can be induced with a price increase.[6]

## 2.9 Why Competitive Prices are Special

Let us consider the equilibrium condition for a competitive producer once again. It goes thus: 'Price equals marginal cost'. This means that price reflects the cost of producing an extra unit. Therefore, when buying the product, consumers pay for exactly what it costs to produce one more unit of the product. This is an admirable property when it holds (we will see that it does not hold in many situations). Foremost, it means that competitive prices are fair—a feature we noted earlier. Competitive prices, therefore, provide a benchmark. They are the fairest prices that a market can offer.

This gives us a way of measuring the extent of a market's imperfection. For any given market, we can find out by how much (in percentage terms) the price exceeds the marginal cost of production. That would be a percentage measure of market imperfection. Note that the measure of imperfection of a market is also a measure of the 'unfairness' of the market price. If we have enough data on prices and costs we can make comparisons across markets to see which ones are more competitive and which, more imperfect.

[5]A producer gets no profit from the last unit produced. But all units produced before the last generate profit as price exceeds marginal cost.

[6]There are exceptions, though. In some cases more can be produced at a lower average cost. This means that marginal cost falls with output. We will discuss this case in the next chapter. For now we comfort ourselves that this cannot happen in competitive markets. If average cost were to fall, a firm that started first in the business would produce more than others, make more profit, outgrow others, and become a monopolist.

We know that buyers try to substitute costly goods with cheaper ones if they serve the same purpose. Since prices reflect marginal cost, consumers unknowingly care about the relative resource cost of the things they buy in competitive markets. They shun products that have higher resource costs in favour of those with lower costs. The same goes for producers. A product can be produced by different methods using different mix of inputs. To maximise profits, producers substitute costly inputs by cheaper ones to the extent that technology permits. When they use more of the relatively cheaper inputs, they promote the use of inputs that cost the society less resources to produce.

When these observations are strung together, they represent an overall rationality of the arrangement of competitive markets. This is surprising because buyers' and sellers' actions are not based on any social considerations. Nor are their actions coordinated. It is this property that Adam Smith described as 'the invisible hand' of the market. The following lines from the *Wealth of Nations* are among the most quoted in economics:

Every individual intends only his own gain, and he is in this, as in many other cases, led by an invisible hand to promote an end which was no part of his original intention. By pursuing his own interest he frequently promotes that of society more effectively than when he really intends to promote it.

The first sentence of the quote summarises what we have already discussed. But the second sentence adds something more. It says that markets allocate resources better than any deliberate policy—better 'than when he really intends to promote it'. In other words, an intervention or a regulatory guidance would make resource allocation worse than what competitive markets can attain. The idea has been developed by later economists who show that any intervention in a competitive market results in inefficiency. Inefficiency means that the economy produces less than its potential given its resources. Hence they claim that regulation and intervention lead to a loss to the society. The loss can be measured by the difference between what the economy can produce when efficient and what it actually produces. This is called the 'deadweight loss' from an intervention.

Common examples of intervention are tax or subsidy on goods, rationing, setting of minimum or maximum price, rent control, wage setting, fixing professional fees etc. These examples should not persuade us that market intervention always comes from the government. Private bodies also intervene in markets. A group of producers or traders may fix the price of an item or items. The Organisation of Petroleum Exporting Countries (OPEC) tries to fix petrol and related prices by manipulating production of oil wells. This is a non-market way of setting price and output and so an example of intervention into markets. Similarly, when a business and its trade union together fix its wage structure, it is a market intervention. Guilds or professional bodies often set up their fee structure unilaterally. All these interventions reduce the output of an economy below its potential.

We may consider a sales tax on a product to see why it produces deadweight loss. When a producer has to pay a sales tax, from its accounting perspective, the marginal cost will include the tax. This marginal cost is, therefore, higher than the true marginal resource cost. So the equilibrium price of the product will increase from the true marginal cost to that plus the tax. Clearly, consumers now have to pay more than the resource cost of the product. As a result, they will use less of it than is warranted by resource cost considerations. They may also substitute it with something else—whose resource cost may even be actually higher! Thus, allocative efficiency will be undermined. For similar reasons, subsidised prices are also inefficient. They lead to greater consumption of subsidised items than is justified by resource cost and hence are wasteful. As we know, subsidised power supply leads to over-use of electricity. The same is the case with free water, subsidised office canteens, free office stationery, free or cheap fertiliser and diesel for farmers, and so on.

---

### Box 2.6: Subsidy, Tax and Income Distribution

Subsidies are often (but not always) intended to help low income families. Economists have no objection to such help but they oppose using prices for providing help, for example, by reducing the price of a good for the

*(contd...)*

*Box 2.6 continued.*

beneficiary. Such price tampering produces deadweight loss. Economists suggest that a target beneficiary should be given cash. This will leave price determination to the market. It will not interfere with the ability of prices to allocate resources. This will also give a beneficiary the freedom to spend the cash on substitute products depending on their relative prices, that is, their relative resource costs.

Taxes also distort relative prices as we have already discussed in the text. With taxes, prices cease to correspond to resource costs. However, taxes are unavoidable because they are needed to run governments and provide for public amenities. Given this dilemma, economists propose what is known as the Ramsey rule,[7] which generates the least possible distortion to raise a given amount of tax money. It is based on the following idea. When there are no taxes, the relative demand for different goods reflects relative resource costs. Taxes change this structure arbitrarily. The Ramsey rule proposes a taxation method that keeps the relative demand structure unaffected. It suggests different tax rates for different goods, such that the percentage fall in demand is equal for all of them. Thus, the relative demand structure after taxes would be the same as it was before. It requires that a product whose demand is more sensitive to price increase be taxed at a lower rate than one that is less price sensitive.

The rule would no doubt minimise the deadweight loss to raise any given amount of tax money. However, you can see that it is not egalitarian. Necessities such as food and medicine respond less to price increases because we cannot do without them. On the other hand, the demand for luxury goods responds to price increase significantly. So the rule would mean higher taxes on necessities than on luxury goods. But poorer households spend more of their income on necessities. The Ramsey rule, therefore, raises distributional concerns.

Advocates of the rule suggest that governments should nevertheless persist with it. At the same time they should provide cash compensation to those they think are being unfairly affected by commodity taxes.

[7]The rule is named after its author Frank Ramsey (1903–1929). Ramsey was a legendary whiz-kid of economics. He lived for only 26 years but made several contributions to theoretical economics that continue to be taught today. He also made serious contributions to the logical foundation of mathematics. Ramsey, an Englishman, is reputed to have picked up enough German in a week to help translate Ludwig Wittgenstein's profoundly difficult book *Tractatus Logico-Philosophicus* into English.

## 2.10 Efficiency versus Fairness

We saw that we cannot produce an extra loaf in an efficient equilibrium without producing less of something else. That raises a very important question. If you or anyone else demanded an extra loaf, how would markets decide if it should indeed be produced by giving up something else? And, who decides what to give up? Do we produce less sugar or less milk to accommodate an extra loaf of bread? To put the question differently, what determines the product mix of a market economy?

Markets adjust continuously to supply and demand decisions. It is from these interactions that the product mix emerges. The price of a good rises when demand exceeds supply and falls when supply exceeds demand. These price changes then feed back into the demand and supply decisions and bring them closer. The process goes on until they match. When the matching has occurred for all products, we have the equilibrium product mix. Therefore, product composition ultimately depends on the supply and demand conditions for all products.

We have seen that producers produce up to the point where marginal cost equals the price. Thus, supply of goods depends on their respective cost situation. That, in turn, depends on production technology and the price of inputs. On the other side, demand depends on consumers' tastes and income.

Suppliers get to know demand from buyers' behaviour. Higher demand shows up in many ways, for example, buyers' offer to pay higher prices, order books with more orders, or perhaps a stampede at a film's premiere. We should, however, note that demand that shows itself up along these routes does not necessarily reflect what people need. What gets revealed to suppliers is only the demand backed by money. Low-income buyers may fail to let the market know of their needs because of their lack of purchasing power. Retailers easily notice an increase in the demand for automobiles when purchase and bookings increase. They report this to suppliers, who in turn inform producers leading to an increase in car production. On the other hand, if people starve because they cannot afford food, their demand cannot show up in food stores. So it is not communicated to producers, nor does it bring about an increase in food production. The marketplace is like a voting system where the production of a good depends on the votes it gets from buyers. But the rule here is neither universal suffrage nor one-person one-vote. Those with low income may not have votes at all, while rich voters may have more than one vote. This results in a situation where items necessary for low-income households have a smaller market demand than their real need, but the demand for luxury items is fully expressed in the market.

To put the matter in perspective, product composition depends on supply and demand conditions, but demand in this case is that backed by money. It is not the same thing as need or want. Markets say 'show me your money first'. We sometimes use the phrase 'effective demand' to emphasise that we are referring to demand backed by money.

Note that this is not an issue of efficiency. It is about fairness. A market may be efficient and yet unfair. This is indeed a major criticism of free market policy. Critics claim that its concern for efficiency makes it blind to fairness and income distribution. A question mark hangs around the composition of GDP. Why do we produce so many cars but so few AIDS vaccines? Most AIDS patients being among the poorest of the world, the answer is a no-brainer. These observations lead to the complaint that markets favour the rich. Criticism about unfairness has produced two types of reactions. One is to complement markets with institutions that care for low income households. We observe this kind of arrangement in most countries today where a ministry of welfare looks after poorer households within an unencumbered market system. The second reaction is more radical. It calls for abolishing markets altogether. In the former Soviet Union the government had virtually replaced the market system with price and output decisions of its own.

How do free market economists respond to the question about fairness? Their reaction is similar to what we saw in relation to tax and subsidy. They advise against mixing efficiency of resource use with the issue of income distribution. They suggest that distribution should be settled with the use of non-market instruments, that is, with tools other than prices and production. If the government is concerned about poverty it should give low-income families cash grants so that they can buy more of what they need. The prices of those goods will rise as a result. Suppliers, in turn, will respond and the output mix will change. This course of action will not interfere with the work of markets and will keep resource use efficient.

Helping low-income households is an attempt to redistribute a society's output in their favour to a certain extent. When redistributing the total output or GDP it is sensible to take care that it remains as large as possible. If the government tries to redistribute income by fixing prices or ordering more output of this and less of that, resource use will not follow any optimising rule. The economy will end up with less than its potential maximum output. This is like reducing the size of a cake in an attempt to distribute it fairly. Free market economists point out that it is wiser to ensure that the economy produces as much as possible by keeping production efficient, and then use non-market methods to redistribute the resulting income.

## 2.11 Competitive Labour Markets

We now have a fair idea of the basics of competitive markets. We should, however, look at the labour market separately because it is very important. Let us discuss how wages are fixed in a competitive economy. Recall that a worker is worth hiring to a firm if his marginal product exceeds the wage. As a firm hires more workers the marginal product of labour falls. The firm will go on hiring until marginal product comes down to the level of the wage rate. At this point, wage per hour equals the marginal product of an hour's work. So a worker gets for an hour's work what the employer and the economy would lose if that hour were not worked. In opportunity cost terms, the wage rate will exactly equal the opportunity cost of labour.

This sounds very fair. But can't employers subvert this deal? What stops a firm from paying less than the marginal product? The answer is that as long as wage is less than marginal product, the firm can make more profit by hiring more workers. So it will be foolish for the firm to stop hiring at such a wage. It is in the interest of the firm to continue to hire when the wage is less than the marginal product. But as it does so, marginal product will fall and eventually become equal to the wage. So in a competitive labour market, the wage rate indeed tends to equal the marginal product of labour. However, subversion is possible if the labour market is not competitive. In such markets employers can collude among themselves and set the wage rate below marginal product. But if the labour market is competitive then this possibility is ruled out.

We can deduce the relationship between employment and the wage rate from the fact that marginal product has to be equal to wage. If the wage is high, employers will hire fewer workers because marginal product has to be large enough to match the high wage rate. And, if the wage is low, there will be more hiring until marginal product falls down to the level of the wage. This explains why demand for labour varies inversely with wage rate.

However this does not tell us what wage rate will actually prevail in the market. That it will equal the marginal product of labour does not clinch it because marginal product is not a fixed quantity. So what exactly fixes the wage rate? Well, wage rate is the price of a unit of labour service. Like all other prices, it depends on its demand and supply. Demand for labour, as we just saw, depends on the wage rate and falls with it. On the other hand, supply depends on the choice or compulsion of workers as the case may be. It increases with wage. If the labour market is competitive then the equilibrium wage rate will settle at the point where the demand and supply are equal. Individual firms will face this wage in the labour market. Being competitive firms, they cannot change it. So, they will take it as given and hire up to the point where marginal product equals this wage.

We saw earlier that in equilibrium a worker gets for an hour's work what the economy would lose if that hour were not worked. Since an economy cannot afford to pay more for an hour's work than what it produces, the competitive wage is the fairest wage. However, as already noted, this is true only of competitive labour markets and not all labour markets work competitively. Unskilled labour markets in most countries have chronic over-supply. Rural workers migrate to industrial towns expecting higher incomes. Industry does not have jobs for all of them. So a pool of unemployed workers gets trapped in industrial towns and hangs out there. These people are not in a position to negotiate properly with potential employers. To be able to hold out for a higher wage, they need a fall-back option. They have to be able to live without a job for a reasonable period. This is not the case, particularly in developing economies. Alternatively, workers can threaten to seek jobs with other employers. This too is ruled out if employers collude. Hence, we find a large number of labour markets operating with wage rates below the marginal product of workers. Labour markets can be imperfect for many reasons as we will discuss later. So, we should be careful not to extend the competitive results to all labour markets uncritically.

Coming back to competitive markets, paying labour its marginal product is the best possible incentive that can be provided to workers. Free labour markets are, therefore, in the position of getting the best efforts from workers by providing the right kind of incentive. If rewards are not based on performance or contribution they tend to demoralise the workers and fail to draw out their best efforts.

## 2.12 Prices as Information

In the former Soviet Union and Socialist Bloc countries, governments used to fix output and prices according to the perceived priority of the product. Products which they held as of a low priority were produced in relatively small amounts. They were priced high to discourage consumption. On the other hand, goods accorded a high priority were produced in greater amounts and priced low. Governments used to plan out the price and output of all products in an elaborate exercise. But they could only roughly guess how much consumers would want to buy at prices they set. Hence inevitably there would be supply–demand mismatches. Some goods were in perennial shortage while others rotted in warehouses. Many items widely used in other countries were frowned upon as unnecessary in a socialist society. They were produced in small amounts and as a result their demand was never met. The approach led to long queues in stores. Buyers would try to get to the stores ahead of others to ensure they got those scarce things. Queues for everything grew longer over time as unfulfilled demand piled up.

Needless to say, all this led to widespread resentment among consumers. You may get an idea of the frustration from this little story from a Soviet Bloc country.

Three friends named Capitalism, Socialism, and Communism[8] decided to meet at a café. Capitalism and Communism arrived in time but Socialism did not. After an hour or so Socialism arrived looking tired and bitter. His friends asked, 'Why are you late?' 'I had to queue up for meat', Socialism's reply was short and curt. Hearing this Capitalism looked puzzled. He asked, 'What is a queue?' Communism, however, knew queues all too well, but he also appeared puzzled. He asked, 'What is meat?'

Could these queues have been avoided? To avoid them governments would have to match supply with demand for all items. At the same time, they would have to align prices with resource cost. You may try to imagine what this involves. First, it requires the knowledge of demand for each product at every possible price. The problem is compounded because demands for various goods are inter-connected. Some goods substitute others (these are called substitutes) and some are used together (these are called complements). Thereafter it is necessary to figure out at what price the demand for a product would match its production if prices were to be set at resource cost. Here too the problem is made more difficult as costs are inter-connected. So the procedure amounts to using a system of simultaneous equations to solve for unknown prices. It is these prices that the socialist countries needed for queue-free markets and proper resource use. The number of equations would be as many as there were products—running into hundreds of thousands. And, just to set up the equations would require a stupendous amount of information on demand and costs. Socialist governments did not realise the enormity of the responsibility when they started price setting as a routine political task. Misalignment of supply and demand became one of the biggest economic problems in

[8]Communism is supposed to be the ultimate goal of communists, socialism being a transitional state between it and capitalism.

these countries by the end of 1950s. However, socialist governments liked to believe that the problem was administrative in nature. They focused on stricter management of the supply chain from production points through warehouses to retail outlets. Similarly, they tried to be innovative about the management of queues.

Oskar Lange (1904–1965), a Polish-born US economist was possibly the first to appreciate both the economic and mathematical problems underlying this form of socialist planning. Large-scale numerical computing was becoming possible by the end of the 1950s. Lange suggested that planning offices should set up computing programs to solve demand and supply equation systems. However, this was never tried. If it had, it would have been discovered that there was an impossible subsidiary task, namely, to specify the equations that the computers were expected to solve. An awful lot of information would be necessary to build up the demand and supply equations. On the demand side, they would require information on how much of the product consumers would buy at every possible price. This relation between price and demand for a product is called the demand function. Similarly, to specify the supply side of the equations, they would need to know the cost at every level of production for each product, the cost functions.

In principle, however, a system of inter-dependent equations can be estimated from past data on prices, production, and purchases. But gathering the information for hundreds of thousands of products would use up an enormous amount of time, resources, and expert manpower. More importantly, in countries where consumers had never been able to buy what they wanted (because of queues and rationing), past data would not have revealed the true demand functions.

The socialist pricing fiasco highlights something very important. It shows the immense service that markets provide. The web of markets gathers supply and demand information and makes it available for resource allocation. It does so without costing time, resources, and manpower or even anyone noticing. Prices carry information about cost and consumers' preferences and disseminate them for producers, buyers, and sellers.

---

**Box 2.7: Oskar Ryszard Lange (1904–1965)**

Oskar Lange was a Polish born socialist economist. He went to the US in the mid-1930s. After teaching for a while at the University of Michigan he became a professor at Chicago in 1938. Lange, however, was not part of the so-called 'Chicago school' and used to describe himself as a Marxian economist. He belonged to a very small group of economists who contributed to both mainstream economics and socialist economic principles. His analysis of socialist economies uses the tools of mainstream economics rather than Marxist jargon. This helped a better understanding of socialist economic principles and systems in the West. Lange had a famous debate with Friedrich Hayek about the economic feasibility of socialism. In course of the debate he presented a model of 'market socialism'. The point of the model was that rational resource use through markets can be combined with social ownership of property and capital goods.

Lange maintained relations with the nationalist Polish government in exile until the Second World War. Towards the end of the war he transferred his allegiance to the 'Polish Committee of National Liberation', better known as the 'Lublin Committee'. It was set up by Joseph Stalin just before the end of the war to help establish a communist-dominated Polish government after the war. Lange also served as a mediator between Franklin Roosevelt and Joseph Stalin during negotiations on post-war Polish government and its borders. His joining the Lublin Committee and mixing with the Soviets isolated Lange in western academia after the war. His academic work, however, did not suffer and he remained as prolific as before.

---

## 2.13 Socialists and Big Business: How they Regard Markets

Though markets evolved through many centuries, towards the end this evolution was contemporaneous with the rise of capitalism. This creates the impression, particularly held among socialists, that the market mechanism is itself a capitalist institution set up for exploitation. This is why socialist leaders did not want markets to work freely and resorted to price setting through administrative decrees. Even outside the Socialist Bloc, left-leaning regimes are generally suspicious of markets and resort to administrative pricing of important items. They also prefer to set up important industries in the public sector so as to control their production and prices.

The competitive market mechanism, however, is an institution for resource allocation which can be utilised by any form of government. Oskar Lange's model of market socialism acknowledged this and proposed that socialist societies should use the optimal allocation property of markets. Mikhail Gorbachev,[9] defending his market-oriented reforms, had remarked in 1990, 'The market is not an invention of capitalism. It has existed for centuries. It is an invention of civilization.'

Socialist economies could have done better if they had tried to attain egalitarian income distribution through non-market means, rather than through price fixing and public sector production. In that case they could have left their markets to function normally. Markets would have generated information about resource costs to help them set growth targets, interest rates, and exchange rates—which they tried to fix on the basis of *ad hoc* considerations. Believing that markets would breed capitalism afresh, they tried to guess and set prices, a task that markets do better. Even putting together all the wisdom of leaders and experts, it was impossible to get adequate information on costs and tastes and hence to run markets without queues and allocate resources efficiently.

While socialists are wary of markets in general, big business in industrial countries is wary of competitive markets. As we saw, competitive markets drive prices down to the level of marginal cost. Big business does not like this. It would like to set prices higher. Higher prices, of course, reduce demand to an extent. But so long as demand drops proportionately less than the price hike, profits would increase. Hence, big business is generally interested in subverting competition. Larger companies try various methods to

<hr />

[9]Mikhail Gorbachev became the General Secretary of the Communist Party of the Soviet Union in 1985. At the party congress next year he announced his policy of *glasnost* (openness) and *perestroika* (restructuring) for the Soviet economy as a package of market-oriented reforms. In the West, Gorbachev is credited for ending the Cold War for which he was awarded the Nobel Peace Prize in 1990. He is also seen by many as the person who brought about the collapse of the Soviet Union.

restrict competition. They make agreements among themselves to rig prices, block the entry of potential competitors into the business, and lobby with governments to enact provisions that make entry of competitors difficult. In the next chapter we will take a look at these practices and how they affect the economy.

## 2.14 Summary

We have surveyed the working of competitive markets. If all markets in an economy are competitive, then the economy is expected to be in efficient configuration. This means that it would not be possible to produce more of anything without reducing the output of something else. Hence aggregate production cannot be increased by reallocating inputs across firms or industries. Second, the price of an item equals its marginal cost of production. This implies that the price of a good reflects the cost of production of its last unit. When consumers buy at these prices they unknowingly act according to the relative resource cost of various goods.

However, efficient allocation of resources alone does not settle all issues, the most important being poverty. Some people may not be able to buy the bare necessities even when markets are a hundred per cent efficient. Free market economics claims that this can be addressed by letting the market system function without intervention, and at the same time helping the needy with cash. This would ensure that the cake that we seek to redistribute remains as large as possible while those who do not get adequate income can buy an adequate slice.

The good properties of markets are good only from the point of view of small players. A small producer, a small buyer, and an individual worker benefit if markets are competitive. But larger players—both large producers and large buyers—can gain by subverting competition. Hence competition is often deliberately undermined. This breeds various forms of market imperfections. Market imperfection is also encouraged by the nature of some products and technology. We will discuss such markets in the next chapter.

# 3 Many Forms of Market: Sellers Big and Small

Even as the theory of competitive markets was taking an elegant shape in the 19th century, it was noted that many important markets were not competitive. Monopolies, that is, firms that sell or buy exclusively in a given market had been in existence in Europe since at least the Roman period. Roman emperors granted monopoly rights to favoured senators for public construction, shipping, and trading in salt, grains, and many other items. Nearer to our time, the British and the Dutch East India Companies were established in 1600 and 1602, respectively with exclusive rights for trading in Asia. They preceded James Watt's steam engine that would power the Industrial Revolution by about a hundred and seventy years. Smith commented in the *Wealth of Nations* that it is in the interest of traders to subvert competition and warned that they should be watched. A hundred years later Marxists argued that concentration of industries in the hands of a few capitalist owners was not just an empirical fact but a compulsive tendency of capitalism. Augustin Cournot, a French engineer, tried to analyse the battle of large firms that can influence prices as early as 1838. Soon other attempts were being made to understand non-competitive markets.

## 3.1 Competition and Entry Barriers

The good features of markets noted in the last chapter arise from competition among firms, among buyers, and between them. Competition checks traders' ability to make indefinitely large profits.

In the real world, however, very few markets are competitive in the textbook sense. So we should not expect the virtues of the free market to prevail in every situation.

Wherever possible, traders and producers work to restrict competition so as to shake off the constraints on their profits. This produces market forms that are generally called non-competitive. In these markets, prices are greater than marginal cost and, therefore, consumers are the losers. Consumers also lose in a more subtle way. When prices do not reflect opportunity costs, resources are not used in the best possible way. Hence the economy produces less than its potential and generates less income and fewer jobs. In this chapter we will take a look at non-competitive markets.

First, of course, we should clarify what a competitive market is. The basic feature of a competitive market is that no buyer or seller is big enough to influence the going price. Sellers and buyers in these markets are called price-takers rather than price-setters. The most important requirement of a competitive market is that individual buyers and sellers should be small compared to the volume of trading in that market. That would ensure that none of them can individually affect the price by its sale or purchase. A few structural features are also significant. Price has to be equal in all parts of the market. Further, market participants in all parts of the market must have full knowledge of the current price. If price is not known in some part of the market, a seller or a buyer can take advantage of the situation and influence price in his favour, locally. Next, the product has to be reasonably homogeneous. If a market sells a range of different types of the same generic product, then each type of product develops a market of its own. Each market would then have a different demand, supply, and price. Each of these markets will have a relatively small number of buyers and sellers even if the market for the generic product has many. So it is important that the product should be reasonably homogeneous across the whole market. Finally, buyers and sellers must not know one another. They must remain anonymous. This ensures that there is no special advantage in buying from the local politician's shop or selling to the police officer's wife. If these advantages existed, then the politician or the police officer could exert an influence on price.

---

### Box 3.1: Adam Smith Once Again

Adam Smith is both credited and criticised for his views on competitive markets—the so-called invisible hand. But it is not well-known that he also observed that competition is widely subverted by traders and hence we need to be watchful of them. This observation was made in *Wealth of Nations* where he had discussed the idea of the invisible hand. He commented on a spate of business laws and regulations that were coming up in the England of his time. These laws granted various rights of association to traders. In this connection he noted, '… the price of free competition … is the lowest which the sellers can commonly afford to take, and at the same time continue their business', and therefore, '… to narrow the competition is always the interest of the dealers … The proposal of any new law or regulation of commerce … comes from an order of men, whose interest is never exactly the same with that of the public, who have generally an interest to deceive and even to oppress the public, and who accordingly have, upon many occasions, both deceived and oppressed it.'[1]

As Smith noted, 'to narrow the competition is always the interest of the dealers'. Non-competitive markets result from narrowing of competition. Generally, though not in every case, collusion among traders or between traders and the institutions such as bureaucracy, political parties, or trade unions gives rise to non-competitive markets.

---

Incumbent sellers in a non-competitive market make it difficult for new sellers to enter the market. This is done by setting up difficulties generally known as entry barriers. However, if a market has no such barriers, it can work like a competitive market even when it does not have very many sellers. In this case even if there are only a few sellers—even if only one—they cannot maintain an artificially high price for long. If they do, potential entrants to the market will sense the extra profit and will surely enter the market and set up shops. Then, not only would the price fall but the number of sellers being now more, each would have a smaller market share. Knowing this, the best move for an existing firm is to keep the price close to marginal

---

[1]The first quote is from Book I, Chapter VII and the second from Book I, Chapter XI of the *Wealth of Nations*. I have omitted words from the quote as shown with ellipsis.

cost and enjoy a large market share. Potential entrants in that case would know that if they were to sell in this market, they would have to sell at marginal cost. Hence they would not find the market attractive. So the market may continue to have a few sellers, and yet price would remain close to the marginal cost. If a market is free of all entry barriers, it is called a contestable market. A contestable market produces a competitive outcome if it has many buyers even if it does not have many sellers.

Therefore, a general recipe for getting markets to deliver the best social effects is to keep them open to potential entry. On the other side, incumbent sellers would like to restrict competition and try to establish entry barriers. Barriers are set up in many ways. Incumbent firms can form a cartel, that is, a formal or informal agreement. When an outside firm shows interest in the market, the cartel manipulates the market price in such a way as to discourage the outside firm. A common practice is to reduce the price. Potential entrants know that if they join the market, they would have to sell at this price and make a loss—perhaps indefinitely. In many countries cartels are prohibited by law; but informal understanding is difficult to prove and stop. Other common methods are acquisition of smaller firms by large ones, negotiated mergers, and control of industry by interlocking boards of directors and ownership.

Incumbents of an industry sometimes lobby with the government for laws and institutions that can make the entry of new firms difficult. They try to convince the government of the merits of these proposals. If and when they succeed, the industry becomes less competitive. For example, an industry or trade lobby can persuade the government to impose licensing requirements. This makes new entry not just costly because of the licence fee, but also difficult because the government bureaucracy has to be 'satisfied' with the merit of the applicant. Public offices that issue these licenses can be 'captured', as it is described colourfully, by the existing clique of the industry. In some cases, the industry itself gets the right to select new entrants. In many countries, guilds of surgeons, pharmacists, paramedics, electricians etc. decide who are qualified to join those trades. Associations of auditors control entry into the profession of external auditing in all countries. Such associations are presumably set up with the intention of assuring service quality. They however restrict competition in the end.

Apart from all these, there are legally created monopolies. Governments give monopoly right to selected private or public firms. This is common in defence production where strategic reasons and secrecy are used to justify the decision. Until recently, public sector monopoly used to be common in post and telegraph, water and power supply, railways and so on. The practice still continues in many countries. In some countries, insurance, banking, and dealing in foreign exchange are also reserved for one or a few public sector companies.

In the real world, a market for a relatively homogeneous product with a large number of buyers and sellers who do not know one another approximates the idea of competitive markets. Wholesale markets for grains, fruits, vegetables, cut flowers, cattle, poultry etc., and stock markets where corporate shares are traded are good examples. Internet trading sites too work like competitive markets. Typically they have many buyers; sellers have no entry barrier except to pay a commission to the site after a sale; the price of the product is posted and is known to all concerned; and buyers and sellers are completely anonymous. Neither a buyer nor a seller can influence the price by acting individually.

## 3.2 Variety of Market Forms

Most markets that we deal with as householders are not competitive. To understand their working, we first need to classify them in ways that might help further analysis. One possible classification is by the difficulty that potential sellers and buyers have to face to enter the market. If entry is completely unrestricted, we have a perfectly competitive market. At the other extreme, strong entry barriers result in a monopoly with a single seller. More generally, industrial markets are dominated by oligopoly with strong barriers. An oligopoly has a few sellers and so each has some degree of control over price. There are also markets with a single *buyer* or a small group of buyers. For example, a small country may have only one large engineering firm. Engineering graduates would then face a single buyer for their services. Governments often give themselves the right of sole buyer for agricultural output, minerals etc. Obviously the single buyer would have a lot of control over the price at which it buys. These markets are called monopsony (one buyer) and oligopsony (a few buyers).

Another way of classification is by the degree of homogeneity of the product. As we have noted, a market with many buyers and sellers tends to be competitive only if the product is homogeneous. Some generic products, particularly consumer goods, can be easily made somewhat different by adding extra features. Toothpaste, for example, is a generic product which can be easily differentiated by adding fluoride, chlorophyll, germicides, whiteners, and so on. After adding the features, a producer tries to represent it as a different product. Thus it develops a niche market for the differentiated product. Though its demand stays closely related to the price of other products of the generic group, the producer can price his product relatively more freely. This kind of product differentiation gives rise to a very common market form called monopolistic competition. The phrase is intended to capture the idea that each producer holds a monopoly of its differentiated product, and yet competes vigorously in the overall generic market. Most industrial consumer product markets are of this kind. On the other side, if a product is fairly homogeneous and difficult to differentiate, then it is sold in a competitive market or an oligopolistic market, depending on the ease with which competing firms can enter the market.

## 3.3 Monopolies and how they Develop

The polar opposite of perfect competition is monopoly. It is a market with only one seller. A monopolist has a lot of control on the price at which it sells. It charges the price that would be most profitable given its cost of production. Recall that it is competition that brings prices down to marginal cost, so price in a monopoly market will surely be above the marginal cost. In other words, monopolies force buyers to pay more than the opportunity cost of the product. This results in less consumption and production than is warranted by the resource cost of producing the good. The economy loses because less is produced. Less production means less income and fewer jobs.

Monopoly also affects the quality of the product. Because consumers have nowhere else to buy from, the producer may become indifferent to quality and service.

Monopolies have very strong entry barriers that arise in many different ways. Sometimes, a monopolist owns a key input so that no one else can produce the product. The input may be a patent right or a crucial part of its manufacturing process. Drug companies owning patented formulations act as monopolists in the market for that drug. There are European firms that own natural water sources *believed to be* indispensable for a particular grade of whisky. Some firms own grape farms in counties *believed to have* unique soil and climate for particular type of grapes. They enjoy monopoly of particular brands of whiskey and wines. Note the words in italics. The resource need not be indispensable in a basic chemical, physical, or engineering sense. If buyers believe that it is indispensable, then they would also be convinced that others cannot produce it. In effect the firm would enjoy monopoly.

Monopoly also results from collusion among sellers. Sellers may form a formal or informal association—a *trust* or a *cartel*. The cartel sets price and output on behalf of the members. It sets the price that a monopolist would have set in this market and thus generates the maximum possible profit. At this price the market is expected to buy a projected amount. The production of this amount is shared among members according to an agreed formula. If outsiders try to enter the industry, the trust cuts the price discouraging the potential entrant. Thus the cartel itself sets up barriers to continue as a monopoly.

The hold of a monopoly on its market cannot be very strong if there are close substitutes of its product. Consumers would switch to the substitutes if the monopoly gets too demanding. Monopolies therefore try to convince buyers that their products are special and cannot be replaced with substitutes. The famous diamond company DeBeers of South Africa controls more than eighty per cent of the world's diamond production. It is a monopolist for all practical purposes because other producers are very small and very many. Surprisingly, De Beers spends a lot of money on ads. You might puzzle, if it really controls the global market, why does it have to spend so much on ads? The answer is that there are many possible substitutes for diamonds for DeBeers' wealthy customers: pearls, sapphires, emeralds, rubies, and so on. DeBeers' runs a very high-profile advertisement campaign which has the bottomline slogan 'a diamond is forever'. The campaign tries to convince the consumers that a diamond is in a class by itself among the group of precious stones.

To eliminate competition from close substitutes, monopolies often produce the substitutes themselves. Global leaders of the breakfast cereal market produce a range of cereal products. Only a few of them are revenue earners. Others are close substitutes. They are made by mixing grains and fruits in alternative combinations that might catch the fancy of an odd novelty-seeking customer here or a health-watcher there. Even though they do not sell much, they adorn supermarket shelves. They simply jam the space for a possible newcomer's breakfast product. They signal a threat to potential competitors that charging into the market with a close substitute will not work.

Early in the history of capitalism, monopolies were created by governments rather than by business itself. In the seventeenth century, European governments granted sole rights to lucrative trade with Asia to their favoured trading companies. Typically, kings and noblemen were the stockholders of these companies or would hold other kinds of stake. The right granted was called a monopoly. Monopoly as a right sanctioned by the government has continued into the present days. Governments can create statutory monopolies by giving exclusive production right for certain products or services. In many countries the government creates companies in the public sector and gives them monopoly right to produce defence related goods and services. Government monopolies in utilities such as power, gas, water, postal service, railways, etc. are common. They were more widespread before the 1990s. Since the mid-1980s, some governments have dismantled them for reasons we will take up below. Governments also grant exclusive right to private firms. This generally occurs when a government is unable to develop its minerals, oil, gas, etc. or infrastructure such as ports, airports, power, and so on. It invites private firms for the job. These firms then demand and obtain exclusive right.

## 3.4 Can a Monopoly Charge any Price?

Is there a limit to a monopolist's ability to increase price and make profit? Surely there must be such a limit; because profit comes from buyers and the buyers' income is after all limited. So price cannot be indefinitely raised and there is a best price for a monopolist. It is the price that gets the highest possible profit in the given market situation. We can easily see how it is decided. When the firm increases price, demand would certainly fall. But that does not mean that its sales revenue would also fall. If price is increased by 1 per cent and demand falls by less than 1 per cent, then clearly sales revenue increases as a result of the price increase. As long as the situation is like this, a monopolist would like to increase price. Note that in this situation revenue increases by selling less! So fewer units are produced, and that saves on production cost as well. Therefore, overall profit increases in this situation as the monopolist raises price. However, the situation cannot continue indefinitely. When price becomes very high, a further 1 per cent increase is likely to lead to more than 1 per cent fall in demand. This would then reduce the firm's sales earning. The firm however will not stop here. It would raise price a bit further beyond this point. Raising the price reduces demand and thus saves some production cost. If the cost saving is more than the fall in sales revenue, it still makes sense to keep increasing the price. The monopolist will finally stop when the fall in sales revenue threatens to exceed the production cost saving.

This means that the limit to market power depends on how rapidly demand falls when price increases. To use economic jargon, it depends on the *price elasticity of demand*. Price elasticity of demand shows the percentage fall in demand when price increases by 1 per cent. It is different for different products. Also, for the same product it is different at different prices. It depends on the availability of close substitutes. If there are close substitutes, then demand will be more elastic, that is, it will fall more for each per cent rise of price. As price rises, buyers switch to the available substitutes. As already noted, a monopoly enjoys a lot of freedom if there is no close substitute in sight.

However, if you think of the world of products and services, you will readily see that there is no product without a good substitute or at least a potential substitute. If a product becomes too costly, potential substitutes which were not commercially viable earlier become so now, and spring up in the market. As we are witnessing right now, increase in petrol price is making it possible for bio-fuel to compete with it. Similarly nuclear, solar, and wind power too have become viable power sources while just forty years ago it was doubted if they would ever be commercially produced. Monopolists have to keep this aspect of the effect of pricing into account. The upshot is that monopolists too have limits to their powers of pricing.

## 3.5 Antitrust Laws

Restricting the entry of rival companies into the market and unfairly blocking their business operations are called anti-competitive or restrictive practices. Many countries have laws against them. The tradition of similar regulations goes back more than two thousand years in India and to the Roman Empire in Europe. In the modern period, the US has the oldest history of actively using anti-monopoly laws which are known as Antitrust Laws. They date back to 1890 when the first US federal law was enacted to curb monopolies. The 1890 act is popularly known as the Sherman Act and is still used as the basis for most antitrust charges filed by the US federal government.

---

**Box 3.2: Microsoft and Antitrust**

One of the most high profile antitrust suits in recent times was that against Microsoft which started in 1997. Microsoft was also dragged to court by Europe's Competition Commission. After a long-drawn legal battle, Microsoft was ruled to have breached competition in both cases and suitable settlements were reached. It was tried for two serious anti-competitive breaches. First, it was 'bundling' other Microsoft software along with Windows. So, a buyer who bought Windows would not need software from its competitors. Windows being virtually the only disc operating system, it would mean that almost all computer buyers would stop buying software from Microsoft's rivals. This practice, known as bundling, is a serious anti-competitive practice. Most prominent of the

---

*(contd...)*

*Box 3.2 continued.*

items bundled with Windows was Microsoft's web browser, Internet Explorer. It was identified as a move aimed against Netscape's browser Netscape Navigator. Netscape's usage share fell drastically, from above 90 per cent to close to nothing, during the period when Internet Explorer was supplied with every Windows system. The other offence, around which the European case centred, was withholding some crucial information about the Windows network needed by other companies' software to be compatible with it.

US courts take the position that certain business actions do restrict competition; but they cannot be prohibited simply because of this. If a business takes such actions, then it is required to satisfy the court that the motive was neither profit, nor harming the interests of its competitors. Suppose an electrical implements manufacturer always buys parts from its wholly owned subsidiary and never from other companies. But other companies sell those parts at a price no higher than the subsidiary. The government can use this behaviour as *prima facie* evidence of a restrictive business practice and bring charges against the company. The company can, however, argue that it uses parts from its own subsidiary to ensure that consumer safety standards are met. If the company can convince the court that parts available in the market do not meet safety standards as rigorously as those from its subsidiary, it will probably get a favourable ruling. Though competition is restricted, courts would probably rule that antitrust laws have not been violated as the motive is consumer safety rather than limiting competition for profit.

## Box 3.3: India's MRTP Act and The Competition Act

The Government of India passed the Monopolies and Restrictive Trade Practices (MRTP) Act in 1969. The stated aim was to prevent concentration of economic power in a few large companies. Though India had very large government monopolies in certain lines, the MRTP Act left the public sector corporations and government departmental

*(contd...)*

*Box 3.3 continued.*

enterprises out of its purview. It also left out trade unions and co-operatives.

In spite of MRTP, Indian industry on the eve of liberalisation in 1991 was far from competitive. Most observers think that the MRTP, together with other features of India's industrial policy, helped rather than curbed the concentration of economic power. India had a policy of industrial licensing at that time. Producers were required to get a licence to install production capacity. The government wanted to use licensing to keep an eye on the size of private business houses and industrial concentration. But in practice, the licence became a serious entry barrier for new business, thus encouraging concentration. Second, monopoly/oligopoly prevailed in many industries simply because the government had set up public sector firms in core industries where private firms were not allowed a licence.

The MRTP Act was also somewhat toothless as it did not incorporate adequate detail to enable legal proceedings. It did not provide legal definitions of a variety of practices such as collusion and price fixing, cartels, bid rigging, refusal to do business with specific parties, predatory pricing, etc. which are common anti-competitive moves. In the absence of clear-cut legal definitions, it was difficult to bring offenders to book.

In the post-reform environment, MRTP was considered obsolete and need was felt for an act with emphasis on promoting competition rather than restricting monopoly. The Competition Act of 2002 resulted from this new thinking. The Act also created a statutory commission called the Competition Commission of India as the successor of the MRTP Commission. The Commission is not only an enforcement agency but also advises the government on competition policy and it has been given extra-territorial jurisdiction.

## 3.6 Natural Monopoly

Until the 1980s, most countries had government monopoly in some of these sectors: power, water supply, postal service, telecommunications, railways, ports, aviation, and defence production. Of these industries, monopoly in defence production is generally justified by considerations of secrecy and national interest. For the others the rationale comes from a peculiar feature common to all of them. They require very large initial outlays. Consider the railways. It requires laying tracks, producing coaches and freight carriages, and setting up rail stations, signal posts, rail-road crossings, and related administration. Power supply requires setting up means for power generation and a network for transmission, and so on. But once the infrastructure has been built, the cost of producing an extra unit of the product or service is quite small. As a result, the average cost of output gets lower when more is produced. A power network supplying to 5,000 households would operate at much higher average cost than one supplying to 50,000 households.

It is obvious that in these industries it is better to have fewer producers than many. Suppose a township has 10,000 households and two power companies supply to 5,000 of them each. They would both have higher average cost than if only one of them operated and supplied to all the households. So it costs a society less if only one company operates. This is then a situation where competition costs the society more than monopoly! The reason is that while average cost increases with output in most other industries, it falls in this select group of industries. These industries are described as *natural monopolies*.

Natural monopolies present a number of difficult problems. Because one firm would produce at a lower cost than many, it is tempting to think that the government should select a good firm and give it a monopoly right. But that does not help. Suppose a firm has been given the monopoly right for production and distribution of power. Then the firm will set a monopoly price and produce the relatively small amount that can be sold at this price. So if monopoly is to be granted at all, the government has to include a pricing formula as part of the deal. But that raises a difficult question. At what price should the company be asked to sell power? What principles should form the basis of pricing?

We have seen that the condition for efficiency is 'price equals marginal cost'. So we might think that the producer should charge a price equal to the marginal cost of production. Because the government would have an estimate of the amount of power consumption of the locality, it can also roughly work out the marginal cost of production at that level. The company may be asked to set unit power price around that benchmark. This would ensure efficiency and optimal use of power by consumers.

But this pricing formula will not be accepted by the company. We noted that in power, as in other natural monopolies, average cost falls when more is produced. So, marginal cost of a unit of power is always less than its average cost.[2] This means that if power is sold at marginal cost, the firm will recover less than its average cost of production for each unit it sells. It will incur a loss. No private company would agree to sell a natural monopoly product on the marginal cost pricing formula.

One way out is to nevertheless ask the firm to sell at marginal cost and then allow it to recover the loss in some way that would not affect resource allocation. The loss plus an agreed normal amount of profit can be recovered through a fixed charge on each consumer. This is indeed done in practice. You might have noticed that there is a monthly rent on the power meter. Meter rent is a fixed charge. It is calculated to compensate the power company for its loss by selling at the government's price formula. There are similar meter rents for water, gas, and telephone sets on land lines. Because the meter rent does not depend on how much or how little power a consumer uses, it does not affect the marginal decisions of users and so does not affect resource allocation.

If a natural monopoly product is produced by a public sector company, it can be asked to use the same principle—marginal cost pricing and a flat charge. Alternatively, its loss from marginal cost pricing can be compensated through the government budget. The government, in this case, gives the company an annual transfer from its budget. This method was common in the past and is still used in some countries. However, it violates a basic value of private economies. It goes against the user-should-pay principle. An example will make this clear. Not all tax-payers have a telephone. Hence, compensation from the budget for the loss of a government telephone company means that those who do not use telephones also pay for the loss. This will be considered unfair. Besides unfairness, transfer of funds from the government budget may condone poor management. Some of the loss may be due to sheer bad management.

---

[2]Average can fall only if the last unit is less than the average. Recall that a cricketer's batting average can fall only if he scores less in the present innings than his average. So falling average cost means that marginal cost is less than average.

Because it is difficult to separate the loss from pricing and that from bad management, the company will recover the entire loss from the government budget. It will then mean that tax payers have to pay for poor management as well. At the same time, by not penalising bad management, the practice helps foster a culture of indifferent management in government companies.

Of late, there has been a lot of change in the way we think about the production of utilities by governments. It is now thought that the government should set up a company to organise production and supply. The management of the company can then be contracted out along commercial lines. In this arrangement the managers and staff of the company would be employees of the entity that takes up the contract. The company has to earn its income from its operations and make enough profit for investment in capacity and quality. It is obliged to follow an agreed price plan and maintain certain specified quality parameters. While formulating prices for the contract, the government should build into it the so-called marginal cost pricing principle and a set of fixed user charges. The contract would be terminated and given to another party if quality falls below the stipulated level. This arrangement called 'outsourcing' is now practiced quite widely. We will discuss the pros and cons of outsourcing below.

## 3.7 Are Natural Monopolies really 'Natural'?

Government monopoly in utilities has come under sharp scrutiny since the 1980s. In many countries these companies were routinely making losses. Governments had to borrow money to cover the losses. Funding of losses and interests on loans often pre-empted spending on health, education, and infrastructure. Added to this were complaints of poor quality and service. Further, some governments were found to be using utility companies for political benefit. They would influence voters with subsidised utility services. The practice would further increase losses and put greater strain on the government budget.

The first round of suggestions from economists at this point was that utilities be contracted out to private companies along the lines we have discussed above. A more radical suggestion soon followed.

It called for selling off the companies to private business. This was expected to save government budgets from perennial losses. But there is no guarantee that a private party would provide any better service or would not raise prices once it buys the outfit. Of course, there would be no entry barrier in the new environment and other firms could set up business and compete. But whoever buys the outfit first would easily fend off potential competitors. Recall that these industries have falling average cost. Whoever comes first starts off by supplying to the entire market. So it would have a much lower average cost than any company which tries to enter at a later date. In fact, no competitor would consider joining the industry because they would know this.

In this backdrop, it was realised in the 1980s that natural monopolies can be operated in a very different way. These industries had changed enormously from the time of their first appearance in Europe. Over more than a hundred odd years, both technology and the market for utilities had changed enormously. These industries had become enormous, serving country-sized markets as opposed to a number of towns and cities in the early days. In the environment of the 1980s it appeared possible to break up the operation of a natural monopoly into a number of component businesses. Not all the components produced from the break up would have the feature of decreasing average cost. Some of them could indeed work in competitive or contestable markets. As an example, think of power supply once again. The older business model was this: a government or private monopoly owned and operated power generation facilities; owned and maintained power lines; connected retail buyers to power; and finally was involved in billing and bill collection. These activities can be easily separated. Power generation can be detached from the rest of the activities and operated by a few competing public or private firms. The government can then lease out or sell off the existing power lines to a number of companies to get rent or one-off revenue. These line companies would allow competing power generating companies to use the lines as grid to which competing retail companies connect up and distribute power to users. In this arrangement, consumers have the choice of buying from a number of retailers who compete with price and service quality. Power generators, when selling to retailers compete in terms of the schedule of price at various hours of the day. The line companies compete by providing cheaper use of lines to power generators and retailers, providing shorter routes and congestion free networks. To make their competitive position stronger they would construct new lines and shorter routes as part of business.

Many countries broke up their utility industries in the late 1980s and 1990s. The so-called natural monopolies of the past disappeared, making room for intermediate industries where business can work on competitive lines. Governments not only got rid of perennially loss-making businesses but got one-time revenue or a source of permanent income from the lease. Consumers gained from the competition that led to better service quality. Overall, the economies gained because resource use became more rational.

---

**Box 3.4: Privatising Utilities**

The transition from government monopoly to the regime of competing private component industries has been a big affair—both economic and political—wherever it has taken place. Government utility companies are large employers. In some countries, the government sector used to be the largest source of organised employment. A condition of smooth transition is that their employees be re-employed by the newly formed companies that replace the government companies. It is, however, certain that all of them would not find re-employment. Government utilities are generally run by more workers and officers than needed. In fact, that is a major reason for their inefficiency. Naturally, private companies would not like to carry the baggage of unnecessary payroll.

Countries that made a relatively smooth transition have relied on a number of measures. First, they persuaded a section of employees to voluntarily walk out in exchange for a sizeable one-off payment. The cost of the deal was partly recovered from private companies who bought the utilities. This option was generally accepted by workers close to retirement or those who feared that they would not do well in the private sector environment. Second, governments persuaded some of the workforce to become self-employed in a related trade in which they had expertise. The government provided financial and technical support for self-employment.

---

*(contd...)*

*Box 3.4 continued.*

> After the voluntary retirees and the self-employment seekers left, the problem became more manageable. Finally, the government provided for a so-called 'safety net', figuratively, to catch those who fell off during the transition. In practical terms, the net was a set of provisions like unemployment benefit, free training with new skills, and help with job placement. Countries that made a relatively smooth transition were those that already had a well-running unemployment benefit system in place.

## 3.8 Monopolistic Competition

The word monopoly creates in our mind an image of a gigantic corporation with all the pomp and glitz of the corporate world. But as we noted earlier, there are many small business units which enjoy a sort of monopoly because they can effectively differentiate their products from the rest of the generic market. They become the sole seller of their own differentiated product. Restaurants in a city make a good example. They all sell the same generic service—dining out. Yet, they all try to make their product special. They introduce differences in food, recipes, crockery, service style, and innovation in the shop's décor. Some might install TV screens for viewing sports as you eat your food to attract sports fans and younger clients. Some may locate at a scenic area, hire renowned chefs, and target the higher income end of the market. Essentially, all of them try to carve out a niche and operate like a monopolist in that niche. To operate like a monopolist means to be able to set the price rather than being forced to sell at the price of other sellers. They escape being price-takers like competitive sellers. However, they are less fortunate than the big monopoly houses because their products substitute one another's fairly closely. A Thai food shop round the corner is a monopolist but its monopoly power is small. The range within which it can set its meal prices is certainly cramped.

The market structure that results from this kind of business is called monopolistic competition. It arises if it is relatively inexpensive to differentiate the product and there is no serious barrier to entering the market as a seller and setting up a shop. Often a seller can differentiate by simply choosing the location of its stall differently.

All ice-cream vendors in a small town would be selling the same ice creams manufactured by the lone ice cream producer in the township. But some would differentiate their product by selling near the school gate and others near the movie theatre. They may be able to charge slightly different prices because of their different clientele.

Monopolistic competition is the dominant mode of business in personal services. Tea and coffee shops, motels, hotels, barber shops, convenience stores, beauty services, massage and physiotherapy, educational institutions, and so on try to differentiate by service features and location to snatch some freedom to set prices. It is also widespread in consumer products when there is no serious entry barrier. Manufacturers try to add features to the generic consumer product. They spend a significant amount to advertise their special features. In turn, consumers may develop brand preference. Once that happens, the producer has a fairly secure niche. Preference for brands is widely cultivated in toiletry and personal products: toothpastes, soaps, shaving items, perfumes, cosmetics, readymade fashion wear, style accessories, sauces, spices, and so on. Similarly, product differentiation and monopolistic competition are prevalent in motor cars, two-wheelers, and personal electronics. Manufacturers spend money to develop the so-called brand loyalty. Apart from boosting current sales, an established brand name is an asset which can be sold.

## 3.9 Product Differentiation: A Waste of Resource?

Because monopolistic competition is so widespread, the total spending on product differentiation is quite large in today's economies. Is this a waste of resources? To go into this issue, we should note that spending for differentiation has two parts: (i) adding or changing features and (ii) advertising that the difference is important. The first part can be seen as an improvement in consumer product and services. Continuous improvement in products and services that we have got used to comes from this line of spending. This spending has made today's cars and personal electronics so much more useful than those that were available only a few years ago. Unless we dismiss features and conveniences as unnecessary frills or flourish, this spending is to be counted as useful. The second part of the differentiation is spent on advertisement and it is this that many have argued to be wasteful. In the US, total advertisement expenditure has varied between 2 to 2.5 per cent of GDP since the middle of 1980s. Assuming that it was 2.5 per cent in 2010, advertisement expenditure would have been about US $ 366 billion, an amount greater than two and a half times the GDP of New Zealand in that year. Is this stupendous spending socially useful or a mindless waste? The question has been raised again and again.

As you can expect, for this type of question, the answer is that some items of the spending are useful while others are not. It is difficult to come up with a clear cut estimate of what proportion is useful. Some advertisements inform consumers about quality, features, price, discounts, and location. It is easy to see that this part is socially useful because it reduces consumers' search cost. But the rest of the expenditure cannot be entirely written off. Brand names often serve a purpose for consumers and hence spending to develop them is at least partly useful in many cases. Brands cannot be built in a day, and an established brand is the result of performance and consumer acceptance over a long period. Hence a well-established brand name signals a reliable product or service. This is often a big help to consumers who are new in a market or those who want to avoid too much search. An American travelling through an unknown town and looking for clean and hygienic food settles for McDonald's or Pizza Hut without hesitation. Buyers who are not technology savvy can buy established electronic brands with confidence. In the absence of brands, consumers might have to spend a significant amount of resources in researching, visiting markets, and contacting fellow consumers, which is saved by branding. So those advertisements that appear to be mindless displays of a brand name or logo are not entirely useless for the society. On the other hand, when two established brands, that the market is well aware of, start an advertisement battle, the resources spent are clearly a social waste.

## 3.10 How Oligopolies Fight it Out

I mentioned oligopoly earlier. It is a market for a relatively homogeneous product with a small number of sellers. So, each seller can influence price to an extent by selling more or selling less. Oligopolies selling the same product share a given market demand. This is what makes oligopoly different from monopolistic competition. In the latter, each seller has a separate demand for its niche product. However, price charged by one oligopoly or how much it sells affects other oligopolies in the same market. An action by one leads others to change their price or sales decisions, and in turn this might lead the first firm to change its action too. Hence an oligopoly decides about its moves, much like in a game of chess, by thinking of the likely effects of its action on competitors.

For this reason oligopoly decisions are called 'strategic'. An oligopoly cares not only about demand and cost, but also about competitors' moves. The analysis of how an oligopoly business goes on, how decisions are made and battles fought is interesting and intriguing. The strategic aspect of their behaviour is analysed by using Game Theory, a branch of mathematics that analyses interactive decision making.

The first analysis of oligopoly appeared quite early. In 1838 a French mathematician and engineer named Augustin Cournot (1801–1877) produced an analysis[3] that is still part of the economics curriculum. Around this time, scholars with mathematics, engineering, and science backgrounds were taking interest in economic issues and formalising them with mathematical reasoning. Cournot analysed a scenario where only two firms shared a market and were trying to decide their best quantity of sale. The two were competing to get the most profit at the expense of the other. The market with two sellers is called a duopoly and is a convenient starting point for understanding oligopoly. Cournot worked out the eventual equilibrium of the market, that is, who sells how much and the price at which the market would settle. The analysis gave us a method which can be extended to oligopoly with more firms. The Cournot Model, as it is called now, is the first idea introduced in a course on oligopoly.

When oligopolies battle it out, they use a variety of weapons. These are not only price-cutting and sale but include signals to competitors about their strength and resolve. Aggressive advertisement is a common signal. So is building up a large

---

[3]Chapter 7 of *Researches into the Mathematical Principles of the Theory of Wealth* by Cournot, translated by N.T. Bacon, Macmillan, 1897.

production capacity. Both require significant investment. By committing investment, a firm sends the message that it is in the market for the long haul; it would not yield to competitive threats or price cuts. Cournot developed a method rather than a realistic model. He assumed that the two firms compete using supply as the strategic variable. If one of them increases supply, it will reduce the price for both because the market is the same for both. That is how the actions of the two firms affect each other. For every supply of firm 1, for firm 2 there would be a supply that gives it the maximum possible profit. Cournot showed a method of working out the supply of firm 1 for all possible supply decisions of firm 2, and similarly the supply of firm 2 in response to supplies of firm 1. Equilibrium is attained when the supply of each firm is its best response given the supply of the other. This idea of equilibrium makes common sense because in this situation there is no reason for either firm to want to change its supply unilaterally.

Models of oligopoly in use today are far more complex. They try to simulate the multifaceted battles of oligopolies. Firms take decisions at a number of stages. For example, entry into a market and the decision of the initial production capacity to be installed are strategic decisions in themselves which must consider the response of other players. This is only the first stage of a protracted war. In the next stage, the firm has to decide about price setting and amount of production. Then or at the same time comes advertising and so on. The models also incorporate other oligopoly weapons. The purpose of these models is to explain observed market events and to help with prediction.

## 3.11 Why don't Oligopolies Co-operate?

It should be obvious that at the end of the day the battle is about market share—who sells how much in the common marketplace. In Cournot's model and in others developed since, duopolies or oligopolies fight out for market share with strategies and counter-strategies. Equilibrium is a configuration of shares that no firm would like to change unilaterally. This kind of equilibrium is called a non-cooperative or competitive equilibrium. It means that firms do not approach one another to work out a market-sharing formula.

Yet, they could be better off by doing just that. If both parties in a duopoly bury the hatchet then they can work together as if they are a monopoly. They can set price at the level that a monopolist would have done for the given demand condition. A monopolist gets the maximum possible profit in any given condition. So at monopoly price, sales will produce the largest profit possible. The two parties simply have to share the sale according to an agreed formula. This kind of arrangement is called a cartel. I mentioned earlier that cartels are banned in many countries. So, when they arise, they develop as informal and un-written agreements.

---

**Box 3.5: Organization of Petroleum Exporting Countries (OPEC)**

OPEC is one of the best known international cartels and has remained in the centre of the news since the 1970s. It was formed in 1960. Its membership has increased over time and current members are Algeria, Angola, Ecuador, Iran, Iraq, Kuwait, Libya, Nigeria, Qatar, Saudi Arabia, the United Arab Emirates, and Venezuela. Indonesia, an ex-member dropped out after 2008 because it had become a net importer of oil and was unable to meet the production quota of the cartel. Like all cartels, OPEC restricts output to keep prices high. If oil producing firms were to behave non-cooperatively, price would fall because of competition. Output would be larger. The cartel arrangement prevents this.

However, OPEC's control on oil price has waned since the first 'oil shock' of 1973. Jolted by the shock, a spate of discoveries and development of oil reserves were started around the world leading to some decline in OPEC's influence. The 1973 shock had produced a large price rise resulting from output restriction by the Organization of Arab Petroleum Exporting Countries, formed by Arab members of the OPEC and a few other Arab countries. It was a political action against the West for its role in the 1973 Arab–Israel war, rather than a cartel's normal economic move. Major reserves have since been found in Alaska, the North Sea, the Gulf of Mexico, and Canada. Also the breakup of the Soviet Union has opened up the huge Russian reserves to the world market. At the end of 2010, about a third of the world's oil supply was coming from the OPEC countries.

Yet cartels rarely form; and when they do they have rather short lives. They do spring up in specific circumstances but then break up almost as a general rule. The reason is that the interests of members run contrary to one another's even after they form a cartel. A cartel sets price like a monopolist. It works out how much the market would buy at this price and then allocates this production among the members. Because the price is like a monopoly price, it is higher than the marginal cost of production in all the firms. The problem begins here. Members would like to produce and sell more than their quota because extra production would cost less than the price it would sell for (as price exceeds marginal cost). They realise that they can make profit over and above what they would get officially from the cartel arrangement. So, they produce and sell more, of course, in a stealthy way. When a number of firms start cheating, the market gets significantly more supply than the cartel had planned for. So price falls below the cartel's expectation and it becomes clear that cheating is going on. Therefore, cartels require serious internal policing and often lead to allegations and counter-allegations and break down. This is why we rarely find co-operation among big firms selling the same product.

## 3.12 The Prisoner's Dilemma

An oligopoly firm would break up a market-sharing cartel agreement because it gains by unilaterally breaking it up. But all firms, including itself are worse off if all of them break it. They know this; yet they break it because they believe that others would break it in any case. Does that sound familiar? Yes, this syndrome is widespread in social interactions. In international forums countries agree about the benefits of reducing tariffs or other forms of trade restrictions. They know that if trade is free, it would significantly benefit all participating countries and increase their GDP and employment. But they rarely uphold such agreements in practice. The reason is that if a country removes restrictions while its partners do not, then the country would lose while its partners would gain big time. Knowing this, the country reasons that if it removes restrictions, others will surely not do so under various pretexts. Since that is certain, it is better off maintaining trade restrictions too. A similar situation prevails in an arms race. Countries know that it will be good for both (and other countries in the region) if they disarm. But they also know that if they disarm and the rival does not, the result will be disastrous for them. So they believe that others will certainly not disarm if they do, and in turn continue to arm themselves. Similar cases arise in politics, the economy, and society; and so they have been analysed in detail.

These situations conform to a pattern of strategic interaction which is called the Prisoner's Dilemma in Game Theory. This colourful name comes from a little story used for introducing the prototype which you will find interesting. The story goes like this. Police has caught two men who committed an armed robbery together. But they do not have adequate evidence that could stand in a court of law. However, they have enough evidence to get the two robbers sentenced for stealing the two bikes they were riding when they were nabbed. This will give two years of jail to each. The police now make the following offer to the two prisoners, who are kept separate:

- If you confess to the robbery and your partner does not, then we will set you free and he will get ten years in jail.
- If both of you confess then we will be lenient and both of you will get only four years.

The prisoners, of course, know that if neither confesses, then the court can give them only two years for stealing bikes, which is the best that can happen. What would they do?

Note first that the best outcome for both prisoners occurs if neither confesses. Both will then get only 2 years in jail. But they are not in touch. So prisoner 1 will think that a better action is to confess no matter what prisoner 2 does. If 2 confesses, then for 1 the better action is to confess, because this gives him only 4 years in jail instead of 10 years if he does not confess. On the other hand, if 2 does not confess, even then the better action for 1 is to confess. In that case, he would get free by confessing. So no matter what 2 does, prisoner 1's best action is to confess. Prisoner 2 will also reason similarly and he too will confess. Hence, the end result is that both confess, and the outcome is 4 years in jail for both.

You must have realised that if the prisoners could trust each other, then neither would confess. Player 1 would think: 2 trusts me enough to know that I will not confess and so he will not confess either. And then, if he does not confess my best action is indeed not to confess. Player 2 would also think similarly. In that case neither would confess and they would get the best outcome of 2 years of jail. But because they cannot trust each other, both would get the worst outcome possible.

There is something remarkable in this. Acting as individuals the prisoners end up with the worst outcome. This is quite the opposite of the 'invisible hand' idea which claims that people acting as detached individuals lead to an arrangement that is socially the best even as the actors realise their individual bests. In both cases, of course, the actors try to further their personal interest. Yet in one case they produce the best outcome for all (invisible hand) and in the other the worst (Prisoners' Dilemma).

## 3.13 Battle of Oligopolies

Decision making in oligopoly often resembles the Prisoners' Dilemma. Here I will give a hypothetical example with two firms. Suppose the only two firms in an industry have decided to set the product price at the monopoly level, which is Rs 100. At this price, the total sale is expected to be 1000 units. The firms have decided to produce and sell 500 units each. If they stick to the agreement each will get half of the monopoly level of profit. Clearly that is the best they can ever get.

What starts after the agreement is similar to the Prisoners' Dilemma. Each firm can either stick to the deal or break it. The first means to sell only 500 units. The second means to cheat and sell more than that. If they both stick to the deal, they would get the maximum profit. If they both cheat, then they would set their individual best outputs. Then they would both get less than the co-operating amount of profit. Finally, the worst for each is to honour the deal while the other does not. Then the other firm runs away with almost all the profit.

Clearly, the best action for each will be to cheat no matter what the other firm does. If one firm upholds the deal while the other cheats then it faces ruin. On the other hand, if the other does not cheat, even then cheating gives it more than sticking to the deal. Therefore, just like the prisoners, they would end up with a sub-optimal outcome. Both will cheat and get less than what they could have raked in by co-operating.

This is the essence of what happens in market sharing agreements. Each firm suspects that others would break the commitment and hence they all break it. Prisoners' Dilemma is a particular type of interaction analysed in game theory. There are many other types of 'games' and their analysis has been found to be very useful in understanding not just business behaviour but many other types of social interactions. Development of this branch of applied mathematics started with fundamental contributions by the celebrated mathematician John Nash in the mid-twentieth century (for the remarkable story of his career see Box 3.6).

---

**Box 3.6: John Nash**

John Nash (1928–) shared the Nobel prize in economics in 1994 with Reinhard Selten and John Harsanyi, two economists who also contributed hugely to the development of game theory. Nash, however, is a mathematician. He happened to take an optional paper in international economics in his under-graduate studies at Carnegie (now Carnegie Mellon) University. According to his own accounts, this exposure gave him the idea of the bargaining problem, which later led to a publication in the journal *Econometrica*. He earned a doctorate in 1950 with a 28 page dissertation on non-cooperative games. The thesis contained the idea and properties of what would later be called the 'Nash Equilibrium'. His doctoral thesis gave rise to four famous papers that are considered basic to non-cooperative game theory. He also made path-breaking contributions in some branches of pure mathematics. The most famous among them is known as the 'Nash embedding theorem'. He also contributed to the theory of singularity and the theory of non-linear parabolic partial differential equations.

---

*(contd...)*

*Box 3.6 continued.*

But much more was expected from Nash by his peers and teachers, many of whom rated him as a mathematical genius. Unfortunately a really tragic development came in the way. His career turned upside down at its prime as he developed acute paranoid schizophrenia in the late 1950s around the age of 31. He was under the care of hospitals for an entire decade. He remained paranoid and inaccessible even after release from hospitals. According to the campus legends of Princeton, there walked a 'phantom' through the Fine Hall (Princeton's mathematics department)—an inaccessible and crazy character scribbling away esoteric equations on blackboards through the night. It was John Nash. It is not clear exactly when Nash started overcoming his schizophrenia. Even in the 1990s, according to some accounts, the Nobel awards committee was not too sure that he would be able to conduct himself properly at the award ceremony. A remarkable feature of Nash and his schizophrenia is that later he was able to describe to people close to him the various phases of his illness and the philosophical and rational struggle that one part of his being was waging to explain and come to terms with the other. After he came out of his mental illness, Nash proposed several hypotheses on the subject of schizophrenia.

When he received the Nobel award at the age of 66, Nash was aware that the best part of his life had been consumed by schizophrenia. He concluded his Nobel acceptance speech with the following touching words: 'Statistically, it would seem improbable that any mathematician or scientist, at the age of 66, would be able through continued research efforts, to add much to his or her previous achievements. However, I am still making the effort and it is conceivable that with the gap period of about 25 years of partially deluded thinking providing a sort of vacation my situation may be atypical. Thus I have hopes of being able to achieve something of value through my current studies or with any new ideas that come in the future.'

The Hollywood film 'A Beautiful Mind' was based on Nash's life. It was nominated for eight Academy awards and won four including the best picture award. The film was based on Nash's biography also called 'A Beautiful Mind'.[4] It focuses on his mathematical genius and his struggles with paranoid schizophrenia.

---

[4] *A Beautiful Mind: The Life of Mathematical Genius and Nobel Laureate John Nash* by Sylvia Nasar.

## 3.14 Is Co-operation Impossible?

Given its set up, the outcome of the Prisoner's Dilemma is quite convincing. But just as mistrust is a fact of life, so also is co-operation. I am here using the word co-operation in the sense of the Prisoners' Dilemma. It means keeping to a commitment while knowing that running away unilaterally is better. In this sense, the instances of co-operation that we see in society are amazingly abundant given the Prisoners' Dilemma analysis. In fact, social life would be impossible without people keeping their commitments in situations where they would clearly gain by breaking them. The economy itself is based on implicit commitments of various kinds among all players. In some cases, the commitments are explicit as written in law books and contracts, and in other cases they are implicit. Even the simplest of economic transactions, say, buying goods from the bazaar, is based on certain implicit commitments among all the relevant actors. The most important is that if I appear in a transaction as a buyer, then I would hand over the price of the good after I pick it up. I would certainly gain by defecting, for example, by picking up a bagful of the good and running. There are, of course, deterrents like the security staff. But they are meagre. It is in the interest of every buyer to defect from the commitment of paying. The fact that the meagre deterrents suffice means that the commitment is broken only as exception.

One reason that we keep to our commitments is that the Prisoners' Dilemma is played in our society again and again among the same set of players. Going back to the prisoners' story, suppose these two partners in crime are serial offenders. They know that they would be caught again and again and the police would make them similar offers ever so often. How would they play the game in that case? Because the game will be played repeatedly, the players would need a strategy based on the other player's behaviour through time. Take a simple strategy: 'Co-operate as long as the partner also co-operates. And, if he once defects never co-operate with him afterwards'. If both prisoners have this strategy and if both of them know this, then co-operation would be a very likely outcome. A prisoner can avoid jail by defection only the first time. But every time he is caught after that, he will get 4 years in jail as the other will not co-operate. But if he co-operates, he will get only 2 years in jail whenever caught. Considering this over the robbers' lifetime, not confessing is a better move whenever they are caught. Hence, co-operation is more likely if similar interactions occur again and again.

Economists believe that many social norms have evolved through repeated occurrence of Prisoner's Dilemma type interactions. The prospect of a re-run of the interaction keeps players interested in co-operation. There is another important way societies try to attain co-operative solutions. It is by making defection, that is, not co-operating, illegal and punishable. When there is a law against it, players know that others are unlikely to defect. Hence they would also not defect thus bringing about a co-operative outcome. Much of constitutions and laws can be interpreted as ways of making co-operative behaviour more probable.

Coming back to oligopoly, firms that have been in business for a long time, develop certain business etiquettes and norms and stick to them. For example, they may not pay wage and salary above the industry average or poach one another's better workers, even though it will clearly increase their profits in the short run. Similarly, when they present a joint front to the government and suppliers, they do not break ranks though it could be individually profitable. Traditional commercial houses used to develop a reputation of honesty through good practice with customers and suppliers over generations of family business. In the short run they would have done definitely better by opportunistic actions. But they did not go along this course because the interactions with customers and suppliers are played repeatedly. We might say honesty is the best policy if the game is repeated.

## 3.15 Monopoly, Oligopoly, and Competition

It is, of course, good news that oligopolists find it hard to co-operate. If they colluded they would charge monopoly price and restrict output to the monopoly level. Therefore, an industry under collusion would produce less. Price would also be correspondingly higher. We are spared this outcome as large firms fail to maintain a cartel. The greater the number of firms in an oligopoly, the higher is the market output and closer is the price to marginal cost. In fact, when the number is fairly large, output and price get very close to what the industry would have produced under perfect competition.

How many firms have to be in an industry so that we can call it a competitive industry? Well, there is no such number. The number of firms in a competitive market is fixed by the process of competition itself. The number is such that the firms manage to make profit at the same rate as prevails in other markets, called 'the normal rate of profit'. If from here demand for the good increases, price will rise and then firms will produce more. Their profit will now climb above the normal rate. This will attract new firms into the industry. When new firms join, total supply will increase and price will fall until profit is normal again. The industry now settles to a new equilibrium with more firms than earlier. This means that the number of firms in a competitive industry changes with the state of demand.

So in order to check if an industry is competitive or not we should examine its average long run rate of profit rather than the number of firms. In a competitive industry, the long run average should be 'normal'—the same as the average in other industries over a long period. This method needs data on profits in the market under scrutiny and elsewhere. Since profit is not always fully or honestly reported and also fluctuates quite a lot, the result of the calculations can be easily challenged. A much simpler method could be to check if entry of new businesses into the market is free. As we saw earlier, if entry is free, it keeps the existing firms in check. They cannot raise prices significantly above marginal cost. So examining the institutions around the market and checking if entry is free is a practical method to verify a market's competitive status. There is yet another way of checking the competitive credentials of an industry (for an example see Box 3.7).

---

### Box 3.7: Internet Service Providers in the US

The market for internet service providers (ISP) in the US is free of any entry barrier, commercial or bureaucratic. Entry also does not require significant investment. Thus the market is expected to be competitive. Can we verify this expectation by an independent method?

*(contd...)*

*Box 3.7 continued.*

---

ISPs in the US operate on local levels, not nationally. Thus the markets of ISPs are confined to the counties or metropolitan areas where they are located. The markets in counties away from large metropolitan areas are small whereas markets in major cities are larger. Measuring the size of a market by the population of the market catchment area, we would expect the number of firms in different markets to be positively related with the population of the market area. It is found to be indeed so. In 1998, the smallest markets with average population of 74,000 had just 1 to 5 providers. On the other end, in markets of average size 943,000 and above, the number of providers was 21 or more. And a steady increase was seen in the number of firms in the intermediate range.[5]

The relation between market size and number of firms can be used to test if a market is really competitive or not. If the ISP markets had hidden entry barriers, and were in fact working as oligopolies, things would be quite different. Big oligopoly firms would corner the larger metropolitan markets, so that the number of firms per thousand people would be fewer in those markets. As a result, there would then be no systematic relationship between market size and the number of firms across the country.

---

## 3.16 Price Discrimination

I want to talk about another market form before we end this chapter. So far we have taken for granted that a monopoly or oligopoly sells its products to all customers at the same price. Often this is not true. Some monopolies sell their products at different prices to different customers. Let us first see some examples.

- A licensed copy of Microsoft Windows operating system is cheaper for individuals than for companies. Further, among individuals, students can buy it cheaper than professionals.
- Most hair dressing shops offer haircuts at lower prices for students and senior citizens.
- Airlines price their tickets differently for the same trip on different days of the week and at different hours of the day. Some give

---

[5] The numbers are from a table presented in Thomas A. Downes and Shane M. Greenstein, 'Do Commercial ISPs Provide Universal Access?' in S.E. Gillett and I. Vogelsang (eds), *Competition, Regulation, and Convergence: Current Trends in Telecommunications Policy Research*, Mahwah, NJ: Lawrence Erlbaum Associates, 1999.

you a cheaper return ticket to big cities if you stay the weekend there!

• Most movie theatres, amusement parks, and holiday parks charge children and seniors less than others.

• Many eating out shops sell the same meals cheaper during day time than in the evening.

If you look around you can spot literally hundreds of such examples. This kind of pricing is known as *price discrimination*. A seller can do this under two conditions. The first is obvious. The seller needs to have control over price so that it can set the price according to its calculation. The second condition is that it should be impossible or prohibitively costly for a buyer to resell the product to another customer. If you get a haircut for 10 rupees as a student, you cannot sell the haircut to another person at a higher price to make a few rupees' profit. So, a lot of price discrimination occurs in personal services that cannot be resold. It also occurs in products that are costly to move across markets or cannot be moved from the location at all. A motel chain provides exactly the same type and quality of accommodation in a small town and a tourist spot, but charges more for it in the latter.

Why do sellers use price discrimination? The answer must be that it increases profit. If resale is not possible, it makes sense to sell at a higher price to one who is willing to pay more, and a lower price to one who would not pay that much. Different buyers are generally willing to pay different amounts for the same product. Sellers take advantage of this when possible. Let us see an example. Suppose a publisher is going to publish a textbook of economics for first year students written by a famous American professor. It has been estimated that if it is priced at $120, it will sell 200,000 copies in US universities. But at that price, it will not sell at all in Asia which is however the largest market for such books. The market there will bear at the most a price of $15. At $15, the price is still above production cost and the firm will make significant profit. But if the book is priced at $15 then the publisher has to forgo the huge potential profit from the US market. This can be avoided if the possibility of the resale of the book from the Asian market to the US can be eliminated. In that case it can be sold at $120 in the US and at $15 in Asia. This is indeed what happens when resale between two markets or parts of markets is not possible.

Resale is not possible if by nature the product is not transferable as in services like medical treatment, surgery, legal services, massages, fitness training, beauty therapy, music lessons, and so on. It is also not possible if transport between two parts of the market is logistically difficult or costly. Significant trade barriers between countries also help in price discrimination across them. Resale can also be prohibited by government order or by formal contracts. Sometimes medicines, nutritional formulations, baby food etc. are sold to distributors in poor countries or areas afflicted by war and natural disasters at a lower price, and care is taken to make them difficult to re-sell. In the textbook example above, copies sold in Asia would be prominently marked as not for sale outside Asia.

## 3.17 Setting the Price

How does a discriminating seller find out the best prices? It follows a few simple rules. I will illustrate them using the book publisher's example. The first rule is a no-brainer. In both markets the price should be pushed up as long as that increases profit. When price is increased sales would of course drop but the publisher pushes along if the price rise makes up for the fall in sales. While prices are being raised like this, the best configuration comes when the following happens. We can call it Rule two: shifting, say, a hundred copies away from Asia to US or *vice versa* should not make a difference to the total sales revenue. If a hundred copies fewer are sold in the US, price will increase a bit there. But because fewer books are sold, overall there will be some loss of revenue. Now if these books are sent to the Asian market, they would reduce the price there a bit but the increase in sales will increase the total revenue by some amount. The rule is that the revenue lost in the US market should just be recovered. This would mean that the distribution of the books across the two markets is the best. If the books gave more revenue in one market then obviously profit could be increased by selling more in that market and less in the other. But when the revenue loss and gain are equal in the two markets, there is no scope of profit by reallocation. The third and last rule is that the extra cost of producing these books should be equal to the extra revenue they fetch when sold in either market. Obviously, if the extra production cost exceeded the extra revenue, that production would need cutting down, and in the opposite case, more production would be recommended. A discriminating business firm of course cannot actually go back and forth with price and sales to figure out the right prices. It calculates them from market data using the above rules.

So when a discriminating seller has the right prices, the extra revenue that it can get by selling a few more goods is equal in the two markets. Price in the two markets will be different for this to happen. It will be lower in the market where the price elasticity of demand is higher. Why, for example, are Japanese cars cheaper outside Japan than within the country? The answer is that the price elasticity of these cars is higher outside Japan. There are many substitutes for Japanese cars in the world market and, therefore, the demand for Japanese cars is quite elastic (that is, sensitive) to prices. The Japanese home market is less competitive. Foreign-made cars do not have a very large presence there. So, Japanese cars do not have many substitutes in Japan. Demand is, therefore, less price elastic there. Hence Japanese cars would sell cheaper outside Japan. In common-sense terms, overseas buyers can react more to high prices than customers in Japan. Hence they also get a better deal.

Students and seniors get low price offers in services because their demand is generally more price elastic.[6] Why do some airlines give a cheaper return ticket to big cities if the passenger stays back for the weekend? The answer to this one is not immediately obvious. Airlines have figured out that they have two types of customers with very different price elasticities of demand. There are business people, company executives and professionals who do not pay for trips from their own income. Hence their price elasticity of demand is close to zero, meaning that a higher ticket price would not affect their demand much. Nor would a price cut increase their demand for flights. On the other side, there are the ordinary fliers whose price elasticity of demand is fairly high. They would cut down travel

---

[6]That is, their demand increases more when the price is reduced.

significantly if prices were higher. Airlines, therefore, want to charge a higher price to the first group and less to others. But how do they make out what kind of customer you are? To classify the type of customer, they have a clever, though devious, method. The chance that business and professional guys will stay back over the weekend is slim. They are expected to have a high opportunity cost of time. Nor will a cheaper ticket appeal to them as others pay for them anyway. Other passengers however care for cheap tickets, may have lower opportunity cost of time, and would try to take the offer. So when the offer is made, customers 'self-select'. Corporate travellers take the high cost tickets, while others take the cheaper ticket if they have a way of staying over the weekend.

## 3.18 In Lieu of a Summary

As we have surveyed here, there is a wide variety of market forms. We discussed the more important ones. How does a particular form of market get associated with a particular industry? Why are some industries oligopolistic while others operate in monopolistic competition? Is it accidental or are there patterns? A branch of economics, called Industrial Organisation Theory, tries to study these questions. It is found that the characteristics of the product, distance between production points and the market, early history of the industry, and many other factors are relevant.

We have discussed the market forms seen in industrialised market economies. Other economies have a 'dual' structure. They have a set of markets in the formal or organised part of the economy. These resemble the types of markets that we have discussed above. But these economies also have an informal or unorganised part. In that part, markets work quite differently and cannot be fitted into the types described in this chapter. The most important difference is that contracts are informal in this part of the economy. Employment, borrowing and lending, supplies, etc. occur mostly on trust and information flows by word of mouth. Informal sectors also employ a significant amount of family labour which is not separately accounted as employing another person. This sector thus avoids a significant amount of hiring cost, the cost of making formal contracts, and taxes. On the other hand, it cannot benefit from statutory protection available to business and employees, nor can it access organised insurance and finance. The study of behaviour in these markets is fascinating. Equally fascinating is how formal and informal markets co-exist in an economy and how they engage with one another.

Typically, developing economies have a very large informal sector. That makes the analysis of a developing economy a specialised subject. We cannot use the market theorems appropriate for advanced market economies to analyse developing economies without making suitable modifications. We will discuss some of these issues in Chapter 9.

# 4  Markets Often Fail and So Do Governments

It would appear from our discussion so far that an economy would sail along smoothly by using resources in an efficient manner if only it could keep its markets competitive. Unfortunately that is not true. There are a number of hurdles to efficient allocation besides imperfect markets. They account for a large part of the challenge of economic management. The first is the problem of externality—a situation where events that arise outside the realm of markets affect people and businesses in economic terms. It is obvious that markets, competitive or otherwise, cannot do much about them. Our understanding of externalities began to take shape early in the twentieth century. The second problem arises from 'public goods'—a term I will explain here. Though a beginning was made in the early twentieth century, the theories developed through the later years of the century. Methods to deal with externality and public goods are evolving even today. This chapter is about these challenges which cannot be handled by simply improving markets and making them competitive or by turning them over to the government.

## 4.1 Externality

We have seen that competitive markets are efficient because in those markets the price reflects the resource cost. Now let us ask an odd question. Will such efficiency prevail if producers get some inputs or resources for free, that is, without paying for them? If some inputs are free, then the cost of production as calculated by the producer would be less than its true cost to the society. We will refer to the cost as the producer sees it as 'private cost'. In a competitive market, the price of a product will be equal to marginal cost as the producer calculates it, that is, the 'marginal private cost'. Therefore, the competitive price will be less than the true cost of the product when some inputs are free. Sold at that price, buyers will consume more than what is justified by the true cost. In common sense terms, things produced using a free resource will be produced and bought beyond the optimal level.

This situation arises whenever a good or service can be got without paying for it. It also arises if someone does not have to pay for an action that costs something to others. For example, a factory that produces air-borne pollutants creates a cost for the people around it. The neighbours suffer from pollution-induced diseases, which cost them health, money, and earning ability. The more the firm produces, the more it costs the neighbours. Obviously, the firm produces more than it would have done if it had to pay for the neighbours' costs. If we could make the factory pay, its private cost would increase and it would produce less. This would take its output closer to the socially optimal production level.

The polluting firm is said to be creating an *externality*. The term *externality* has been coined to remind us that the cost occurs without the intermediation of markets; that is, it is external to the system of markets. Because it does not occur through market channels, it plays no role in price formation. Therefore, it prevents prices from reflecting the true cost of a product. As a result, when users compare product prices, they cannot see the true costs. Hence markets are no longer efficient. They are then said to *fail* to allocate resources efficiently.

A characteristic example is the use of air. Factories exhaust fumes into the air but do not pay for it. Nor do consumers pay for releasing automobile fumes. The resulting pollution has medical and other costs. If we could price the use of air, that price would reflect the cost of fighting the pollution-driven ills. It would not eliminate air pollution but would reduce it to an economically optimal level. A factory would operate up to the point where extra payment for pollution cost cancels what it will get by selling the extra product. This is obviously less than what it produces when it does not pay for pollution. Air would be used for dumping fumes only to the extent that the price paid for dumping is matched by the benefits of production or transport that cause it. Because there is no such price, the true cost of using air remains much higher than the benefits. Externalities are widespread in the use of environment and ecological resources. Here is a common example of ecosystem abuse: we catch more fish than is optimal because we do not pay for the loss of catch for the next season from disturbances in this year's breeding cycle.

Externalities, of course, are not necessarily negative. Sometimes we also get benefits without paying. We may term them 'positive externalities'. If my neighbour plays cricket commentary a trifle loud, I can get to hear it for free. When a coal mine pumps water out of the mine, it lowers the water level in neighbouring mines because underground water tables are connected. If a bee-keeper farms more bees, it helps the neighbouring mango orchard, because more bees help to pollinate more mango flowers. These are positive externalities. Taking a cue from these examples, negative as well as positive, it is easy to see that there are myriad cases of free inputs and unpaid costs which markets fail to price. In all these cases output or consumption will be either more or less than the true best. Is there a way of handling the problem and bringing outputs closer to the optimal level?

## 4.2 Tax and Subsidy for Correction

A common method is to set a tax on what generates a negative externality. We noted that in a negative externality, the private cost of the producer is less than the true cost of production. A tax simply increases the private cost. If it is calculated so as to increase it to the level of true cost, then the producer will automatically produce the right amount. These taxes are called corrective taxes as the idea is to correct the pricing distortion. They are also called *Pigovian taxes* after Arthur Pigou, the British economist who explained the theory and purpose of these taxes.

We have noted that externalities are not always negative. When someone's action brings unpaid gains to others, it is a positive externality. In this case the producer does not get paid for some part of what he produces. So he produces less than what is socially warranted. For example, a bee-keeper raises fewer bees than is socially optimal. He gets money only by selling honey, but no return for his bees helping in the production of extra mango output. He would raise the right number of bees only if he could get the part of the mango orchard's profit that he contributes. We can get him to farm more bees by promising extra money for each unit of honey he produces. The arrangement is called a production subsidy. It is the opposite of taxation.

---

**Box 4.1: Arthur Cecil Pigou**

Pigou (1877–1959) was perhaps the most respected British economist during the period between two outstanding economists Alfred Marshall (1842–1924) and J.M. Keynes (1883–1946). He was a favourite student of Marshall and took over the leadership of the market-oriented Marshallian tradition at Cambridge University. Pigou discussed the difference between private and true cost in his book *Wealth and Welfare* (1912) and used this to explain corrective taxes. These taxes were widely used during his own life time.

But Pigou had to face serious attacks on his Marshallian views, particularly on the analysis of the labour market and unemployment. Keynes, another prominent student of Marshall, broke away from Marshall's teaching. He often used Pigou's *Theory of Unemployment* (1933) as the whipping boy for all the alleged mistakes of the market-oriented tradition. With the rise of Keynesian economics, the Marshallian tradition of Cambridge went on retreat for a long, long time.

---

The idea of taxes and subsidies to combat externalities appears reasonable. But their use is an administration's nightmare. First of all, how do we figure out the right amounts? To set the right tax for a factory spewing a noxious gas, we need to know the neighbours' medical bill per unit of gas ejected or per unit of its output. If we set the tax too high, we force the factory to produce less than the 'best' amount. We will, of course, want to avoid that. Governments are unable to assess the money value of externalities accurately enough. So corrective taxes or subsidies are generally *ad hoc* amounts, which may indeed reduce the efficiency of resource allocation. Typically, the corrective tax for gas emissions is imposed on the product of the factories. To avoid administrative and legal complications, all producers of the good would be subjected to the same rate of tax. This means that the tax does not discriminate between a factory polluting more and one polluting less. Factory owners, therefore, would have no incentive to invest in green technology. Further the tax rate can be challenged creating costly litigation. The main contention of these law suits is that the tax is greater than the cost of pollution and hence unfair. Because it is impossible to establish the true costs, the proceedings continue for years. In the end, settlement at an *ad hoc* tax rate is arrived. Note that nothing ensures that the settlement rate is in fact the socially correct one.

## 4.3 Some Markets are Missing

The root of the externality problem is that either producers or buyers get something without the mediation of markets. To put it differently, externality arises because a relevant market, which would be useful, is in fact missing. If that market did exist then it would impose the due price and align private commercial decisions with socially optimal decisions.

Let us discuss an example. Suppose a chemical factory dumps effluents into a lake and this reduces the output of a fishery that catches fish from the lake. The more the factory's output, the more the effluents flow, and the more is the fishery's loss. The chemical factory takes production decisions on the basis of its own private cost. Therefore, it produces more than it would if all costs were considered, including the fishery's.

It sounds a touch odd, but if there was a market for 'polluting the lake water', things would be quite different. To see this, suppose that we could indeed start such a market. One possible way is this. The government sells or leases the lake to a third party. Let us call it the Lake Company. This company would use the lake commercially. So it will allow the fishery to fish in the lake for a price. It will also allow the chemical factory to discharge effluents for a price. But when discharge is allowed, the lake's potential catch will fall, and the fishing company will be willing to pay less for fishing in the lake. As more and more discharge is allowed, the fishing company will also want to pay less and less. So the Lake Company will charge higher prices for additional discharge as discharge increases. Effectively, the chemical factory will have to pay for the loss of catch, that is, the cost it produces to the fishery, and this cost will increase when it produces more. The externality it was creating earlier is now 'internalised' through this new arrangement. The chemical factory will now include in its private costs what it has to pay to the Lake Company and will, therefore, produce the socially optimal amount. The example makes it clear what is meant by 'missing markets'. In this case the missing market is that of 'polluting the lake'! In many situations, it is possible to establish missing markets and make the external costs and benefits internal to the cost accounting of the relevant business firms.

This method of resolving externalities is better than simply clamping a tax on the chemical factory. To fix a tax, we require data on the cost created by the chemical factory at every level of its production. That information will be inaccurate and can be challenged. Establishing the missing market bypasses that requirement as the market assesses the cost and prices it as appropriate.

Economists suggest that we identify the missing market in a given scenario and use our imagination to establish it. It may not be always possible to create an arrangement that looks like a normal market. But a *market-like* institution that imposes the right cost on the offending party can be created. A number of such institutions are now in place in various countries and some more have been proposed. As the world becomes more conscious of the costs of externalities, innovative institutions are expected to arise.

Here is another possibility. In the above example we can encourage the chemical factory and the fishery to become a single company. One may be encouraged to buy the other out. Profits of the merged firm would then depend on both activities. To maximise profit, the output of its chemical department would be increased only if its profit increases more than the extra loss it creates for the fishery department. The merger creates profit accounting that automatically extracts the right price from the offending wing of the firm. Note that the profit of the merged unit will be more than the sum of the two firms' profits when they existed separately. Therefore, the merger or buy out is also commercially profitable.

## 4.4 A Bargaining Solution

Merger or buy-out decisions depend on owners or on the stock market. Governments can hardly induce these moves. But there is a kind of solution to externality where the government can play an active role. When a firm complains of another firm inflicting external cost to the government or the court, the latter can direct it to start a negotiation with the damage-creating party. Let us go back to the case of the chemical factory and the fishery. Suppose the fishery starts a negotiation with the chemical factory. It can propose that the factory reduces production by a certain amount, and offer it compensation for the resulting loss of profit. The fishery can afford to do this if it gains more from the chemical factory's production cut than the chemical factory's loss. In that case it can retain a net gain after paying compensation. The chemical firm should agree if it gets adequate compensation; and if it is offered a little extra, it would agree all the more. What output cut can be agreed to in this manner? To begin with, when the chemical firm is producing a large output, a cut in its production will bring a significant gain to the fishery. But as more and more output is cut, the additional gain of the fishery falls at each step. The reason is that initially when the chemical firm is producing a large quantity, the pollution level in the lake is serious. Some cut in production can go a long way in de-polluting the lake. But later, when it is producing a smaller amount, the release of effluent is also small, and cut in production does not have as much effect as earlier. The fishery will push the bargain until its extra gain from chemical production cut falls and becomes no more than the extra loss of the chemical firm. If the chemical firm were to cut production any more, then the increase in the fishery's gain will not be enough to pay for the chemical factory's additional loss. The bargain will stop there. This point is the best combination of the two firms' outputs, that is, the best social output.

In this example, the negotiations actually started a market for effluent dumping and bargaining established the right price. These negotiations are expected to work no matter who owns the lake. Neither party owned the lake in the example. But the two parties can reach the right solution through bargaining even if one of them owns it. Consider a situation where the fishery owns the lake. In that case it will prohibit all discharge by the chemical factory. This will completely stop chemical production. When that happens, the chemical factory may start a bargain with the fishing farm. It can offer to compensate the fishery for dumping some effluents. It can do this as long as its profit increases more than the loss it brings to the fishing farm. In that case it will pay for the fishery's loss and retain the rest of the profit. At low levels of chemical production, the effluent will not cause much damage. The gain of the chemical producer will exceed the damage to the fishery. So compensation will work. But as more chemical is produced and more effluents are disposed, the damage to the fishery will at some point equal the gain of the chemical factory. The chemical factory will not be able to compensate for any more discharge. Bargain will stop, and at this point the society attains the best combination of output of chemicals and fish.

A notable feature of these bargains is that they generate the right price for externality because the bargaining parties know how much the other's action costs them. Hence they end at the right point without the help of any external information or intervention. Bargains end at the point where the extra gain of one party is entirely used up to compensate the extra loss of the other. From the social point of view, this is the best position. At this point, any increase in output by either of them would reduce the output of the other by exactly the same value. So there is no net gain for the society by increasing the output of either.

## 4.5 Tradable Pollution Permits

Relatively recently, a novel method for pollution control is being tried out around the world, notably in the US. It is best to illustrate it with an example. Suppose an industry consisting of a number of firms generates a polluting gas. The government can impose a tax on their output. But we know that this method does not provide the polluter with any incentive for adopting less-polluting technology. Taxes also do not discriminate between a small and a large polluter because the tax rate is uniform. Now consider this alternative. The government decides to sell a fixed number of 'permits' for pollution to this industry. One permit is needed for a specified amount of discharge. The government decides to allow a certain amount of discharge for the whole of this industry in a given year. It then calculates the total number of permits necessary for this and puts them on sale. At the start, firms have to buy the permits through auction. Later on they can buy or sell these among themselves in a secondary market. Because the supply of permits is fixed, the industry as a whole cannot generate more pollution than the sanctioned amount. But those firms that pollute more have to procure more permits. This will increase their production cost more than that of other firms. What a firm spends on permits is a sort of tax. Note that it will be higher for a firm that pollutes more. If the demand for the industry's product increases, the permit price will automatically rise in the secondary market because firms will try to buy more permits from a fixed stock. As a result, the price of the product will increase, thus moderating the demand for the pollution-generating product. Substitute products that do not generate pollution would gain a competitive advantage. If the permit price becomes high, a firm will be better off by spending on pollution-reducing technology than buying permits. At the same time, a firm that pollutes less can sell its permits to others or buy fewer permits to start with. This gives it an advantage over others. So these tradable permits make a polluting product less competitive in relation to substitutes and encourage investment in cleaner technology. They have caught the attention of policy-makers in many countries and are being tried out for establishing missing markets to prevent many other kinds of externality.

## 4.6 Public Goods

Market failure, however, is not always the result of a missing market. There are some peculiar goods and services that induce market failure by their very nature. These are called public goods and they are very important in a modern society. They have one or both of two peculiar features. The first is that once the good is produced it is not possible (or is extremely costly) to prevent anyone from benefitting from it. It sounds strange, but there are hundreds of examples. A country's defence service defends everyone in the country and no one can be selectively excluded. Services such as law and order, governance, clean air, greenery, cleaner cities, street lighting, clean beaches etc. are obvious examples. We sometime refer to ordinary goods as private goods to distinguish them from public goods. A seller can refuse a private good like a pair of shoes if someone does not pay for it. But this is not possible or is very costly for a public good. Further, there are some goods that are partly public and partly private. Take, for example, the case of vaccination. It is not a problem to stop someone from getting a shot if he does not pay. In that sense vaccination is a private good. But when more people get their shots, the disease is contained and it is not possible to stop others from getting the benefit of less contagion. So vaccination is also a public good of sorts. Similarly, a school can exclude a student who does not pay school fees. But when more students are educated, we get a better society, the benefits of which cannot be held away from anyone.

There is another type of goods, also called public goods, which have a different feature. Once they are produced, the marginal cost of allowing an extra unit of consumption is zero for all practical purposes. A road or a bridge illustrates this. Once the road has been constructed, there is no extra cost if another person walks along it. Public goods have at least one of these two features.

It is easy to see that markets will not produce the right amount of either type of public goods. If consumers cannot be stopped from using an item, there is no easy way to make them pay for it. Even if they are made to pay some amount by appealing to their social or civic sentiments, it is impossible to make them pay the *right* price because we do not even know what the right price is. For a private good, markets establish the so-called right price because they bring together producers who are hard-nosed about costs and buyers who are willing to pay up only to the amount they think worth. In a public good market, producers of course would know what it costs to produce. But buyers do not reveal how much they are willing to pay or how badly they want the good. When a private firm produces such a good, it will be inevitably under-produced. In the case of a vaccine, consumers would pay for their direct benefit but not for the indirect gains of others. Market demand for vaccines will therefore be less than what is socially best. Responding to market demand, producers will produce less than the socially optimal number of vaccines.

It is now easy to see why infrastructure, governance, environmental and eco-system services, public health, education etc. would be under-produced if they are left to private business and markets. More of these things are needed than what buyers are willing to spend on them. Private business would produce only as much as the buyers spend. Hence we cannot expect the right amount of production.

Because private business fails the job, we may suggest that governments should produce these goods. But that begs the basic issue. The issue is, how to find out the right amount required. The problem that markets face in getting this information does not disappear when the government takes over. Just as a market cannot produce this information, neither can the government.

The problem is a bit more tractable for *local public goods* that are used by people living in the neighbourhood rather than the entire country. Examples are a city's parks and its neighbourhood streets. This type of item is generally funded by local authorities from local taxes and levies. Users are more forthcoming in showing their preference and willingness to pay for these goods. Typically, an authority would propose the details of a project and send mails to residents asking how much extra tax they would be willing to bear for it. If the tax offer is enough, the project is taken up. Otherwise, a lower-cost alternative is proposed and the method repeated. The users being local, there is greater involvement and they reveal more of their willingness to pay. Obviously, this method is not a solution to the nationwide public goods problem.

## 4.7 Free Riding

Under-revelation of preference for public goods is a widespread phenomenon. Quite appropriately it is called 'free-riding'. The phrase comes from the analogy of using public transport without paying the fare. The transport system will not have enough funds to operate if too many people are free riders.

Think of a group of students living in a flat together. They want to buy a fridge. The initiator of the proposal starts by asking each flatmate how much he or she is willing to pay to the kitty. Once it has been bought, the fridge will be there for all flatmates to use. Hence we may find the flatmates trying to free-ride on others. Each will understate his or her preference and offer to pay less than the actual extent of preference. In the general case of public goods, it means that tax-payers would offer to pay less than what they actually think a project is worth. This results in insufficient funding even of projects that all tax-payers think are important.

We encounter free riding in unexpected corners. When a trade union negotiates higher wages or more benefits, they are available to all workers in a given organisation or industry or even nationwide. The fruits of the negotiation are public goods for workers. Many workers do not become union members to avoid fees, responsibilities, and trouble but do of course get the benefits. A classic case of free riding is the defence services, which people avoid as a poor job market option even though they are aware of the necessity of defence. Many governments use compulsory enrolment as a result. There is significant free riding on mass-collaborated internet sites where ideas and information are added and shared by a large number of people. Many visitors regularly use these websites but do not add anything to them.

Can free riding be overcome? In some cases governments simply override the behaviour by not asking for public opinion. They decide on the expenditure and fund it from taxes. While that is accepted in some cases, for example, defence, law and order, crime prevention, and emergencies, it will meet with protests in the case of other public goods.

Though our explanation of free-riding seems to agree with observed behaviour, it may be somewhat simplistic. It is possible that the economic account is not the entire explanation and we need to look into its sociology. This suggestion arises because we find that free riding is less of a problem in smaller and closely held population units. We noted earlier that local public goods suffer less from free riding. The smaller and more closely-tied the population unit, lesser the free riding tends to be. It is rare inside a properly functioning family. Village communities fund local libraries, sports, fairs, and cultural events from voluntary contributions by residents. The method used is to agree on the major features and expected cost of a project at the village level, and then just ask for voluntary contributions. This behaviour extends even to smaller towns, or specific communities in larger towns. Not only monetary contribution, but voluntary labour is also provided to build local infrastructure. It appears that individualistic interest is often overruled by group interests, but we may not yet understand the mechanics of it well enough.

---

**Box 4.2: Seva Café**

Seva Café is located in a central area of Ahmedabad in India. It offers its guests free vegetarian food of very good quality in a nice ambience. If the guests want, they may donate towards the meals of others who come to eat there. But it is entirely voluntary. To keep it really voluntary, guests' donations are not opened until they have left; so there is no embarrassment for not paying or paying small amounts. The establishment has been running since 2005 and, amazingly, it is not financially strained. A precursor to Seva Café is a vegetarian restaurant in Singapore called Annalakshmi which has been functioning since 1986.

These and others examples of a similar nature raise doubts about the universality of free riding expected on the basis of unmixed selfish behaviour. We should further note that Seva Café and Annalakshmi are not parts of any religious organisation. Behaviour in religious organisations and occasions is known to be different from pure economic behaviour and is more easily explained.

---

I will end this section now. We started the chapter on the trail of problems within a market system that may lead to market failure. We saw that externalities lead to market failure because in these cases economic interactions bypass the web of markets. We have also seen that there are goods with peculiar features—the public goods—that make it impossible to produce them efficiently and optimally. In the case of public goods not only do markets fail but governments too cannot effect optimal and efficient production. In the next section we will discuss another important source of market failure.

## 4.8 Asymmetric Information

We take it for granted that market actors are fully aware of products and prices. But there are markets where buyers and sellers have different amount of information about the product. Asymmetric information affects market behaviour and its efficiency and optimality. As an example, professionals know more than their clients about the service they sell. Doctors, surgeons, dentists, opticians, lawyers, electricians, plumbers, auto mechanics, and almost all other professional groups know more about their services than the persons buying them. The possibility is open that a doctor or a lawyer can advise a patient into accepting a more costly procedure than is required. An auto mechanic can thrust unnecessary checks or replacement of parts on the buyer. This is not to suggest that it happens in every instance, but that the buyer is potentially at risk.

Markets with information asymmetry cannot function as efficient markets. It is obvious that if buyers are duped because they are ignorant, then they do not get the best for their money. But the problem extends beyond this. Even when sellers do not take advantage of asymmetry, these markets generally fail. They fail because buyers behave differently fearing that they can be taken for a ride. They take various precautionary measures. This costs them resources which could have been used elsewhere. They may tap into their social networks to check the credentials of professionals before visiting them. Or they go for a second opinion after consultation. If the advice is for costly procedures, sometimes buyers simply avoid them assuming that they are being misled. All of these lead to in-optimal choice and unwarranted costs of time, resources, and well-being.

Information asymmetry does attract government regulation. Generally governments try to devise measures to allay buyers' fears. Some types of behaviour are declared as cheating and made punishable. But behaviour—and particularly intention—are difficult to establish. Specialised laws are often required to facilitate the proceedings. In some countries, professionals are required to join associations that regulate members' behaviour. The associations keep an eye on members' conduct and handle complaints of sharp practice. But on the other hand the associations may breed favouritism and cliques. Further, they may reduce competition by restricting entry into the profession.

Insurance markets have serious asymmetry issues. In these markets it is not the buyer but the seller who faces difficulty. A health insurer cannot have full information on the medical history of its clients. So when selling insurance, the company has only a very rough idea of the probability of expenses it is promising to pay for. Auto insurers are also in a similar position. They do not know how risky a particular driver is.

Asymmetry creates two tough problems for insurers. The first is called *moral hazard*. It is the effect of the insurance itself on the client's efforts to reduce the chance of the insured event. Once a person gets comprehensive medical cover he may become less careful against small ailments. We may not lock our cars or park them in unsafe places if they are fully insured. People may be less wary of drinking before driving when they have a comprehensive insurance. In case of moral hazard, it does not help to gather information on a client before insuring him. Because, once the client gets insured, the probability of the damage will increase.

Insurance companies try to cope in a number of ways. One is to make clients share the cost of damages to keep them careful. They offer policies at a lower premium if the client is willing to bear a part of damage costs. For example, the client may have to pay the first 3000 rupees of the repair cost of the vehicle after any accident. He can pay a significantly smaller premium on this policy than on a policy that reimburses the full cost. Another method is to reduce the premium if the client makes efforts to reduce the chance of the hazard. Home and contents insurance buyers, for example, can save on premium if they install fire and burglar alarms. Similarly, auto insurance buyers can get a lower premium by installing an electronic surveillance system.

The second problem that insurers face is known as *adverse selection*. It tends to create a sort of no-win situation for them. An insurance market contains potential clients with a range of riskiness. For an auto insurance company, clients may be good and careful drivers as well as poor or rash or drunk drivers. They have different accident probabilities. Because the insurer cannot know the driver's type in advance, it would use the average probability of the market to set the premium. But at this premium, low risk drivers find insurance too costly. Some of them would therefore stay without insurance. On the other hand risky drivers would find the premium quite attractive. They would go for it. The company would, therefore, get more bad drivers and fewer good ones than the actual market proportion. Having set the premium according to the overall market probability, it can get normal profits only if it gets good and bad clients in the market proportion. But with a higher ratio of bad drivers, it will get less than normal profit or even make a loss. The problem cannot be eliminated by raising the premium. If the company raises the premium, it will drive away those clients whose risk level is now less than what corresponds to the new premium, and thus the average riskiness of its clients would not fall. The insurer is in this sense in a no-win situation.

A number of methods are used for tackling this menace. The foremost is to acquire and use statistical information to the fullest extent. Potential clients in any given market fall into various demographic, social, and ethnic groups. Insurers engage statisticians to analyse if the risk profile is systematically related with these groups. Is it the case, for instance, that women drivers are less accident-prone than men, or people above fifty than those below fifty? If yes, what are the probability differentials? Can the groups be further narrowed down? Among women, is there a difference between housewives and working women, between single and married women, and so on. Average risk of groups is then used as the basis for premium calculation. The insurer asks the client to provide information on social or demographic features when applying for cover. These features are then used as a proxy for the client's potential riskiness. This is why a smoker pays a higher premium than a non-smoker for identical health insurance coverage.

Insurers use another interesting technique called *screening*. They offer a number of alternative insurance products for the same kind of events. The products are so designed that clients with low risk would prefer to go for one product, while more risky buyers would prefer another. Suppose an auto insurance market has two types of customers, one with a high level of risk and the other with lower risk. An insurance company may offer two policies in this market. One will have an attractive low premium but it would not cover the full value of the car. If the car is valued Rs 300,000, the insurer may provide cover for, say, up to Rs 150,000. At the same time the company sells another policy that would cover the full value of Rs 300,000 but at a substantially higher premium. Low risk drivers would find the premium for full cover too high because they know that their chance of a car bash is very small. So they will buy the cheaper policy with less than full coverage. Because they reckon their chance of an accident as low, they do not mind partial cover if it comes cheap. High risk drivers however would not like incomplete cover even if it is cheap. They would be comfortable only with full coverage and would buy the more costly policy. What these two products achieve for the insurer is obvious.

We may take stock of the discussion so far. Markets fail not only because of lack of competition, but also because of externalities, public goods, and asymmetric information. These instances are widespread in a modern society. When markets fail, resource allocation is no longer efficient. We have looked at the methods used to patch up the problems and realise that they are inadequate. A normal reaction is to suggest that where markets fail the government should be involved. We will take a look at the merits of this suggestion below.

## 4.9 Government Failure

Until fairly recently, it was customary to consider the government as a decision-making unit sitting above the economic process, untouched by its goings-on. It was taken to have no self-interest. Economists explored how such governments would improve things using tax, subsidy, spending, and regulation. The idea resembled a disinterested trustee looking after a community for the benefit of the trust members.

However, a government is anything but a disinterested trustee. It is a collection of real persons—politicians and bureaucrats—who themselves have personal and ideological agendas and career interests. The collective decisions of this group of people need not coincide with the so-called interests of the economy. Second, 'the interests of the economy' by itself has no meaning because the economy is made up of people with different and, often, opposite interests. The so-called interests of the economy acquire shape through a process in which politicians and bureaucrats themselves play a role. Questions about government's economic policy should be recast to reflect this. It means that we should first ask what the assortment of persons comprising a government is likely to do when faced with a particular economic situation. Once that has been understood, we may explore how to make the government take some other measures that we think are better.

This way of looking at the problem is called the 'Public Choice' view. It emerged in the late 1950s. The view increasingly gained ground, particularly after 1986, when one of its two founding theoreticians, James Buchanan received the Nobel Prize in economics.[1] The public choice view draws attention to the fact that just as markets are prone to fail in some situations, so also governments systematically fail to respond in the required way. The failure arises because the decision-making and execution are guided by the players' personal interests. Government decisions are made by committees within a relevant ministry or by inter-ministerial groups. In a democracy these committees are formed with representatives of those who are to be potentially affected. Outcomes result from bargains among the stake-holding groups determined by their bargaining strength. Besides that, typically some groups remain unrepresented. Unrepresented groups are most likely to be economically deprived sections with least political clout. Hence remedial action for market failure cannot be just to leave it to the government believing that it will do what is best for society as a whole. It is necessary to devise mechanisms with checks and balances along the line from decision-making to execution so as to drive decisions towards optimality or fairness. This line of thinking has given rise to a lot of research in the political economy of government decision-making. We now look at political constitutions, contracts, and business laws as potential mechanisms which can be improved to ensure better economic policy.

## 4.10 Market *versus* Government

The role of markets and the government in a production system is one of the most debated questions today. Should markets be given

---

[1] The other theorist is his colleague Gordon Tullock. James Buchanan set up the Center for Study of Public Choice at George Mason University which is the most important centre of public choice research.

a free hand in production? The opposite of the motion is that the government should produce the more important things and at least have a say in the production and prices of other items. Because the subject is tinged with ideology, answers tend to be strongly polarised: an emphatic 'No' or 'Yes'. We need some groundwork to sort out the issues. Let us examine the question separately for production of private goods and public goods.

## 4.10.1 *Private Goods*

Recall that a private good is easily denied to a person who does not pay for it. These are the goods on which we spend most of our income. For these goods we do not have any compelling reason for production or price setting by the government. If new firms can freely enter markets, then private producers are expected to produce at prices close to marginal cost. This assures efficient resource use. A government cannot add anything to this scenario. If government production is entirely guided by commercial motive then it will not achieve anything different from a private business. If on the other hand it has non-profit considerations, as is generally the case, then that would distort resource allocation. Therefore, governments' attempts to produce private goods would either create no difference (if they seek profit) or would lead to waste (when they have non-profit objectives).

However, many governments own factories and facilities that produce private goods. These are often the legacy of the past and politically difficult to dismantle. As we have argued, if production and pricing are decided by bureaucratic fiat, the result would be a waste of resources. To avoid that, the producing unit can be made to work like an ordinary business. It should form a corporation and conduct its business without any special privileges. For new investment it should rely on profits, stock markets, and borrowing and not the public budget. Its management should be independent of the political system but should be responsible to the government as shareholder.

However, even when production of private goods for sale is avoided, governments often tend to produce private goods for their own use. Large governments have a tendency to produce some of their own inputs. They print forms, produce stationary, build and maintain office buildings, repair furniture, maintain security, service office equipment, run employee canteens, maintain and service a fleet of cars, and so on. This kind of production inside the government is generally inefficient. It means that if the government picked up these goods or services from the market, it would save itself money and save the economy some real resources.

We can easily see why. How much of such a good is used in a government department is a bureaucratic decision. Department employees who use the good need not care about the cost. On the other hand, those who produce it inside the department need not care about reducing cost. Money for production is sanctioned as long as the department wants the goods produced. Therefore, the overall result is a loss of efficiency from not having a yardstick for costs and benefits. It is not surprising to find governments employing auto mechanics and electricians who remain unutilised most of the day. We should add to this, some inevitable loss through pilfering and private use by the bosses and employees. All in all, there is no case for the production of private goods by a government, either for the market or for itself.

## 4.10.2 Public Goods

The situation is different for public goods. Private producers go by market demand. So they end up producing less than the optimal quantity. Does this provide a reason for the government to produce? The problem that demand cannot be assessed remains whoever is the producer. It does not disappear if the government produces a public good. But the government has one advantage. It can use the political route to decide how much to produce. For example, a cabinet committee of the government may decide that a four lane road costing X billion rupees is needed and ought to be produced. It is not possible for the private sector to come up with any such idea because it knows that the money cannot be raised from road users. The government, on the other hand, can raise those billions from the general budget or through additional taxes and allocate them for building the road.

The government's advantage, however, ends there. It is not a good builder of roads or producer of any other good for that matter.

If it constructs the road with its employees and bureaucracy, it is expected to build a poor road and spend more than such a road should cost. We have discussed the reasons for that earlier. A better solution is that the government pays for public goods, but gets them produced by private firms that specialise in producing them. This can be done using a number of business models. Contracts can be awarded through competitive bidding among road building firms of repute and experience. The contracts should incorporate the issues of time and cost over-run, quality, future maintenance, and so on. Alternatively, the government can set up its own road construction company. But it has to be fully outside the government's political reach. The government should own it as shareholder but the company should be a profit-seeking company with a clear-cut accountability structure. The government could also set up joint ventures with private construction companies. If the government is short of money required for the road, it can go for other business models. For instance, it can approach private builders to build the road, operate it for a specified number of years and collect toll, and finally transfer it to the government. But in all cases it is best for the government to not take up the task of building the road.

The same principle applies to most public goods but not to all. There are cases such as defence, internal security, policing, prison services, and a few similar items where private production is ruled out by extra-economic factors. Inefficiency inherent in any production whose cost is not compared with the outside world is also present in these cases. But other considerations dominate and the inefficiency has to be accepted.[2]

### 4.10.3 Education and Health care

Education and health care have some special issues. If education is provided only by private institutions, it will be produced to satisfy its market demand. There are two problems with this. First, as we noted, education not only benefits the students who pay for it, but it gives us a better society. So we all benefit from the education of

---

[2]Note, however, that we are talking about condoning poor economic efficiency, not the effectiveness of these organisations in doing their tasks. A police force may be economically inefficient but needs to be effective in crime prevention.

others. But few would pay for the benefit that education brings to others. Therefore, less education will be produced than optimal. The second problem, special to education, health, and a few other services, is that they are 'merit goods', that is, a basic premise of a modern society is that everyone should have access to them. You may not have an iPod if you cannot afford one, but we do not like to say that you may not have education or health care if you cannot afford it. If merit goods are produced and sold like private goods, then generally there would be many people unable to afford them. People below a certain income will have to go without them.

Education and health care have been organised in many ways in different countries at different times. But none has proved to be entirely satisfactory. Governments, not-for-profit organisations, and private providers are in search of the right model and approach. Hence experiments and innovations abound. Let us discuss some of the options that have been tried.

In the former Soviet bloc countries, the government produced and provided for health care etc. in entirety. The principle that the State should be responsible for merit goods cannot be disputed. But production by the government results in a system that is not just inefficient but also ineffective. The government becomes the sole employer of health professionals. So, the professionals' salaries, benefits, and work conditions tend to stagnate. That, in turn, reduces the incentive for joining the profession. It shows up as a serious shortage of health professionals after a generation. Second, the quality of care deteriorates from the lack of competition and mechanisms to set incentives for quality. Further, as demand increases with population growth, the expansion of facilities is not automatically driven by demand as in a private system. It waits for bureaucratic orders creating a serious lag between demand growth and supply increase. On the demand side, there is abuse of services because they are free. Taking pills and diet supplements without sufficient reason not only increases the government's health bill, but also damages national health. Patients would demand and get costly physiotherapy, long medical leave, and paid leave in health resorts when not necessary. The Soviet bloc countries faced all these syndromes.

Many countries have what we may call a dual system. Private organisations provide health care for a price just like any other private good or service. The government also provides health care for free or at subsidised price. This arrangement too has some inherent problems. If health care is available freely as well as at a price, why would anyone buy it at a price? So, to make the system function, there must be some way of keeping some people away from availing the free stuff. Much depends on the method used for this rationing and how well it is managed. In many countries income is the rationing criterion, that is, you get free care if your income is less than Rs X. Families with less income are given membership of the public system. This model has been widely adopted by developing and middle income countries. The procedure, however, has a weakness. Lower income people generally have less political and social clout. Hence the quality of service in the public system tends to decline unless a well-planned mechanism is established to arrest this. Also on the supply side, wages, incentives, work environment, and responsibility structure have to be managed to prevent migration of better professionals to the private sector.

Another way of rationing is by waiting or queuing. In this case the government leaves it to the patient to choose if they would be treated in the private or the public system. Because there will be more demand for the free service, the public system develops a waiting list. Public hospitals advise the expected date when someone applying for a medical procedure today would be admitted for it. It is by considering the expected wait and the cost of the procedure in a private clinic that patients decide about their choice. You may wonder why waiting time cannot be eliminated by capacity expansion of public hospitals. It can of course be done. But then the private sector will be squeezed out of business. The government will then become a monopoly provider and we have discussed the problems of that system already.

Another variation is that the government withdraws from provision of health care altogether but gives financial support to some patients. The government may develop the criterion for such support through public discussion. Once the criteria are established, cost of treatment would be provided to those who qualify. In this scenario, health care is produced only by private establishments. There would be many providers and patients would choose among them based on service quality. The system would give rise to a competitive private health care sector and yet everyone would be cared for. A snag is that if the government simply picks up the bill of the patients, then providers would love to jack up the prices. This can be avoided if cash is handed out to the patients instead of directly paying their bills. The government has to produce a schedule of the amounts it would provide for various medical and surgical procedures on the basis of existing prices. Patients will surely shop around to save a bit of the money that they get from the government. In the process they will induce price competition among producers. The competition, however, may be undermined if providers collude. Recently, there has been a suggestion to form regional consumer organisations to bargain collectively with health providers on behalf of their members and set prices for various medical procedures.

As I remarked earlier, we do not really have a fully satisfactory health care system anywhere. In some countries it is relatively trouble-free but not without flaws. Considerations relevant for health care are also relevant for education. In addition to the issues discussed for health care, we have another problem in the case of education. It arises when the government provides cash support to tertiary students. In the case of health care we saw that giving patients cash is a good solution. In the case of education, when students shop around for tertiary education, institutions can compete along various lines. Tuition fees, library and computers, class room gadgetry, residence facilities, better teaching, accreditation to professional bodies, and placements are some of the items of competition. It is good to have competitive improvement of these features. But it is also possible that institutions would attract students by lowering academic standards—that is, making it easier to pass and get a degree. Courses can be thinned down, level of rigour reduced, percentage of pass and $A$ grades raised—all of this could be competitive tools as well in the cynical world of private production. Academics have indeed complained of this in many countries where education has been recently privatised. In those countries the universities fund themselves from students' fees. The government provides students with a specified sum of money and the universities compete to get more students. It is clear that the government has to ensure that a mechanism is in place to arrest the fall of education standards if this model is adopted.

In a globalised world, the problem affects not only the country itself but other countries as well. Third world students are vulnerable to privatisation of education in some of the western countries. Given the job market value of a western degree, third world students try to acquire such degrees from the relatively cheaper providers in the western world. These would be typically the universities that economise by paying less to their academic staff. As a result, better academic talent bypasses these institutions. Overseas students who get their degrees in these universities obviously do not get a good education in spite of their expenses and hardship overseas.

## 4.11 A Summary

We have now seen that markets fail to allocate resources properly in many situations. These cases arise from some inherent features of production and the peculiarity of a few goods and services. So, production by the government does not necessarily offer a satisfactory solution. Second, government decisions are taken by people who are no less motivated by self-interest than public interest. This adds to the possibility that governments would fail to do the right thing.

Now, because markets and governments are both prone to failure, 'market *vs* government' is not a very useful general debate. A better approach is to debate if a given good or service will be better produced/provided by the government or private producers. Markets function well for private goods and in situations where there is no overwhelming externality. Hence market allocation and private production should be allowed to function unobstructed in these areas.

In the case of public goods, the government should step in as a provider though not as a producer. By and large, governments have poor records as producers. It is not because we have had necessarily bad governments everywhere, but because governance procedures work against efficient production. Given this, governments should raise the money for public goods and get them produced by private producers. There are, of course, exceptions where extra-economic considerations dominate, for example, defence, the police, and so on.

Merit goods, especially health care and education, present a special problem. Governments have to ensure universal availability of these goods. We do not have a fully satisfactory method of providing for and producing these goods. Hopefully, trials and errors around the world will give us the appropriate institutions in the future.

So far we have examined how individual business units work in competitive and other forms of markets. We have also tried to understand the outcome in individual markets given the type of good, private or public. While these microeconomic questions are important, they do not give a complete idea of the economy. We also need to understand the bigger picture. How are the overall income of the economy, its growth rate, and the price level (as opposed to individual prices) determined? How do economy-wide events like recession and inflation occur? These system-wide questions are a part of macroeconomics which analyses the economy as a whole. We will turn to macro questions in the next chapter.

# 5 Unemployment and J.M. Keynes

## 5.1 Unemployment and its Ups and Downs

Unemployment and inflation are the two central economic problems as they touch the lives of almost everyone. In this chapter we will discuss unemployment and how its perception has evolved. First of all we need a way to measure unemployment. The basic question to be answered is 'who all make up the workforce of a country?'—some of whom may be the unemployed at any given time. For this, a specified age bracket is taken as the working age. It differs somewhat across countries. It begins at some age in the teens and ends at some age around or above sixty. However, we do not count all working age persons as workforce because all of them do not want a job. Some wish to be housewives or house-husbands; some want to be self-employed or work on their land, property, or business, and some may be simply unwilling to, or incapable of, work. The workforce is made up of those among the working age people who want to do paid work. The percentage of working age persons who want a paid job is called the participation ratio. This ratio varies across countries.

Unemployment rate is the percentage of workforce without a job. It is found out by a sample survey of households across the country and is subject to significant fluctuation. So, strictly speaking, the rate found by a survey refers to the date of the survey. However, it is used until the next survey. Unemployment rate moves up and down around a long-run trend value. The movement is irregular, that is, periodicity and the amount of fluctuation are not the same through time.

Those found to be unemployed on the survey date have different reasons for being without a job. Some are not interested in a job at that time. We can call them unemployed by choice. This sort of unemployment is more a feature of richer countries where people want to take time off from work once in a while. Second, there are those who have left a job and are looking for another one. They may want a change of location or are looking to improve their career and so on. Their unemployment is called *frictional*. Frictional unemployment, like mechanical friction, cannot be eliminated but can be reduced. Better job search mechanisms and skill matching by job exchanges can cut down transit time between jobs and hence frictional unemployment.

However, some among the frictionally unemployed workers face a challenge. They are those who have lost jobs because of structural changes in the economy. Structural changes occur as some industries recede or die out and new ones come up. As a result, workers in the declining industries lose jobs and look for employment in the emerging industries. This type of unemployment, called *structural unemployment*, is tougher than other forms of frictional unemployment. It requires re-orientation of workers in many ways such as learning new skills and migrating to new industrial centres. It may disrupt the worker's family and life cycle.

There are two other components of unemployment. The first is seasonal fluctuation. In countries with a large agricultural workforce there is huge variation of unemployment reflecting the seasonality of principal crops. The second is a component that moves up and down in tandem with the downs and ups of business called business cycles. Seasonal factors and business cycles contribute large variation to unemployment.

Statistical methods are used to separate out the various components from the data on total unemployment. The part that fluctuates within the year with temporal regularity is attributed to seasonal influence. Seasonal influence need not be from agriculture alone. It may reflect a busy season for various reasons, for example, November to January in Christian countries. From the remaining unemployment we can separate out a long-run trend component. What remains after this is the variation around the long-run trend. We attribute this part to business cycles.

Policy makers are less worried about frictional unemployment if it does not arise from structural change. Some workers will always be in the process of changing jobs and the policy is to shorten the duration with better job-matching facilities. But serious concern centres on the long-run trend of unemployment, particularly, if it is large. It would be sizeable if those losing jobs due to structural change do not find jobs easily. These workers may remain jobless for years in some cases and finally drop out from the workforce believing they are out of sync with the new developments. This is a regrettable development and can disturb social life in industrial neighbourhoods. The second major concern is cyclical unemployment due to the ups and downs of business. Policies to address the long-run trend of unemployment and that due to business cycles are, as you would expect, quite different. Business cycles result from variations in demand. To reduce the short-run unemployment due to business cycles, we attend to the demand side of the economy. But to reduce long-run structural unemployment an economy has to focus on the structure of production. Policies that focus on these issues are called supply side policies.

Unemployment is at the centre of much of the troubles of a modern economy. Theoretical understanding is necessary to help policy intervention. We will explore how economists have tried to understand unemployment and developed measures to deal with it.

## 5.2 How the Classical Theory saw Unemployment

Let us recall the classical idea of unemployment that we have discussed previously. Employers hire up to the point where the worker's marginal product equals the wage rate. If there are some unemployed workers at this stage, it must mean that their marginal productivity is less than the prevailing wage. This is why employers are not willing to employ them. If these unemployed workers are keen to get jobs, they would offer to work below the current wage.

The wage will then come down and the unemployed—some of them at any rate—will get jobs. If it still leaves some workers unemployed, they would bid down the wage further. The process would go on until all those who want work have got it. Unemployment would thus disappear after some wage adjustment. In this story, the labour market has to be competitive and wage should be flexible. If these conditions are met, we should expect the market to employ all those who are looking for jobs.

Given this analysis, if unemployment persists then it can only mean that those who are without jobs are not keen to work at the current wage. Classical theory would call them unemployed by choice or voluntarily unemployed. Classical economists, of course, knew that involuntary unemployment could also arise from time to time. But it would last for a short period—the time it would take for wage to adjust downwards. It would be considered to be a passing state that would be short-lived. The labour market mechanism was expected to work unless something were to clog the wage adjustment process. If, for example, a minimum wage law fixes the minimum wage above the productivity of many workers, then many would remain jobless. Similarly, involuntary unemployment can result from trade unions blocking the fall of wages. The competitive market theory did not admit the possibility of involuntary unemployment unless there were such obstructions. It expected that wage would adjust to a level where all those who wanted a job would be hired.

---

**Box 5.1: Henry Ford and Efficiency Wages**

Is it possible that an employer would pay more than the marginal product or more than the average wage of the industry? Henry Ford did. In 1914 the Ford Motor Company started paying its workers $5 a day when the prevailing wage rate was between $2 and $3. Years later Ford claimed that this was a major reason behind the enormous success of the Ford Motor Company.

Many companies now pay more than the industry average for strategic reasons. The practice is called 'efficiency wage'. It helps companies to get workers more skilled than the average. These workers would also work

---

*(contd...)*

*Box 5.1 continued.*

better and shirk less, knowing that if they lose this job their income will fall to the industry average. This reduces supervision and monitoring costs for the firm as well as turnover and recruitment costs. In developing countries, multinational enterprises generally pay substantially more than the industry average for blue collar workers. They believe it ensures their workers are well-nourished, healthy, and have a relatively better family environment. The companies tend to have a grateful and loyal workforce that is more efficient than others.

## 5.3 Keynes: Why Things are not as in the Classics

It is very likely that you would doubt the above claims about employment and the labour market. Though they sound logical, they do not fit observations—the long periods of unemployment and recession that arise from time to time.

J.M. Keynes was one of the first economists well-versed in the classical theory to doubt and challenge it from within the tradition. The classical theory boils down to saying that if unemployment and the corresponding loss of income persist, then it means that workers chose it that way. As he watched the Great Depression of the 1930s, Keynes found it unbelievable that a quarter of the workforce in so many countries chose penury and starvation rather than a lower wage. Table 5.1 shows the stupendous drop in consumption in the

Table 5.1: Consumer spending on selected items, 1929 and 1933 (in billion)

|  | 1929 | 1933 |
|---|---|---|
| Food | $19.5 | $11.5 |
| Housing | $11.5 | $7.5 |
| Clothing | $11.2 | $5.4 |
| Automobiles | $2.6 | $0.8 |
| Medical care | $2.9 | $1.9 |
| Philanthropy | $1.2 | $0.8 |
| Value of shares on the NYSE* | $89.0 | $19.0 |

*Source*: *Historical Statistics of the United States*, the Millennial Edition.
*Note*: *NYSE is New York Stock Exchange.

US between 1929 and 1933. It was obviously not possible to view this drop as the result of deliberate choice. Nor was it possible to call it a passing disequilibrium. It lasted too long for that. As mentioned in Chapter 1, in 1936 Keynes published the book titled *The General Theory of Employment, Interest and Money* which presented a very different analysis of the labour market and of the economy.

Keynes argued that a depression strikes when *aggregate demand* is insufficient. Aggregate demand is the sum of demand from all sources. Part of it originates inside the country from households, private firms, and the government. A significant part also comes from outside—it is the demand for exports. A recession is triggered when any of these components takes a dip and aggregate demand falls below the normal level. If firms still hire as usual, they won't be able to sell their output. So they lay off workers even though their marginal product is still the same.

When we state it this way it sounds fairly simple. You might even say it is simplistic as it does not take into account the features of various relevant markets. You may think, surely jobs are lost when demand falls, but that can't be the end of the story. For example, you may ask why wouldn't the wage mechanism work? It is surely expected that laid off workers will compete for jobs and bid down the wage rate. This in turn should restore some jobs and if that is not enough then wages would fall further until all jobs are restored.

However, Keynes' argument was anything but simplistic. A lot of reasoning went behind his apparently simple conclusion. He examined all the possibilities of market adjustment in a recession and found that they would not be able to restore full employment automatically. He was in effect saying that a sizeable drop in aggregate demand starts a recession and that may indeed be 'the end of the story'. Read 'end of the story' to mean 'an equilibrium state'—a state that has come to stay.

Though it was clear that Keynes had a new method of analysis, economists seriously differed on its interpretation. Different scholars emphasised different aspects as central. As a result many schools of Keynesianism have developed much like the many sects of a religion. Each emphasises a different set of 'fundamental reasons' for the failure of the market system, drawing on some parts of the *General Theory* and Keynes' other writings. Part of the problem is that Keynes used concepts and terms of economics of his time to discuss ideas that did not exist then. That made the *General Theory* a very difficult book and open to many interpretations. Second, the language of scholarly writing of the time is very different from what it has since become. That introduces further difficulties in reading the book today. 'What Keynes really meant' continues to be the subject of essays in economic journals, though their frequency has abated. It appears that the disagreement has now narrowed down to a few dominant interpretations.

## 5.4 Sticky Prices and the Recession

I will use a simple interpretation to proceed with Keynes' ideas on unemployment. It is based on his observation that prices and wages are not as flexible as classical scholars thought.[1] If we check how prices get fixed in the real world, we will find that most of them are fixed by short term contracts. Factories sign contracts with input suppliers at prices fixed for the contract period. On the selling side, they enter into contracts with wholesalers with pre-agreed prices. Wholesalers, in turn, have contracts with supermarkets to supply at agreed prices for a specified period. These contracts range between three months to a year or more depending on the product. Supply and price contracts in construction, exploration, research and development, and other long term activities are even longer. Contractual prices cannot be changed in a costless manner during the contract. So prices are flexible only over a period long enough for contracts to expire. In the short run, markets are generally stuck at the given prices. Therefore, markets work differently in the short run compared to the classical hypothesis.

---

[1]This is called the 'sticky price' interpretation of the *General Theory*. Those who suggest it are often labelled 'New Keynesians'. They believe that business keeps prices fixed in the short run in a modern economy as changing of price reduces short-run profit. They reason that several strands of the *General Theory* logically imply this and once it is accepted, Keynes' model is very easy to understand.

To appreciate the scenario let us follow the events after a drop in aggregate demand. Retailers are affected first. They cannot lower prices to boost demand, not much at any rate, because they are committed to buying their supplies at fixed prices. So they continue to sell at the same price. Unsold goods would soon pile up with them. When unsold stocks grow, they cut replacement orders. Their suppliers cannot offer significant price discounts to stop these cuts because they, in turn, have to buy inputs at previously contracted prices. So they react by reducing production. That is how the drop in demand moves up the supply chain because prices cannot be adjusted so soon. Therefore, any significant drop in aggregate demand turns into a similar drop in economy-wide production. In turn, this would lead to lay-offs and involuntary unemployment.

This sequence shows why demand does not get restored through price adjustment. But we may ask, what about the labour market? As workers are laid off, they would surely bid down the wage rate and get themselves hired back. That would stop the recession. The question however is why this did not happen in the Great Depression and doesn't happen in other recessions too?

Keynes himself raised and answered this question. He found that the wage mechanism works if there are job cuts in only a few industries. But it cannot work if unemployment prevails in all or most industries. When there is unemployment in most industries, a wage cut has to occur in all of them. It would then produce a significant drop in the economy-wide wage income. Note that wage income is the source of consumer goods demand. So an economy-wide wage fall will add to the demand problem rather than curing it.[2] Thus, the labour market mechanism does not provide any automatic way out.

There is, of course, no doubt that it is profitable to produce more if wage falls. But the firms have to sell the output and not just produce it. They know that selling more at the current price is just

---

[2]Is it not possible for number of jobs to increase more than the fall in wage rate? In that case, the total wage income would increase and demand for consumption goods would increase as well. Well, this is not a likely scenario. Suppose that were to happen and a firm were to restore the pre-recession jobs and production. Because it now pays a larger wage bill it will make less profit than previously. But a firm would hire more only if the wage cut was to increase its profit.

not possible as they are struggling to sell even the current level of output. So more output will only increase the burden of unsold goods. Unsold goods are not welcome—not even if they can be sold at a future date. They have storage costs. Also when goods do not sell, firms cannot pay their banks for the working capital loans they have taken for production. The bottom line is, even if wages showed a tendency to fall, employers would not employ more people or produce more.

## 5.5 Would it be Better if Prices were not Sticky?

The sticky price story is simple and makes sense. It gives us the basic reason why recessions do not go away on their own. But as I said earlier, it is just one possible interpretation of the *General Theory*. The book uses many pages arguing that even if prices were fully flexible, markets would not ward off a recession. We might ignore the stuff saying that prices are not flexible anyway. So what is the point of debating what would or would not happen if they were flexible? But that discussion is useful because it provides insights which were glossed over in the classical theory. I will discuss some of these issues very briefly.

Imagine a big fall in demand and assume that the goods market responds exactly as expected by the classical market theory. A large-scale fall in demand would mean a large amount of unsold goods and the price of goods would start to fall. The price should fall enough for firms to sell what they had been producing. If they produce as much as earlier, they would also employ as many workers as before. So the recession would be over. This is the price mechanism of classical theory.

Note that for this to work, some wage adjustment is required at the same time. The fall in prices automatically increases the real wage rate as the same rupee wage now buys more. At this higher real wage, firms would not employ the pre-recession number of workers. Employment of the pre-recession level can be restored only if the real wage rate is also at the pre-recession level. For that to happen, wage rate has to fall in the same ratio as the price of goods. That fall may also be expected because workers would not mind wage cuts to save their jobs. So wage will fall at the same time as price. When wage has fallen in the same ratio as prices, the real wage is back at its old value and employment should be restored. This is what we would expect if prices and wages were all fully flexible.

This sequence means that the price mechanism will ward off recession if prices and wages are flexible. It means that the classical reasoning was not wrong. If recessions persist because prices or wages are not flexible, then that is a separate matter. We would then say that the Classicals were wrong in considering prices to be flexible. That is a fault of observation, not a failure of reasoning. But Keynes did not accept this. He spent a lot of time arguing that the classical reasoning itself was wrong. Recessions would occur and persist even if prices were perfectly flexible. The fact that wage and price are rigid is not, therefore, the only reason for recessions.

He pointed out—and we have seen this already—that real wage has to be at the pre-recession level to restore the pre-recession jobs. So wages need to fall as much as prices in this process. Now recall that wage is the source of income for most buyers. If wage falls in the same ratio as the price of goods, why would consumers buy any more than at the beginning of the recession? We buy more if goods get cheaper. But if income falls at the same rate, there is no reason to buy more. So, when price and wage fall, demand will not turn around. Firms would find that they cannot sell what they sold prior to the recession. Hence, the price mechanism can correct the demand–supply imbalance in one or a few markets. But it is a fallacy of aggregation to expect that therefore it will do so for all markets at the same time.

Of course, wage income is not the only source of demand and nor are consumption goods the only goods produced. So we should ask, what about other demand? The most important is the demand for investment goods—plants and machinery, buildings, and warehouses etc. They are financed by loans from financial institutions or from business profits. So investment does not depend on wages and it need not necessarily fall when income stagnates. However, it is driven almost entirely by the business sector's confidence about the state of the economy. In a bad recession the outlook is bleak. So businesses do not go in for new projects and previously started projects may be put on hold. Here too, Keynes pointed out that there is no automatic market device to pull it up. Poor investment may reduce the price of investment goods, but price alone cuts no ice in a bad recession. So the price adjustment does not recover investment demand either. The only part of aggregate demand that may respond to a drop in prices is exports. When goods become cheaper inside a country, they become cheaper for overseas buyers if the currency exchange rate does not change meanwhile. However, except for a few countries export is a relatively small part of the GDP. So it is unlikely that exports alone would restore GDP to the full employment level.

When Keynes was advancing his theory, A.C. Pigou at the University of Cambridge (UK) was the most renowned neoclassical economist in England. Keynes often used Pigou's work to highlight the alleged failures of the classical school. During those days of heightened controversy, Pigou elaborated on another possibility of automatic adjustment. He noted that price fall increases the real value of wealth. For owners of wealth, this is like a windfall, equivalent to getting richer. So, it is expected that price fall in a recession would increase their consumption spending. The possibility was later named the 'Pigou Effect'. It is also called the 'wealth effect'. Keynes did not dispute that such an effect exists, but he believed that its magnitude is insignificant. He ridiculed the idea of expecting this slender effect to provide a way out of recessions.

---

**Box 5.2: Is Wealth Effect Significant?**

This controversy can be resolved only empirically, that is, by checking against facts and numbers. So, can we statistically estimate the Pigou effect and assess if it is large enough? To do this, we can first postulate that aggregate consumption depends on GDP (that is, aggregate income), total wealth of all owners, and a few social and demographic variables. The question then would be to what extent these factors influence aggregate consumption; particularly, how much does wealth influence it. To answer this question, we can collect data on GDP, consumption, wealth, and the demographic variables for as many years as we can. Statistics for the same

---

*(contd...)*

*Box 5.2 continued.*

variable over a number of years (or months, weeks, days etc. depending on the variable) are called time series. Time series data for important variables are collected and made available by governments. We can get time series data on GDP, aggregate consumption, and other variables that we need for this exercise for most countries.

Recall that our postulate means that year to year change in consumption is the sum of effects of change of a few specified variables. The effect a variable produces on consumption is called its coefficient. We can try alternative values of the coefficients of our variables and work out aggregate consumption for all the years. We can then pick up the combination of coefficients that gives us a series of yearly consumption closest to the actual data. These coefficients, that is, the ones that fit best, are then taken to describe our postulated consumption relation. The best fit is picked up by a statistical method called Regression Analysis. The coefficients describe the effect of a unit change in a variable on aggregate consumption. For example, one of them would describe the effect of one billion rupee increase in GDP on the society's aggregate consumption if wealth and demographic variables remained unchanged. The one that we are interested in is the effect of a billion rupee increase in aggregate wealth on consumption when other variables remain unchanged. This quantity would be our estimate of the wealth effect. If it is too small, we would agree with Keynes and if large we would go with Pigou.

The method of regression analysis is not difficult to use. There is user-friendly software that guides us through the steps beginning with the first step of entering data. But we face a problem in this exercise on the data side. Wealth, as you know, can be of two kinds. Some are real things such as machines, factories, goods in one's warehouse, buildings, land, gold, and so on. The other kind is financial wealth. It is a claim held on other people or institutions. If I have lent money to a company, then I hold a claim on it for that amount. That claim would be part of my wealth. I will certainly feel richer for it and it may prompt me to spend a bit more on consumption. But while the financial claim held by one person is her wealth, at the same time it is the liability of another person or institution. So when we sum up the total wealth for a whole country, most of the financial wealth owned by its people cancels out with liability or 'negative wealth' held by others. Aggregate financial

*(contd...)*

*Box 5.2 continued.*

wealth will show an increase only if people own debts by people or institutions of other countries. But we do know from observation that aggregate consumption spending goes up when there is a financial boom. This happens in spite of the fact that such a boom increases financial wealth as also liability. Thus financial wealth introduces a conceptual difficulty into the exercise and we must find a way of handling it. It has been handled by researchers with a number of *ad hoc* methods and none seems to be entirely satisfactory.

Another possibility is to look for periods in which the price level has fallen for a fair number of years. A price fall means a corresponding increase in the real value of wealth. So, the price fall for a significant number of years increases real wealth substantially. We can check if price fall over the years induces any significant increase in consumption. If Pigou was right then the price fall for a fair number of years should raise aggregate consumption by a significant amount.

A natural experiment has been provided by Japan recently. Japan's prices fell continuously between 1995 and 2006 during a long period of stagnation. There was, however, little to suggest that this price fall boosted consumer spending. Consumption remained low, stubbornly prolonging the stagnation. However, market interviews of Japanese consumers revealed some interesting issues which complicate our simple experiment quite a bit. Japanese buyers reported that they preferred to delay big ticket consumption purchases expecting that prices would fall even further.

## 5.6 The Interest Rate Mechanism

The conviction that recession cannot persist for long was based on the general belief in the price mechanism. The idea is that the price of a good or resource will adjust to generate enough demand to use the available supply. Accordingly, prices of goods and wage rates would change to generate enough demand for all that the economy produces and all of its labour supply. We have already seen why Keynes argued that price and wage adjustments are unable to cure a recession. Like wages and goods prices, interest rate adjustment is another important price mechanism. We will briefly examine if it can be effective against recessions.

To keep things simple, think of a 'closed' economy, that is, one with no imports or exports. To make things even simpler, assume that there is no expenditure by the government. In such an economy, one part of GDP is bought for consumption and the rest is for investment. There is no other type of demand or expenditure. In the course of producing the GDP, firms pay out wages, the income of workers. And then when the products are sold, firm owners get profits—their income. Total income earned by workers and owners is the total of all wages and profits. Note that this is also the value of the GDP.[3] Workers and owners would spend a part of their income on consumption. The remaining part is the economy's saving. If all output is to be sold, then the part of GDP that has not been bought for consumption has to be bought for investment purposes. This means that the value of saving must be equal to the value of investment. Hence, in order for all goods to be sold, saving and investment have to be equal.

The financial market is involved in the job of making saving and investment equal. Savings are deposited in the financial system, say, with banks. On the other side, business firms want money for investment, which they borrow from banks. If the saving with banks exceeds investment demand, banks reduce the interest rate to make it more attractive to borrow. They raise it in the opposite situation. This interest rate variation ensures that in the end the supply and demand for funds is equal, that is, saving and investment are equalised. It means that income not spent on consumption is eventually spent on investment.

Classical economists thought that because of this mechanism, if the economy produces to its full capacity, it will find no problem selling it. This is another reason why they expected that a recession would only be short-lived. What is not bought for consumption would eventually be bought for investment. Apart from asserting that recessions can be cured by interest rate adjustments, this idea has a further implication. It means that the growth of an economy depends on its supply or production capacity. Because all supply is sold, income or GDP will increase if supply capacity rises. This is referred to as the supply-side

[3]GDP does not include the value of materials that are processed into goods. So it equals the sum of only non-material costs like wages and profits which form the price of goods. Thus GDP is equal to the income of the participants of the economy.

view of economic growth. As per this view, a recipe for growth is to mind the supply side factors such as technology, infrastructure, skills, production organisation, and material resources.

---

**Box 5.3: Say's Law**

'Full employment output' is the output produced when all workers willing to work at the going wage rate are employed. Business likes to produce at this level because it brings them the maximum possible profit. It would produce less only if it fears that selling would be difficult. As we have noted, classical theory believed that this possibility does not exist. Flexible prices, wages, and interest rates would ensure that all that is produced will be sold in the end. This is behind the classical belief that an economy would utilise all its production resources and operate at the full employment level.

This idea was forcefully reasoned by J.B. Say (1767–1832), a French economist, in his 1803 book *Treatise on Political Economy*. His contemporary in England, James Mill (1773–1836) later summarised Say's position in a pithy sentence, 'Supply creates its own demand' which is often referred to as Say's Law.

It is possibly because of Mill's one-liner that Say became the symbol of the classical supply-side view. As a result, more often Say rather than any other classical economist has been taken as the exemplary wrong-doer by anti-classical authors—notably by both Karl Marx and J.M. Keynes. From the severe criticism of his work by Marx and Keynes do not, however, conclude that Say was a conservative member of the nobility. He was a zealous republican and was overjoyed by the fall of the Bastille and the French Revolution. In 1792 he had even served as a volunteer in the military campaign to force the Allied armies from France.

In fact, Say's vision was wider than supply–demand oriented economics in terms of which he is interpreted. Around his economic reasoning he had woven a grander idea: if a good thing is begun its acceptance is ensured in the end. That supply creates its own demand was an illustration of this optimistic message.

Say's Law does fail in the short run as we now know from experience. An economy fails to attain its best output and full employment every so often. As we have seen, the reason is the rigidity of prices and wages. However, the law remains a good approximation of the long-run state of affairs in industrial capitalism because prices and wages do adjust adequately if they get enough time.

Keynes did not doubt that interest rate variation equalises saving with investment. But he pointed out that this does not mean that it restores full employment. To do that, banks must be able to raise investment *adequately*. But this is beyond their ability in bad times when investment does not increase much even when interest is reduced sizeably. A serious recession can be cured only if investment increases by a large amount. This increase is generally not achievable even by cutting interest rate down to zero.

In recessions, saving is relatively small because people are saving from a relatively lower income. Interest rate variation equalises investment to this relatively smaller saving. So the financial mechanism does work but it does not lead the economy out of the recession.

Was Keynes right? Is there any evidence that central banks pushed the interest rate down to zero or near zero to fight a recession and yet investment did not pick up? There seem to be many such examples during the Great Depression. Box 5.4 lists some episodes nearer our time.

---

### Box 5.4: Zero Interest Rate

Several countries have found that interest rate cuts do not induce much investment in case of serious recessions or long-term stagnation. During Japan's long stagnation of the 1990s, its central bank kept reducing the interest rate till it was brought down to zero in 1999. It stayed there till 2006 except for a brief interlude. The zero-rate policy did little to stimulate investment or consumption.

During the US recession that started with the 2007 financial crisis, the US Federal Reserve (that is, the US central bank) kept reducing its key interest rate. It began from above 5 per cent in 2007 when the crisis started. Interest rate was cut in steps, at each step hoping to get an investment response. There was no such response. It came down to 0.25 per cent in December 2008 but there was no sign that the near-zero rate had any effect.

On the other hand, interest rate cut does work in mild recessions and is used as an effective instrument. Demand management with monetary

---

*(contd...)*

*Box 5.4 continued.*

> policy depends entirely on the variation of key interest rates by the central bank. Therefore, it appears that the relation between interest rate and investment is not the same at all times. It depends on the overall economic situation and the state of business confidence.

## 5.7 Recessions Start in so many Ways

What kinds of events bring about the demand dip that starts a recession? Well, events can strike any component of demand and a recession can start. Most often, however, they have started with a slump in investment. Investment is very sensitive to the outlook for expected profits. Therefore, any news, prediction, fear, or rumour that suggests a fall in profitability hits investment adversely. A drought, a flood, fear that the central bank may raise interest rate or the parliament may pass an unfavourable bill, forecast of an oil price hike, are a few of a myriad examples. Further, the scare need not be from the economy. It may start from the political arena as well. Examples are: fear that a pro-business government might lose elections, a left of centre coalition might come to power, possibility of a hung parliament, tension with a bordering country, political uncertainty in a neighbouring country, and so on. In the normal course, business outlook and investment fluctuate within reasonable limits because both good and bad news arrive in a random fashion. But when bad news is plentiful and good news is scant, investment takes a big dip.

A slump may also be 'imported'. The Great Depression had started in the US. When the US income fell, its demand for imports fell too. On top of that, the US Government tried to protect domestic business by imposing import restrictions. The Smoot–Hawley Tariff Act of the US was passed in 1930 for this purpose. It imposed tariffs on many imports which hit Europe's exports significantly. As a result, aggregate demand fell in Europe. Europe thus imported the depression from the US. When European countries faced the slump their demand for one another's imports fell too. This is a general syndrome in any recession. As the income of one country falls, its need for imports falls automatically. At the same time, each country uses a 'beggar thy neighbour' policy to protect its jobs and incomes by restricting imports. In the Great Depression, this process started a downward spiral, travelling from one country to another. The sequence travelled to Japan as well. The value of world trade in 1933 shrank to one-third of what it was immediately before the depression.[4]

A slump can start from the households too. Household consumption is a large part of demand. In rich countries people buy a sizeable part of their consumption with borrowed money, from banks, sellers' credit, and credit card agencies. Much like investment, this consumption is sensitive to the outlook for the future. Consumers' confidence improves when unemployment is low and wages are rising. This increases spending on big items such as housing, holidays, and air travel with borrowed money. A grim outlook can jolt the smugness and bring about a sudden dip in consumer spending.

---

### Box 5.5: GDP and GNP

GDP is a summary measure of economic activity. We calculate it by totalling the market value of all *final* goods and services produced in an economy in a year. Final goods are those that go into use directly, for example, bread, meat, cars, and machinery. They are distinct from *intermediate* goods which are used as input for some other production. Intermediate goods are not included in GDP. Market prices of final goods contain the prices of the intermediate goods used in their production. So if the intermediate goods were included, then we would count them twice, once separately and once as part of some final good. This is why GDP sums up the value of only final goods.

GDP is all that is produced in a country understood as a geographical area. But some of this is may be owned by foreigners. Similarly, some of its nationals and companies may be earning income in foreign countries. If we are interested in the income of the nationals of our country, we would add to GDP the income earned by our nationals and companies in other countries and subtract the income of foreign nationals and companies earned here. The resulting quantity is called the Gross National Product (GNP).

---

[4]*Source*: Kindleberger, Charles, *The World in Depression*, University of California Press, Berkeley, 1973.

## Box 5.6: The Liquidity Trap

Keynes doubted that interest rate cuts could enthuse business investment in a bad recession. He further claimed that it might not be in the powers of a central bank to reduce interest rate below a certain low value. The latter idea came to be known as the Liquidity Trap. Keynes used the 1930s experience of the UK financial market to make his point. This idea was abandoned after the initial enthusiasm about the *General Theory* died out. It was thought to be a theoretical possibility of little practical relevance. But it has come back into circulation after the Japanese recession of the 1990s which evidenced the liquidity trap according to some economists. How does a liquidity trap develop? Here is Keynes' version.

A central bank reduces interest rate by pushing more money into the economy through 'open market operations' (OMO). In these operations the central bank buys and sells government bonds. To force more money into circulation, the bank buys government bonds from commercial banks and others. The money that the commercial banks and the public get by selling the bonds adds to the existing amount of circulating money. This increase in money in circulation reduces the interest rate.

To induce the public to sell off their bonds the central bank offers a higher price. As it tries to push more money into circulation, it raises bond price continuously and the interest rate also drops continuously. When the interest rate is very low and bond prices are close to the highest level in public memory, banks and the investing public start fearing that the bond price cannot go up any more. From here it can only tumble down. So at this stage they sell off their remaining bonds to avoid loss. An offer of higher bond price cannot draw any more customers now, because no one has any bonds to sell. Hence open market operations now fail to work and interest rate does not fall any more. Thus at a very low interest rate, a central bank may not be able to reduce it any further. The name 'liquidity trap' derives from the idea that at very high bond prices, investors want to keep their assets 'liquid', that is, in the form of cash. Though bonds may give them some interest income however small, they fear that their price will tumble down. It is therefore wiser to stay liquid.

Recently some economists have suggested other possible ways to the liquidity trap based on more recent experiences of financial markets.

A third route through which a recession can start is a large drop in foreign investment. Foreign investment has become an important part of GDP in many countries as economies get more connected to the world—the so-called globalisation. A common cause of sudden drop in foreign investment is the fear that the host country may change its policy towards foreign business. Local political developments often lead to such scares. Such fear can also arise from the foreign exchange market. If it is feared that the host country's currency would lose value soon, foreign investors withdraw their funds. Particularly traumatic are episodes where the host country currency is 'attacked' by currency speculators. The fall in currency value in these cases is spectacular and leads to a complete halt in all foreign investment leading to serious economic crisis.

---

### Box 5.7: Attack on Currency

A currency speculator starts an attack on a currency by selling off a large amount of it from its own stock. This brings down the price. Other market participants get panicky; they conjecture that those who are selling such large amounts must have good information that the price is going to fall. Some speculators may even plant articles and stories in financial journals and newspapers with apparently reasoned analysis why the currency is expected to fall. All this triggers a secondary wave of selling by others. Soon the currency loses a lot of value. This provides confirmation that the fear has merit. So, more people sell in panic, and the currency loses more value. At this point, the speculator who had begun the game buys the currency back. It makes handsome gains by having sold at high price earlier and bought at lower price later. It is obvious that the initiator must be a large player in relation to the size of the market. Smaller players keep a watch on such large players. If they sense that the latter are initiating an attack, they too start selling in order to make a gain by repurchase later on. This tends to accentuate the speculative attack.

In 1992 George Soros, the manager of Quantum hedge fund, noted that interest rates in UK and Germany were misaligned in relation to their relative exchange rates. At that time the exchange rate between the two

---

*(contd...)*

*Box 5.7 continued.*

currencies was fixed by their central banks.[5] Soros found that investors could borrow money in UK, sell pounds for deutschemarks and lend in Germany at a rate higher than what they borrowed for in the UK. They could then bring back the profit to UK and overall make a significant profit. If this happened in a big way then UK would have to lower its currency value. Before this happened, he started selling his fund's British assets and also at the same time wrote articles explaining that the pound was unsustainably over-valued. This encouraged a sale of the pound and eventually the pound got devalued. In the end Quantum fund bought British assets back at lower prices and made a handsome gain.

Currency speculation as in this example is a legitimate business operation. Whether a speculator attacked a currency in a given episode cannot be generally ascertained. An *ex ante* motive of attack cannot be attributed only because a firm happens to make a large gain. Yet large currency price movements often create suspicion and unofficial blacklisting of currency speculators and firms. For example, some people, including the Malaysian Prime Minister of that time, Mahathir Mohamad, had alleged an attack on the Malaysian currency during the Asian financial crisis of 1997. By nature these allegations cannot be proved unless the alleged firm itself or its employees acknowledge the act.

## 5.8 The Keynesian Revolution

By the end of the Second World War, majority of influential economists and statesmen got converted to the Keynesian view. Keynesian economics became 'mainstream' rather than unorthodox. The practical message of Keynes' writings was that the government has to get involved when an economy is in recession. It should take up programmes of large scale spending to create demand. This can be financed through taxes, by borrowing, or by creating money through the central bank. This view is the opposite of the classical *Laissez Faire*, which holds that governments should stay away from the economy.

[5]That is, the exchange rate was not determined by the relative supply and demand of the two currencies.

## Box 5.8: The Multiplier

A recession results from a drop in demand and hence there is a suggestion for demand creation by the government. But can we quantify the amount of demand injection necessary in a given situation? Suppose the UK was in a state of full employment and its GDP was at £2000 billion. Suppose GDP then drops by £100 billion due to an investment scare and a recession starts. How much should the government spend to avoid the recession and get back to full employment? We might like to answer £100 billion because income or GDP dropped by that much. Interestingly, a much smaller expenditure will do.

To see why, start by supposing that the government spends, say, only £10 billion. In practical terms this means that it orders £10 billion of various goods and services from the market. For example, it can order new roads and bridges costing £10 billion. This order will be met by the producers of steel, cement etc. and construction firms. As these activities occur and the government pays for them, £10 billion will flow from the government to factory owners, contractors, and workers. So, this will create £10 billion of extra private income.

What will people do with this newly-received income? They will use a part for consumption spending and save the rest. Suppose on average the people of UK spend 80 per cent of any extra income on consumption. Then the new income of £ 10 billion will create £8 billion of extra demand for consumption goods. Producers of consumption goods will welcome it and meet it with production of £8 billion of consumption goods. In the course of this production, they will pay £8 billion in wages, rents etc. and the rest as profit. In other words they will create an extra income of £ 8 billion.

This £8 billion of extra income should now lead their recipients to spend 80 per cent, that is, £6.4 billion on consumption goods. This would be met by that much more production of consumer goods. Hence, so much more income as wage and profit etc. is created.

In this story, £10 billion of government spending has so far created three 'rounds' of income. The first is £10 billion straight from the government's purchase orders. The next is £8 billion of consumption good production; and the third is £6.4 billion more of consumption goods. In all £24.4 billion of income has been created as a result of government spending of £10 billion. It should be clear that demand creation leading

*(contd...)*

*Box 5.8 continued.*

to income and again demand, and again income would continue in this way beyond £24.4 billion. Theoretically speaking, the sequence should continue forever. But each round of income will be smaller than the last because each time people spend only a part of the new income and save the rest. So the chain practically stops after a few rounds. But as we saw, government spending of £10 billion creates more than £24 billion in income! Thus the government can fight a £100 billion drop of investment by spending much less than £100 billion.

The ratio of eventual income rise and the initial spending is called the Keynesian Multiplier. The example I gave here makes it clear that the multiplier will be larger if people spend more of their income on consumption. The precise relation is, multiplier = $1/(1-a)$, where $a$ is the part of extra income that is spent on consumption. If people on average spend 80 per cent of an extra pound then the multiplier is $1/(1-0.8) = 5$. In that case if the government comes out with a programme of buying £1 billion of goods, it will create income of £5billion.

The number $a$ is an important parameter of the economy. We were not aware of its importance before Keynes, who gave it a name, 'the marginal propensity to consume'. The name has stuck to scare economics students forever. Marginal propensity to consume (or MPC), is a fairly stable parameter of an economy and so we can base a lot of useful policy and calculations on it.

Economists and policy makers of the time were charmed by the idea of the 'multiplier'. When the government increases purchase by a certain amount, GDP is expected to increase by a multiple of the purchase. Hence if the government taxes the public and then spends the proceeds, there is going to be a net increase of income and jobs. It is even better if the government does not tax, but funds the spending by borrowing or money creation.

Governments soon invented myriads of ways of spending in order to set economic expansion in motion. They learned to spend directly as also to provide incentives to private spending. Direct spending initially included construction projects: roads, bridges, government buildings etc. As imagination flowered, governments learned to spend big on their own consumption as well. Government offices acquired snazzy looks; they got better furniture and equipment, transport and telephones for more bureaucrats. Left of centre governments got a wonderful excuse to set up public sector industries. Right of centre governments got no less a wonderful excuse to spend on defence and arms.

To induce private investment, governments perfected the art of giving tax breaks, free or cheap land, duty exemption, and subsidies. To boost consumer spending, they started unemployment support, old age pension, free or subsidised health care etc. Income tax cuts were seen as a policy tool for boosting personal consumption. Cut in interest rate became a standard instrument for providing incentive to business and consumers. Exporters got their share too: export subsidies, duty-free import of inputs, subsidised shipping and insurance from government companies and so on. Within a decade after the end of the war, government spending and inducement for private spending became standard tools of economic management.

These measures are known as expansionary measures. Collectively they are known as expansionary policy. The opposite, where a government deliberately reduces demand (in order to rein in inflation) is known as contraction. These terms arose and became popular during the period. Policy for expansion and contraction also uses interest rate as a tool. Interest rate cuts induce business and consumers to spend more, while an increase in interest rate curbs expenditure.

---

**Box 5.9: Government Spending, UK**

Government expenditure was less than 15 per cent of GDP in UK at the beginning of the twentieth century. It rode the Keynesian revolution to reach 50 per cent of GDP in 1975. This level of government expenditure was not sustainable as we will see in the next chapter. The UK and other European economies that went through similar trajectories, had to pay a price for the so-called long boom engineered by sustained government spending through deficit financing. In the face of unrelenting inflation they were forced to change their economic policies radically in the late 1970s and early 1980s. By 1998, the general government expenditure fell to the neighbourhood of 39 per cent of GDP in the UK.

In all these cases it is ultimately the government that spends money or forgoes tax money. This is quite obvious when the government spends directly on infrastructure or departmental purchases. It may not be so obvious in other cases. But when it offers tax breaks or free land, it loses potential revenue, and when it provides welfare support it costs the government an equivalent amount.

In an important sense, this also describes the essence of Keynesian policy. When a recession is on, incomes of consumers and business fall and so they reduce spending. It is not possible to make them spend more without putting money into their pockets. But who can do so in a recession? Well, the answer is obvious. The government alone has the ability to spend, recession or no recession. It is true that a government too suffers a loss in a recession, for example, tax and non-tax receipts fall. But that does not reduce its ability to spend. It can spend from its reserve, borrow from commercial banks, or borrow from the central bank. Borrowing from the central bank is another name for money creation. So a government alone can increase spending in a recession, and if it does so in adequate amount, it can spend its way out of it. Governments across the world seemed to understand this message pretty well and spent aggressively in the following decades.

The policy of spending was adopted by governments across the left–right spectrum. Centre-left governments spent more on health, education, and other welfare areas, while the centre right spent to support private business and beef up military capability. Governments that had used unemployment dole during the Great Depression as a temporary measure were persuaded that unemployment support makes sense as a permanent feature. If an economy has unemployment dole in place, those who lose jobs do not have to cut down their spending. This keeps the severity of a business downturn in check by keeping consumer goods industries insulated. Unemployment benefits are hence known as 'automatic stabilisers' (see Chapter 6).

The world of governance changed beyond recognition in a few decades. Gone were the pre-war governments whose only preoccupations were policing and defence. In came the big governments with many ministries—some with multiple departments and each with a significant budget. Table 5.2 shows the evolution of government spending since 1870. Note the steady rise in spending as a ratio of GDP. The GDP itself has grown steadily. So the absolute amount of spending has increased much more than what the proportions reflect. By 1960 the governments of the world had changed the way they used to think of finance and public budgets before the Great Depression. Germany, Italy, and Japan—the countries that lost the war and faced serious restructuring of economy and government—were the exceptions in the general movement. Among the others, Switzerland stands out as the lone country whose government spent less of its GDP in 1960 than in 1937, the year after the *General Theory* was published.

Until the war, money for government spending used to come mostly from taxes. Governments did of course borrow from merchants and banks from time to time. But they borrowed as little as possible

Table 5.2: Government spending as percentage of GDP

|  | 1870 | 1913 | 1920 | 1937 | 1960 | 1980 | 1990 | 2000 | 2005 | 2009 |
|---|---|---|---|---|---|---|---|---|---|---|
| Austria | 10.5 | 17.0 | 14.7 | 20.6 | 35.7 | 48.1 | 38.6 | 52.1 | 50.2 | 52.3 |
| Belgium | NA | 13.8 | 22.1 | 21.8 | 30.3 | 58.6 | 54.8 | 49.1 | 52.0 | 54.0 |
| Britain | 9.4 | 12.7 | 26.2 | 30.0 | 32.2 | 43.0 | 39.9 | 36.6 | 40.6 | 47.2 |
| Canada | NA | NA | 16.7 | 25.0 | 28.6 | 38.8 | 46.0 | 40.6 | 39.2 | 43.8 |
| France | 12.6 | 17.0 | 27.6 | 29.0 | 34.6 | 46.1 | 49.8 | 51.6 | 53.4 | 56.0 |
| Germany | 10.0 | 14.8 | 25.0 | 34.1 | 32.4 | 47.9 | 45.1 | 45.1 | 46.8 | 47.6 |
| Italy | 13.7 | 17.1 | 30.1 | 31.1 | 30.1 | 42.1 | 53.4 | 46.2 | 48.2 | 51.9 |
| Japan | 8.8 | 8.3 | 14.8 | 25.4 | 17.5 | 32.0 | 31.3 | 37.3 | 34.2 | 39.7 |
| Netherlands | 9.1 | 9.0 | 13.5 | 19.0 | 33.7 | 55.8 | 54.1 | 44.2 | 44.8 | 50.0 |
| Spain | NA | 11.0 | 8.3 | 13.2 | 18.8 | 32.2 | 42.0 | 39.1 | 38.4 | 45.8 |
| Sweden | 5.7 | 10.4 | 10.9 | 16.5 | 31.0 | 60.1 | 59.1 | 52.7 | 51.8 | 52.7 |
| Switzerland | 16.5 | 14.0 | 17.0 | 24.1 | 17.2 | 32.8 | 33.5 | 33.7 | 37.3 | 36.7 |
| United States | 7.3 | 7.5 | 12.1 | 19.7 | 27.0 | 31.4 | 33.3 | 32.8 | 36.1 | 42.2 |
| Average | 10.4 | 12.7 | 18.4 | 23.8 | 28.4 | 43.8 | 44.7 | 43.2 | 44.1 | 47.7 |

*Sources:* Tanzi and Schuknecht;[6] IMF; OECD.
*Note:* NA = not available.

[6]Tanzi, Vito and Ludger Schuknecht, *Public Spending in the 20th Century: A Global Perspective*, Cambridge, Cambridge University Press, 2000.

limiting it to the occasions of war, famine, and other emergencies. Because income and output fall in a recession, a government's tax collection also drops. So a government with traditional views on budget would try to curtail spending in a recession. The Keynesian revolution brought the message that it should be the other way round—governments should spend more in a recession, not less. They should spend by borrowing if necessary.

In the modern context, a government can borrow from commercial banks and financial institutions, or from the country's central bank. Borrowing from the central bank results in new money creation. The government hands over to the central bank government securities or evidence of the loan. The central bank creates an equivalent amount of deposits in the government's bank account. The government then uses those deposits as it spends. In the process, the government gets money to spend without reducing money held by anyone else. Spending more than revenue is called deficit financing. The majority opinion of the time agreed that deficit financing was not only harmless but good in a recession. The policy of deficit spending in a recession gradually changed into routine deficit financing even when no recession was in sight. The idea was that large spending keeps up the aggregate demand and hence recessions can be stopped even before they arise.

Keynesian ideas had a significant effect on public finance everywhere. Two very important long-run effects should be noted. A long-run tendency in all countries was an increase in government spending as part of GDP. The other applies more to Europe, where there was a second tendency, an increase in deficit spending as a ratio of total government spending and GDP.

---

### Box 5.10: Michal Kalecki (1899–1970)

Three years before the *General Theory* was published, an essay on business cycles appeared in a Polish journal. The title of the article, later translated into English, is 'An Essay on the Theory of the Business Cycle'. It saw the ups and downs of business cycles as the characteristic dynamics of how capitalist economies work. In its view, a recession is a phase of this dynamics and is a regular, not an accidental, event.

---

*(contd...)*

*Box 5.10 continued.*

The method of analysis foreshadowed Keynes' work. The author of the paper, Michal Kalecki was a little known employee of the Research Institute of Business Cycle and Prices (RIBCP) in Poland. He was an engineering student but could not complete his studies and turned to writing for newspapers for a living, and then got the job at RIBCP. He was a socialist by persuasion and had a political interest in the working of capitalism. At RIBCP he became familiar with economic data and empirics. This complemented his interest in the economy. He had read the Marxist literature on capitalist economies of his time. Because of his background, his method of analysis was novel and he was not constrained to use the jargon and concepts of academic economics like Keynes would do a few years later. It is remarkable that working with very different perspectives and premises, Kalecki and Keynes arrived at similar conclusions.

Kalecki wrote several versions of his 1933 paper as well as a number of other essays as he later interacted with economists from the English speaking world. His interest in the economy stemmed from his political interest. This took him beyond the capitalist cycles and he tried to develop macroeconomic frameworks for understanding socialist as well as developing economies. At various times he worked at the London School of Economics, University of Cambridge, University of Oxford, and Warsaw School of Economics. He was an economic advisor to the governments of Cuba, India, Israel and Mexico, and advised a perspective plan for Poland for some time.

## 5.9 Countercyclical Demand Management

We have already noted that GDP and employment go through ups and downs because of business cycles. Keynesian economists believed that it was possible to vary government spending to counter these movements. The idea was to increase spending during the downswing of the business cycle, and reduce it during the upswing. To be able to fine-tune government spending for these operations, economists required extensive knowledge of various types of spending—in the government and the private sector—and their quantitative effects. Driven by this interest, national level accounting of economic activities and spending became a focus of intense research. Classification and collection of data on national accounts and macroeconomic variables were standardised. Newly available data boosted interest in using them for both policy and academic research.

Economists with Keynesian persuasion got into advisory and administrative positions in most governments and treasuries of the time. They took active part in promoting demand management. Supporting facilities had to be developed for this:

- in-house expertise in the treasury and the central bank for handling national accounts and statistical data and to make short-run forecasts;
- tools of intervention for the treasury and the central bank;
- legislation to empower the ministry of finance and the central bank to act as necessary; and
- human resource and research infrastructure for continuous monitoring of the economy and design and execution of intervention.

These were done in the 1950s and early 1960 along with the development of macroeconomic theory that would guide government intervention.

## 5.10 Fiscal and Monetary Policy

Demand management and countercyclical policy are conducted using a government's budgetary and monetary powers. The ministry of finance, in some countries called 'the treasury', uses its power to set the public budget. The budget sets the amount of government's purchase of goods and services. Second, it fixes income tax and other tax rates. And finally it can alter the amount of 'transfer payment' to the public. These are items such as unemployment benefit, cash subsidies etc.—amounts passed on by the government without any exchange of good or service. A government's annual budget announces its intended purchases, taxes, and transfers for the year ahead. The items that the budget deals with influence the aggregate demand. The use of the budget for influencing the economy is called fiscal[7] policy.

[7]Derived from 'fisc', meaning the royal or state treasury, which comes from the Latin word *fiscus* meaning treasury as well as a moneybag, a basket, or a bag.

Economic activity is also influenced by using a government's monetary power. If there is more money in circulation, banks have more to lend and the interest rate drops. At lower interest, firms and households borrow more. Firms use cheaper loans for investment, and households for durable goods, housing, travel, or just plain consumption. Contraction can be induced by making money 'dear' rather than 'cheap'. This is done by reducing money supply. Central banks are entrusted with the management of money supply. So, monetary policy—making money cheap or dear—is operated by the central bank.

## 5.11 Cheap Money in the Post-war Period

As discussed earlier, monetary and fiscal policy are handled by different agencies. A treasury's task becomes easier if it has a good relationship with the central bank. When treasuries want to run deficits, they are more comfortable if they have a co-operating central bank. If the central bank does not lend, then treasuries have to turn to commercial borrowing. If deficits grow, commercial interest rate would increase and so would the cost of loans and of servicing old debt. This reduces a treasury's ability for deficit financing. This can be avoided if the central bank lends the required amounts. Hence, the relation between treasury and the central bank is of interest in policy making.

The association between the two institutions is still evolving. Looking across countries we find three broad types. In some countries the central bank is fully within the government, that is, its head is the minister of finance or a cabinet minister. In another group, the central bank is under an autonomous management but there is a close informal connection between the bank and the government. The relation is sustained through bureaucratic and political ties, and also because the government selects the board of the bank. In the third group, the central bank has real autonomy from the government which is formalised by the statutes of the country. In this set-up the government contracts out the operation of the monetary system as per certain contractual guidelines. The contract specifies what the government may and may not ask from the central bank. The contract also provides for possible reasons and circumstances for termination of the contract.

Central banks were closely tied to their governments in the aftermath of the Second World War. This ensured that central banks always obliged when governments wanted to borrow. So the treasuries were not constrained in their spending. Thus, the decades of 1950s and 1960s saw the swelling of cheap money. Money supply grew rapidly as governments borrowed from central banks and spent as a matter of policy. Large amounts of money kept interest rate low which sustained private spending. Economies performed close to full employment. The economies were on a long period of boom.

There was a widespread belief that the long boom was the result of sound economic policy which, of course, meant Keynesian policy. It was believed that armed with the new 'science', the world's economies could function in a state of permanent full employment. Many believed that the problem of business cycles had been permanently overcome by economic science, much the same way that malaria and small pox had been eradicated by medical science. We will see in the next chapter how this complacency would be shaken by the experience of the next decade.

## 5.12 A Summary

Classical economics did not spare much thought for unemployment because it believed that it always ends through the normal functioning of markets. It is generated by a temporary drop in demand for labour. And once jobs are lost, corrective forces become active. Competition leads to fall of wages and this makes the re-employment of jobless workers profitable. So unemployment was seen as an out-of-equilibrium state that would be over in a reasonable time.

The Great Depression raised doubts about this complacent position. Keynes gave a theoretical explanation of unemployment as a possible equilibrium state. His explanation was complemented by policy suggestions of aggressive government spending. He explained that all forms of autonomous spending are helpful in a recession, not just government spending.

Keynes' theory and policy were widely accepted and led to what is known as the Keynesian revolution. It led to a radical change of emphasis in economics towards short-run analysis. Keynes[8] emphasised on many occasions that the classical preoccupation with long-run equilibrium is of little practical use, if not entirely misleading. The following is a famous quote along these lines:

'The long run is a misleading guide to current affairs. In the long run we are all dead. Economists set themselves too easy, too useless a task if in tempestuous seasons they can only tell us that when the storm is past the ocean is flat again.'

The revolution also transformed budgetary philosophy and practice. Besides all this, there was a drastic change in views on saving and consumption. Consumption became a virtue. Governments promoted consumerism. The effect of consumerism on social values has been significant since the Second World War and it continues to be an important element of our social philosophy today. The revolution also institutionalised government transfers as permanent features in the form of unemployment, old age, and other supports. The process was taken further in some countries where the government would provide a very wide range of benefits and welfare measures for the public. All this changed not only the economies but also the nature of society and politics.

[8]Keynes, J.M., *Keynes: A Tract on Monetary Reform*, Chapter 3, p. 80, Macmillan, London, 1923.

# 6 After Keynes

## 6.1 End of the Euphoria

Industrial countries persisted with large public spending and budget deficits up to the end of the 1960s. It was a period of unbroken prosperity with no major recession. As I noted earlier, the credit was attributed to Keynesian policy. It was believed that economic theory had found the way to control business cycles. The new economics was most pervasive in Europe: governments, academics, and bankers alike accepted it zealously.

Initially, the atmosphere was less charmed in the US. President Franklin Roosevelt was not impressed with Keynes when he saw him at the White House in 1934. He is reported to have sniffed, 'I didn't understand one word that man was saying'. [1] Keynes had not yet written his *magnum opus* and was not as well-known in the US as in Europe. But as the years went by, his ideas became more influential. Some of Roosevelt's economists found it very convenient to use Keynesian reasoning to justify the huge government deficits that Roosevelt was running as part of the New Deal (see Box 6.1). By the time, the Second World War started, US policy makers had become quite serious about Keynesian ideas. And after the war, the White House was dominated by Keynesian economists for a long time. Milton Friedman, a would-be Nobel laureate who spearheaded the revival of the classics, famously lamented, 'We are all Keynesians now'.

[1] Frances Perkins, Roosevelt's Secretary of Labour, gave this account in the book *The Roosevelt I Knew*, Viking, 1946.

---

### Box 6.1: How Novel was the Keynesian Spending Idea?

The New Deal, started in 1933, was US President Roosevelt's package for recovery from the Great Depression. The package was surprisingly 'Keynesian' even though the *General Theory* had not been written yet. The Deal provided for large amount of spending and put in place a number of benefits (transfer spending) for the first time. The programmes emphasised the so-called 3 Rs: relief, recovery, and reform. The first two took the form of transfer spending and spending on goods and services for job creation. The New Deal, however, did not openly go in for significant deficit spending as many of Roosevelt's administration were staunch supporters of a balanced budget. The Deal was based on the practical wisdom of Roosevelt and his administration rather than any theoretical conviction. Spending programmes were carried through making administrative and political compromises on the way.

Similar large-scale public spending on roads, infrastructure, and armament production was seen in Hitler's Germany in the 1930s in an attempt to come out of the recession. This too occurred before the *General Theory*. The idea that a government (previously the monarch) should spend in bad times in order to support its subjects is, in fact, a very old idea. Time and again kings and queens of the past have spent large amounts in times of drought and famine to provide employment. Keynes himself observed, in the *General Theory*, that the construction of pyramids in Egypt and cathedrals in Europe were methods of creating large-scale employment in bad years.

Looked at from this perspective, the advocacy of public spending in bad times was not such a new idea. What was, however, novel was the theoretical support provided to such spending and the idea of the multiplier. Those ideas managed to overcome the financial orthodoxy of administrations whose first instinct used to be to balance the budget.

---

However, amidst all the cheer and the celebration of a new science, a new problem made its appearance, gradually but surely. The price level started creeping upward in these countries. Europe found itself facing inflation.

---

**Box 6.2: 'Boondoggling'**

The American-English word 'boondoggle' is defined by dictionaries as 'work of little or no value done merely to look busy' and thesauruses associate it with words such as 'unnecessary', 'wasteful', 'superfluous', 'redundant' acts. It is not unfair to say that public spending did take the form of boondoggling in most countries and occasions.

The first use of the word is noted around 1935 in the US during the New Deal. Here is how Franklin Roosevelt, the US president during the Depression used the word: 'If we can "boondoggle" ourselves out of this depression, that word is going to be enshrined in the hearts of the American people for years to come.'

---

Inflation means a sustained rise of the price level. Price level is measured by an index which is a weighted average of all prices. In making the index, different goods are given weights according to their importance or proportion in use. The idea can be applied to all commodity groups in the GDP, in that case the index is called the GDP deflator. Or it can be used to focus on the prices of a specific group of items. The Consumer Price Index (CPI) is an example; it is constructed with only consumption goods using weights in accordance with the average person's consumption. Often, separate CPI series are constructed for urban and rural areas. There are many price indices in use, each for a specific purpose, for example, index of producer goods prices, wholesale price index, and so on.

The price rise in Europe was initially small and was, therefore, ignored. But it could not be disregarded any more as the 1960s progressed. In the early 1970s many European countries were witnessing double digit inflation rates. In the UK the retail price index (RPI) more than doubled in the decade of the 1970s and annual rate of increase touched 24.2 per cent in 1975.[2]

## 6.2 Inflation in a Time of Peace

Of course, inflation was not an unknown phenomenon. Europe and many countries outside Europe had seen significant price rise during

[2]*Source: www.statistics.gov.uk.* Inflation rate is based on RPI series.

the Second World War. In course of the war, many things went into short supply. Supply chains were broken or disrupted; in other cases there was diversion of goods for the use of the army. The war time inflation was easily understood in terms of supply and demand for individual goods. But the peacetime inflation of the 1960s could not be explained away by a simple supply–demand story.

This inflation was initially explained by using the goings-on in the labour market. The claim was that when an economy moves close to full employment, the labour market becomes very tight. Wage rises because businesses compete among themselves to get workers. The increase in wage increases the cost of production which is partly passed on as higher product price. Thus inflation was considered to be the result of wage increase which happened because the labour market was too tight. At first this was just a piece of reasoning trying to explain the ongoing inflation. But soon convincing statistical evidence came up in support of this idea.

Statistical data showed that unemployment and wage increase were systematically related. This relationship was first observed by A.W. Phillips in the UK labour market data over a very long historical period. Soon the association was verified using data for other countries. The relationship was found to be true wherever investigation was made. The graph of this relationship between unemployment and wage increase was named Phillips curve and it became a part of economic theory. The Phillips curve helped explain the inflation in the two decades following the Second World War. Because Europe maintained close to full employment the labour market had indeed become 'overheated'. Wage rose everywhere and this led to inflation.

## 6.3 Stagflation? Never Heard of it

However, the 1970s brought in some real surprise. Inflation continued but it could not be fitted into the labour market explanation. Associated with inflation was a touch of stagnation and unemployment, rather than full employment. This peculiar combination characterised many economies and soon a term was coined for it, 'stagflation'. Economic theory had no explanation for this baffling phenomenon.

Even when Keynesian views reigned supreme, there were a few prominent economists who were not in agreement with Keynesian policy. Milton Friedman of the University of Chicago, who would get a Nobel prize in 1976, was one of them. In a famous paper[3] written in 1956 he reminded the Keynesians that 'money matters'. This cryptic reminder acquired meaning from the following context. All over Europe large government spending was being funded by money creation using central banks. Economists did not appear uncomfortable about the large amount of money creation. On the contrary, they reasoned that deficit financing was a smart corollary of Keynes' theory. In the eyes of some economists, the triumph of Keynes over the classics was symbolised by the triumph of deficit budgets over conservative concern about budgetary balance. Friedman's paper addressed this context. He reasoned that the growth of money supply, any faster than the growth of the real economy, would produce inflation; if not right away, then most certainly in the long run. Friedman's warning proved to be prophetic.

## 6.4 Quantity Theory of Money

Friedman's warning was based on an idea called the Quantity Theory of Money. It was not a new theory but a classical idea. However, it had been abandoned as passé in the days of the Keynesian revolution. Classical economists had noted that the quantity of money in circulation mediates transactions in an economy by moving from person to person during transactions. How many times the average money unit, say a rupee, changes hand in a year depends on institutional factors. It depends, for example, on how often people are paid their wages, for example, daily or monthly; how often people do their shopping, and similar factors. These factors are fairly stable and change only slowly. So the 'velocity of money', a name for the number of times the average rupee moves from one person to another, can be taken as fixed in the short run.

Now, if money in circulation increases by 5 per cent, it would be moving around with the same velocity as earlier. So 5 per cent

[3]"The Quantity Theory of Money: ARestatement', in Milton Friedman (ed.), *Studies in Quantity Theory*, Chicago: University of Chicago Press, 1956.

more money would now appear in transactions. If the output of the economy has meanwhile grown by 5 per cent, then the extra money will do the extra transactions on the additional output. But if output has not grown, then the extra spending will drive up prices by 5 per cent. The increase of output and price together must be 5 per cent to absorb the increased money supply. The increase of output in physical terms is called an increase of *real output*. Quantity Theory stated that the increase in real output and the price level together has to equal the increase in money supply.

Any increase in GDP is the result of either an increase in prices or an increase in real output. If real output does not change, then price rises just as fast as money supply. Inflation will then equal the rate of growth of money supply. And, if there is some growth of real output, then inflation will be less by that extent. It would equal the rate of money growth minus the rate of real output growth. These ideas were presented as early as 1752 by David Hume and we might find older discussions as well. Most economists before Keynes accepted the Quantity Theory as a long-run theory of price level and inflation. Keynes criticised classical theories quite generally. As a result, all classical ideas were discredited in the aftermath of the Keynesian revolution including the quantity theory.

Milton Friedman continued with a series of theoretical and empirical studies to re-establish the wisdom of the Quantity Theory in the context of the twentieth century. Friedman's words that 'money matters' were meant to warn that money created by years of deficit financing would come back to haunt the economy as inflation. This was simply because real production of goods was not increasing as fast. In his later work, Friedman attacked the logic of Keynesian policies more generally, challenging the wisdom of government spending as a stabilising policy. He argued, and many others joined him later, that given its technology and resources an economy can optimally employ so much of labour and no more. If the size of the workforce is more than that, there is bound to be a certain amount of unemployment. In this sense, every economy has a 'natural' rate of unemployment. It is the unemployment that prevails when employers employ the most appropriate number, given their production parameters.

When demand increases beyond natural limits, employers do employ more workers in the short run to take advantage of it. But this response is not the best for them. Higher production has higher marginal cost, and hence they would like to increase price to match it. They cannot do so immediately because of contractual prices. But to expect that they will forever bear the costs that they can pass on as price increase, is not realistic. Hence, the demand created by the government to push beyond the natural rate will lead to price increase sooner or later.

Friedman's work and that of others like him made slow impact on the Keynesian-dominated scene of 1960s. But as inflation gathered momentum, these ideas acquired more force and currency. By the beginning of the 1970s, inflation had become a serious problem. John Hicks, a British Nobel Laureate in economics and a Keynesian, used the title '*Crisis in Keynesian Economics*' for a book he published in 1974. The view that there was a crisis, or at least that something was seriously amiss, had been accepted. The newest addition to business school jokes was:

Question: How many Keynesian economists does it take to screw in a light bulb? Answer: Only one. He will make sure to screw it.

## 6.5 What could be Wrong

The diagnosis of what was wrong, of course, differed widely. Many believed that it was the interpretation of Keynes that was wrong rather than his formulations. So they tried to reconcile the experience of inflation with possible reinterpretations of Keynes' writings. This produced a number of alternative interpretations and a few different schools of Keynesians.

A second group believed that Keynes' model was just a special case of the classical model. If a set of special assumptions like inflexible price were grafted on the classical model, it would produce most of what Keynes wrote. Those assumptions in fact held true immediately after the Second World War and hence Keynes' policies worked so well. But the configuration ceased to hold later leading to the failure of Keynesian policies. All in all, it was accepted by the majority of the profession that Keynesian macroeconomics was not adequate. Either a lot of structure had to be added to it, or it had to be discarded in favour of a new theory.

One simple thing that was ignored in the Keynesian story should be noted now. It claimed that when the government demands more, the rest of the economy produces more to meet the demand. In the process income and jobs are created. And, while all this happens, prices do not change. Let us focus on the last part that prices do not rise during the economy's response to government demand. That is, demand increases and in response supply increases, but prices do not increase!

This flies in the face of what we would expect from standard economic reasoning. Suppose there is demand–supply equilibrium. If now government purchase increases, it would create excess demand. Standard economic considerations suggest that it will lead to price increase for goods that are in excess demand, which will induce some increase of supply and some fall of demand. The process would continue until demand and supply are equal again. So government spending is expected to lead to more supply no doubt, but not without some price increase. Contrast this with the Keynesian claim that government's demand would increase production or supply alone.

This, as we have seen, can be justified by the idea that prices are sticky in the short run. As we have discussed, supermarkets fix shelf prices and publish them in advertisements and mail fliers, advising a period over which these prices are valid. Obviously they cannot change them before the period is over. Second, they enter these prices into the computer system and barcode readers, and stick the price labels on the shelves. These actions cost money. We call them menu cost, like the cost of printing the menu for a restaurant. Menu costs are significant in modern business. A supermarket will change prices only when the expected profit from doing so exceeds the menu cost of putting in place a new set of prices. Other businesses too have significant menu costs, even though they may come in different forms.

In all these situations, if demand increases and the seller wants to take advantage of it, the best course is to increase supply, rather than raise prices. This is the sticky price situation that we discussed in the previous chapter. However, some price increase should still be expected. First of all, marginal cost is higher when a firm produces more. Hence if it is to supply more at the same price, it bears the entire increase of marginal cost. If that is more than menu cost or the penalty for price increase provided in supply contracts, the business would surely increase its price. Second, prices of all things are not sticky even in the short run. Stickiness is more a feature of industrial products and services. There are important products outside the industrial sector such as food grains, vegetables, and other agricultural products where an increase in demand leads directly to price increase. In primary commodities, too, for example, metal, minerals, and crude oil etc. price response to demand is quite rapid.

Given this, we cannot escape price increase when government spending increases. Short-run price rigidity will moderate the increase but will not eliminate it. Part of the demand created by the multiplier will, therefore, get dissipated through price increase. The real output gain will be less than what the multiplier formula claims. So would the number of jobs created. Additionally, some inflation will accompany the process.

## 6.6 The Aggregate Supply Function

The question here is about the behaviour of aggregate supply. Aggregate supply, as the name suggests, is the supply of all production units taken together. Earlier we came across the concept of aggregate demand. The Keynesian model assumes that when aggregate demand increases, aggregate supply will increase to meet this demand and this will not affect prices noticeably.

This is like reversing the classical position, 'Supply creates its own demand' and saying, 'Demand creates its own supply'. In Keynes theory, supply appears to be a perfectly flexible quantity. It has no role in the story because it is expected to rise or fall according to demand. This is why demand is all important in Keynesian economics and it is called demand-side economics.

But if producers do not produce more without some price incentive, then price increase has to accompany any increase in aggregate supply. We would then expect aggregate supply and the general price index to move together. The relationship between the price level and aggregate supply is called the aggregate supply function. We expect it to be an increasing function of the price level.

## 6.7 A Kiwi Connection: The Phillips Curve

The nature of aggregate supply had to be ascertained to keep economic policy on a sure footing. So, it became urgent to verify the issue properly. This verification advanced hugely with the Phillips curve that I mentioned earlier. A.W. Phillips (1914–75) of the Phillips curve fame was a colourful character, who, we might say, happened to stray into economics. He was born in rural New Zealand in the family of a dairy farmer. He left for Australia before finishing school and worked on a variety of trades, including crocodile hunting and managing a cinema hall. Before the Second World War he set off for China, which would be soon invaded by Japan. Through a series of adventurous journeys through China and Russia to escape being captured, he finally reached the UK in 1938 and started studying electrical engineering. When the war broke out, he joined the Royal Air Force; was captured as a prisoner of war (POW) and spent more than three years in a Japanese POW camp in Indonesia.

Phillips came back to the UK when he was released after the war. This time he joined the London School of Economics (LSE) to study sociology. But he soon moved on to economics. From various accounts it would appear that he attracted a lot of attention at LSE for several off-curriculum reasons and became a popular character. Even as he was studying, he made what we might call a 'hydraulic computer'. The machine ran liquids through a number of channels representing the flow of various components of GDP in the British economy and could be used to answer computable questions on national income and its components. The flows and their relationships were based on a Keynesian model. This interesting machine and its colourful inventor naturally attracted the attention of Keynesians at LSE.

After some time Phillips started in earnest a study of the British labour market. His famous paper was published in the British journal

*Economica* in 1958.[4] He reported that wages in UK had generally increased when the unemployment rate exceeded 4 per cent, and had fallen when unemployment was less. His study did not consider any specific industry but the economy as a whole for the period 1861–1957 for which he had data. This would imply that there was indeed something like a 'natural' rate of unemployment around 4 per cent.

Because wage increased when unemployment fell, it was expected that price level would increase when aggregate supply increased. The reason is: more aggregate supply requires more employment; and more employment increases wage and then price. Therefore, Phillips' observation meant that the price level and aggregate supply always increase together. The assumption used in demand management that supply would increase while prices stay unchanged could not be supported any more. The finding was soon borne out by research in other countries. The curve was accepted as a general feature of all labour markets and economies.

Once it was understood and accepted, economists used it to explain inflation in the demand management years. They agreed that price does rise somewhat with aggregate supply rather than staying constant and this happens because of wage increase. Hence there would be some price rise when governments use demand side policy.

These developments, however, left the idea of demand management intact. It just required some revision of the amount of spending necessary in a given situation. Suppose before we heard about the Phillips curve we calculated that government purchase has to increase by Rs 5 billion to create 1000 extra jobs. Then, after we learnt about the curve we would revise spending to a higher figure. The reason is obvious. If price rises during the multiplier process, the increase in output is smaller, and hence smaller is the number of jobs created. So to produce the same number of jobs, more spending would be required.

[4]Phillips, A.W., 'The Relationship between Unemployment and the Rate of Change of Money Wages in the United Kingdom 1861–1957', *Economica*, Vol. 25, No. 100, 1958, pp. 283–99.

## 6.8 Inflation–Unemployment Trade-off

The curve, therefore, became a part of the extended Keynesian model. Apart from all the revision in economic theory that it brought or would bring later, it revealed some unsuspected features of our political economy. Suppose we state the Phillips relation in terms of unemployment and inflation: unemployment below the natural rate tends to breed inflation. Further, lesser the unemployment the higher would be the inflation rate. Stated thus, it means that if we want to reduce one, we have to accept more of the other. This is an unsavoury fact of life that there is a trade-off between inflation and unemployment—the two worst evils of our system. If we want to reduce unemployment more, a higher rate of inflation has to be tolerated. If we want to reduce inflation, we have to suffer some rise in unemployment.

We might ask: how much inflation for how many jobs? We can answer this if we estimate the curve using statistical data. Then we can plot it on a graph paper with unemployment rate and inflation rate on the two axes. From the plot it is possible to read off how many jobs are saved by accepting 1 per cent more inflation. The rate at which the curve slopes down tells us how much inflation would increase when unemployment is reduced by some amount. Economists and governments often estimated the Phillips curve and stated the trade-off using numbers. During those days we would hear statements such as, 'to reduce inflation by one further percentage, we have to accept the loss of at least five thousand jobs'. Policy makers would use these estimates to mull over their best political move. Should they leave inflation where it is and reduce unemployment at the moment, because the election is just round the corner? Or should they rather attend to inflation which is hated by business that funds their election campaign?

Considerations of this kind can create business cycles originating in the government! Workers want less unemployment which we can have with the easy money policy. Easy money keeps interest rate low, so that the government and business can invest more and create jobs. On the other hand, the well-to-do classes want higher interest rate because they own more wealth. They also like stable prices because inflation reduces the real value of their wealth. Closer to an election, governments use expansionary policies to increase employment, because the bulk of voters are workers. However, after the election the governments try to raise interest rate to keep the pre-election promise made to the moneyed classes that contributed to its election campaign. But high interest rate and dear money will increase unemployment. Thus over the term of a government high employment /low interest rate and low employment/ high interest rate often cycle through. We are likely to see policy cycles of this kind period after period.

## 6.9 Aggregate Supply and Inflation Expectation

The discovery of the Phillips curve, however, did not end the deepening doubts about demand management. More curious discoveries were to follow soon. It was found that aggregate supply depends not only on price or inflation as we would expect; but also on the public's expectations about price or inflation. We need to look into the aggregate supply curve more closely in order to follow it.

Imagine an economy with no government spending at all. A general equilibrium is currently prevailing, that is, there is equilibrium in all markets. Firms are producing their most profitable outputs and their sum is the current GDP. The economy is expected to produce this GDP if markets work unhindered. This may be called the economy's 'natural' output. Individual firms would also want to continue to produce their 'natural' outputs if the relationship between the price of their products and inputs (that is, the relative price) does not change.

Now suppose that this economy has been witnessing inflation for some time. In that case buyers, sellers, and workers would expect some inflation over the year. They would base economic decisions on the inflation they expect. Generally, inflation leaves the relative prices largely undisturbed; all prices rise roughly at the same rate. So if there is an expectation of 5 per cent inflation at the beginning of the year, and during the year business finds that inflation is indeed at 5 per cent, they would produce their natural output. This is so because they would conclude that relative prices have not been disturbed.

Given this, something very interesting happens if the actual inflation rate differs from the expected rate. Suppose business expected 5 per cent inflation but the actual rate is 10 per cent. When prices start rising by 10 per cent, producers would first notice their own products' prices. The information on other prices comes slowly and later. So the fact that the general inflation rate is 10 per cent will become known only at the end of the period. Until then producers would believe that their product price is increasing faster than what they had expected, that is, at 10 per cent rather than 5 per cent. They take it as the price of their product improving against inputs and substitutes. So their optimal production will now be greater than earlier. They will produce more than the natural output. The reaction will be similar for all producers. Overall, the economy will produce more than its natural output if actual inflation exceeds the expected inflation.

The opposite will happen if inflation is less than the expected rate of 5 per cent, say 3 per cent. Again producers will see the price of their own products first. Producers will conclude that their price is increasing at only 3 per cent, while other prices are increasing at 5 per cent. They will consider this as a fall in the relative price of their products and will produce less than the natural output.

Together, we have a surprising behaviour of aggregate supply. It is less or more than natural output depending on whether actual inflation is less or more than the expected inflation. And, the natural output is produced only when the actual inflation rate is the same as the expected rate.

We can now check what would happen if the government tries to cut unemployment below the natural rate. Suppose the economy is producing the natural output and so employment is at the natural rate too. Assume that there has been 5 per cent inflation for a number of years so that producers are expecting it to continue at 5 per cent. They will, therefore, produce their natural outputs if inflation turns out to be 5 per cent.

Now suppose the government increases spending to raise aggregate demand. Producers will respond to the higher demand. They will produce more than their natural output. But since supply will increase with some price rise, as we have seen before, inflation will be pushed above 5 per cent. The government will no doubt be able to reduce unemployment. But it will come at a cost: an increase in inflation. The Phillips curve could be used to calculate how much inflation would rise if unemployment is cut by a proposed amount. And then it would be up to the government to decide the mix of the two.

## 6.10 Milton Friedman, Once Again

So it would appear that if a government wanted to keep up high employment, it could do so by tolerating a certain level of inflation. Subsequent developments would, however, show that to be wrong. Milton Friedman cautioned against this by calling it short-sighted. He made some predictions about the likely long-run result of expansionary policy. Let us go back to the last example where the expected inflation was taken as 5 per cent. The government increased spending, lifted aggregate demand, employment increased above the natural rate, and inflation rose above 5 per cent, say to 7 per cent. Friedman warned that this was only a short-run equilibrium. Business would get used to the new rate of inflation and soon start expecting 7 per cent rather than 5 per cent inflation. When they expect 7 per cent inflation and the inflation is indeed 7 per cent, they will have no reason to produce above their natural output any more. They will revert back to the natural rate of production and employment will fall back to the natural rate.

So, the jobs created by expansion will last only for some time. They will be lost as soon as everyone gets used to the higher inflation rate. If the government wants to keep those jobs, then it will have to start over again. It will have to inject some more demand. This time the spending has to be more than last time, because prices have increased meanwhile.

The same sequence will be repeated. The government raises demand and induces some output increase and some increase of inflation. Increased output will keep the jobs that were at risk. But when everyone gets used to the new inflation that becomes the expected rate. When that happens, business will find that the actual inflation is equal to what they are expecting, and they will produce the natural level of output again. Unemployment will increase back to the natural rate.

So to keep unemployment permanently below the natural rate, as the European economies were trying through the 1950s and 1960s, governments have to inject demand again and again. Each time the injection would be greater than the last. The economies would thus face a sequence of accelerating inflation. This was Milton Friedman's warning. To keep unemployment below the natural rate, governments have to inject demand and raise inflation not once, but as often as people get used to a new inflation rate. Each time the spending will be larger and inflation will continuously increase. The gist is that the effect of demand side policy on unemployment is transient but it increases inflation permanently.

## 6.11 How Inflation Expectation is Formed

It is important to know how long a country takes to revise its inflation expectation. Is it five years, or one year or even a shorter time? Is it a fixed amount or does it vary? There are a few conjectures about how expectation is formed and there is substantial disagreement on the issue. But at the empirical level it has been found that inflation expectation is affected by the recent history of inflation. If a country has had a period of stable prices, its inflation expectation will be low; and it will be high if it has been passing through high inflation. Therefore, the same amount of price disturbance, say from an oil price hike, will affect inflation expectations in different countries differently. We might describe this as 'expectation inertia'. Just as a moving body keeps moving by inertia, so is the case with inflation expectation.

Another feature is that we actively learn from the effect of events and policies relevant to prices. And this learning seems to influence expectation. We expect prices to rise in a year of bad harvest because we have seen that happening many times in the past. This kind of social learning occurs in the case of other economic events and policies as well. If expansionary policy has fomented inflation in the past, then whenever the government spends more, people would expect inflation to rise.

## 6.12 The 1950s and 1960s: A Possible Story

The above ideas can be used to construct an explanation of the events of Europe between the 1950s and 1970s. Of course, it is just a possible story and we cannot claim to have 'the' explanation about anything economic as you must have figured out by now.

The story goes like this. It starts in the early 1950s. An economy has a large production capacity built up during the Second World War which is just over and much of it is now idle. So is a large part of the workforce. The government decides to spend money to generate full employment and help utilisation of the production capacity. This creates demand directly and also boosts consumer demand indirectly. Industry, suffering from idle capacity, supplies the extra demand gratefully. Because of the existing unused capacity, extra production *does not* increase the marginal cost initially. Indeed in some industries it reduces marginal cost because it allows the industry to utilise its fixed overheads more fully. Extra income and new jobs are created. The process is repeated in the next year's government budget and the year after, and so on. This part of the story, call it the first part, is very much like the uncomplicated Keynesian multiplier story.

After a number of years, the economy starts moving to a second phase. Demand has increased over the past few years to the extent that industry is producing at or above its best capacity now. Marginal costs, therefore, start increasing and so do prices. We can say that unemployment is kept low at the cost of some price increase. The economy experiences the trade-off on the Phillips curve.

However, even though price increases a bit, people do not initially think of regular inflation. They lived in a stable price situation before the war. War-time inflation was understood as the result of dislocation. So, people look upon price rise as a random event which would pass. This situation however starts changing. As price effects of successive budgets accumulate into perceptible inflation by 1960, people start taking note of it.

The economy now enters the third phase. As inflation increases people start revising their inflation expectation quickly. This happens for two reasons. Since inflation is a regular feature, any increase in inflation rate is now absorbed into the expectation sooner. Second, it is now known that government spending has been fuelling the inflation. So, increase in government spending is now taken as a fore-sign that inflation is indeed going to increase.

So after a round of government spending, jobs increase and inflation rises. The new inflation rate soon becomes the expected inflation. After that the inflation fails to stimulate production and the economy goes back to the natural rate of unemployment. Jobs created are lost. The sequence now winds out fairly fast. The government has to spend even more and inflation increases faster and faster. Though the inflation rate is high, employment is generally not more than the natural rate of unemployment except for very short periods. The economy is in a state of stagflation.

This is a probable account of the 1950s and 1960s. It explains why inflation was absent or low early after the war even though the economies maintained full employment. It also clarifies why we saw accelerating inflation later even though economies were never significantly above the natural rate.

## 6.13 What happened to the Phillips Curve?

The Phillips curve describes the trade-off between unemployment and inflation. But the story told in the last section would mean that it is not a lasting trade-off. It works only in the short run. Over the long period there is no such trade-off as inflation keeps rising but unemployment stays at the natural rate. Further, the 'short run' gets shorter as time passes. The length of the short run depends on how fast the public gets used to inflation. This is what Friedman had predicted when he claimed that there is no trade-off in the long run.

The Phillips curve was based on empirical observation that in the past inflation had increased when unemployment fell. Friedman's prediction was that this relation would not hold in any prolonged period of inflation. He believed that the trade-off was stable in the past because inflation during those days used to be near-zero and sporadic. Hence people would expect low inflation on average—close to or equal to zero. But when inflation becomes the norm, people expect positive rates of inflation. If inflation rises, expectation rises too. So the trade-off cannot exist for long. If inflation is forced up by easy money again and again, inflation itself becomes the norm and fails to induce any extra production or jobs.

Friedman's claims were based on theoretical reasoning and hence did not attract much credence at the time. But the predictions appeared to be true in a few years' time. Generally economic theorists construct models of observed phenomena. Friedman's theoretical model was an exception in that sense. He had a theoretical model that predicted events that had not happened yet. Arguably, it was the first time in economics that the prediction of a future event based on theoretical prediction was proved true by subsequent events.[5]

We can interpret Friedman's claims somewhat differently. His reasoning means that the natural output is a centre of gravity for the economy. The level of activity gets pulled towards it all the time by business and market forces. Government policy or business cycles can pull the equilibrium away from the natural rate temporarily. But the pull prevails in the end. The natural rate of output in this sense is the stable long-run equilibrium.

## 6.14 Supply-side Policy

Faith in Keynesian policy waned significantly in the late 1970s. In the 1980s many governments were rethinking economic policy. *Laissez Faire* was becoming fashionable once again in academic discussions. But governments could not take their hands off policy making entirely. First of all, governments' economic institutions and bureaucracy had proliferated since the war. They employed substantial numbers; in many countries the government had become the single largest employer. There were countries where the government employed more people than the rest of the organised sector, leaving out agriculture and primary production. Employees cannot be summarily given the good bye. Nor would the bureaucracy like to lose its importance and relevance. Second, post-war politics so evolved that most countries had governments based on coalition of political parties rather than single party rule. Negotiation among

---

[5]Some appreciative scholars have compared this with the discovery of Neptune, which was predicted to exist by calculations before it was actually discovered.

coalition partners typically uses ministerial berths as bargaining chip. Arguably, governments and political parties needed a large number of ministries for their very formation and continuation.

Third, unemployment remained as much an issue in the 1980s as it was in the immediate post-war period and it is evident that it will remain so in the foreseeable future. Popularity of a government depends very much on how unemployment is handled. There were also other economic issues such as balance of payments and inflation. Governments were required to do something about them and be seen to be doing so. So the issue was not whether to withdraw from policy making but to find the appropriate alternative to demand management.

The central question was how to handle unemployment accepting that economists now proclaimed demand management as problematic. One answer that came up was supply-side policy. It is a way to increase the natural rate of output itself. If this can be increased, it will reduce the natural rate of unemployment. Natural rate of output depends on resources and technology. So supply-side policy tries to raise the productivity of resources and improve the technology in use.

Supply-side policy involves a longer time horizon and gestation period. Resource productivity can be raised by investment in infrastructure, health, education, and governance. Education and skill directly contribute to 'human capital' that is, capital embodied in the people. Better health increases labour productivity. Infrastructure and better governance improve the productivity of all factors used in production. Improvements in business management, supply chains, retailing, banking, and other services make important contribution to productivity.

To step up technology requires research and development (R&D), technology purchase, licence agreements, and a better patent regime. Foreign investment can be utilised for these. Several alternative modes of foreign investment have been established over the years and in the increasingly globalised environment, modalities of foreign investment are becoming more standardised. Joint ventures, licensing of foreign technology, and international franchise agreements are useful means of getting foreign technology. Supply-side economics advises countries to sort out foreign investment laws and utilise foreign technology as much as possible.

Management of supply-side policy is presenting new challenges. An important issue relates to the extent of government involvement. Is it advisable for governments to directly start R&D and infrastructure building? If not, what is the best formula or model to incentivise the private sector? Second, these policies involve long-term forward vision on behalf of the governments. Therefore, political and constitutional mechanisms must be in place to make plans work through successive governments of different persuasion and shorter tenures.

## 6.15 Countercyclical Economic Policy

Though it is now widely conceded that demand management does not help in the long run, many, perhaps a majority of economists nevertheless believe that it has to be used as a short-run tool. Particularly when a recession is imminent, injection of demand by the government remains the foremost policy.

In the early decades after the Second World War, econometric techniques for estimating and forecasting macro relations were developing fast. Economists were optimistic that soon it would be possible to use policy in a perfectly countercyclical manner. In their vision, the government would increase spending as the business cycle dips and reduce spending in step as the cycle moves up. If the phases of the cycle can be forecast and the effects of spending on income and jobs are accurately calculated, then business cycles could be virtually eliminated by counter-cyclical policy.

Unfortunately, intervention with that level of refinement has remained elusive, then or since. To the contrary, many now believe that countercyclical intervention should actually be abandoned. They point out that the government has to correctly predict the phase of the cycle in advance. Unfortunately our knowledge and skills fail this requirement. A government cannot be sure that income and employment have started to decline before quite a few weeks after the event. As you can guess, this is because the state of the cycle is a system-wide property. It has to be inferred from surveys of different areas and sectors. Second, because the judgment is based on statistical inference, a small change is not taken as convincing. Analysts would pronounce a change only after significant change has taken place. Furthermore, after it is definitely known that a downward tendency has started, the government has to decide about the nature and quantum of intervention. Typically, it will require a number of meetings to decide the principles and a few more to fix the modalities. As a result of all this, the time lag between the start of downward movement and the introduction of a policy is substantial.

There is another kind of lag that adds to the difficulty. It is between the time that the government acts and when its actions produce effect. Employment does not start increasing as soon as the government starts spending. It takes a series of events to create new jobs after, say ten to twelve weeks. You may recall the discussion about the income generation rounds of the multiplier process in Chapter 5. These rounds represent the time that income goes from employers to employees and then to consumption goods producers.

Critics claim that in most cases when an intervention starts producing effects the phase of the cycle is no longer appropriate for those effects. An expansionary measure may start having effect when the economy has already started an upward movement. Rather than checking the downswing the intervention then adds to the upward movement and produces inflationary pressure. Critics, therefore, claim that stabilisation policy actually destabilises the economy as it accentuates rather than smothers the ups and downs. There is some truth to this criticism. For successful stabilisation a government has to forecast the ups and downs rather than reacting to them after the event. But short-run forecasting of the state of the cycle is generally inaccurate.

There is an interesting suggestion in this connection about forecasting. Rather than relying on econometrics, we might search for 'leading indicators' of the state of the economy. These are things that happen a few weeks or months before the rise or fall in income and thus give an indication before the event. For example, the tourism sector gets a good indication of the coming business several weeks beforehand from the booking of airline seats and hotel accommodation. Airline and hotel booking are two leading indicators for the tourism and hospitality business. Where tourism is an important sector, these indicators are useful information about the coming state of the economy. Take another example. Builders need to apply for consent of the local authorities to build dwellings and commercial units. The number of consent applications and the total worth of buildings in the applications is a fairly accurate indicator of construction activity to start after the average period for clearing of applications. Construction is a very important component of investment and raises GDP by more than itself. So building consent applications can be used to forecast the direction of the economy in the next few months. Order books of large sectors, export orders, advance booking of railway wagons etc. are indicators in other countries. Obviously, indicators will be different in different economies. If research can uncover them for a given economy, governments would be in a better position to foresee the state of the economic cycle.

Another suggestion is the use of 'automatic stabilisers'. They are things that are automatically triggered against the phase of the business cycle. We have at least two such stabilisers in most countries. One is the unemployment allowance. When a business downturn starts, those who lose jobs automatically qualify for benefits and start getting them. This means that aggregate consumption is substantially protected against downturns. The interesting feature of unemployment benefit is that it is triggered off automatically and does not wait for forecasts or the government's response. Another automatic stabiliser is progressive income tax. Income tax is progressive in most countries, meaning that the proportion of income to be paid as tax increases with income. With progressive tax, when GDP increases the economy as a whole pays proportionately more tax, which means that private income growth is slower than GDP growth. This moderates spending and keeps the inflationary pressure under check to an extent. On the other side, when GDP starts falling, the public has to pay a smaller part of income as tax. Private income does not fall as fast as GDP and this arrests the possibility of a rapid fall in consumption.

## 6.16 Can Policy be guided by Pre-set Rules?

Some observers have reservations about short-run policy from non-economic considerations. We saw in Chapter 4 that it does not help to think of a government as a neutral persona. Yet, so far we have been doing exactly that. A government is a collection of real persons—politicians and bureaucrats—who have their own agenda or objectives. So, it is naïve to expect that a government, even when it has all the expertise and instruments, will use policy in the best interest of the economy. Note that most economic issues involve a trade-off of the interests of some people against others'. The inflation–unemployment trade-off is one example we have already come across. It is realistic to expect that those in the government will resolve such issues in a way so as to advance their political goals. Further, policy can be used for personal advancement or wealth creation. Given this, some have called for curbing the discretion of governments over economic policy.

This is not a call for abandoning short-run policy. It calls for a method of curbing political discretion over policy. One way of doing this is to devise rules of policy and get them passed as law. In the 1990s, a few countries passed 'fiscal responsibility acts' which limit an incumbent government's ability to spend by creating deficits. Typically they prohibit the government to run a budget deficit continuously for more than a certain period, for example, six months.[6] These acts allow a deficit only under extraordinary circumstances like war or disaster and prescribe stringent conditions for allowing it, for example, the president's permission or that of two-thirds majority of the parliament, etc. A fiscal responsibility act is an instance of a policy rule that limits political discretion.

Friedman was an early proponent of monetary policy rules. He observed that part of short-run economic volatility results from short-run policy itself. Second, uncertainty about government's future policy creates uncertainty for investment, borrowing and lending, and business in general. Investors need to read the mind of the government and anticipate political developments. This uncertainty not only hampers growth but also wastes resources that are spent on reading the government and lobbying politicians. Friedman suggested that central banks should announce rules about the conduct of monetary policy and stick to it. This would reduce

---

[6]It is not possible to insist on a balanced budget on a day to day basis. Receipts and expenditure on a given day are beyond a government's control.

uncertainty for future-oriented decisions and cut down short-run economic volatility.

What would monetary policy rules look like? One could be that a central bank 'targets' a growth rate for the economy. What it means is this. The bank may calculate that it is possible to maintain the average long-run real growth of the economy at, say, 2 per cent. Further, growth above this rate would produce inflationary pressure. The bank may then adopt the rule that money supply will be increased annually at 2 per cent plus or minus an amount depending on the income growth in the last year. For every basis point[7] that income growth exceeds 2 per cent, money supply growth would be reduced by a specified rate. And if income grows less than 2 per cent, then money growth will be increased by that specified rate. Such a rule will provide monetary stimulus when growth is less than 2 per cent and discourage overheating when growth rate starts exceeding 2 per cent. The central bank should also fix a calendar when these adjustments would be done, and the income growth index that will be used for the purpose. This is qualitatively not different from what a central bank does any way. But the amount of adjustment in a given situation and the timing are usually not known beforehand and they create uncertainty and speculation.

A variety of monetary and fiscal policy rules have been proposed by researchers. Fiscal policy rules, however, have not been made into laws anywhere yet, with the exception of the fiscal responsibility acts in several countries. But Friedman's targeting rule did catch the attention of central banks in many countries; many of them use some variant of targeting voluntarily.

## 6.17 The Present Scene

Alternative theories about the economy are bewilderingly many. But their stance on policy falls into just two groups. Either they strongly support the government's demand-side role or strongly oppose it. Schools claiming Keynesian origin support government activism. They believe that markets comprise a poor mechanism that fails to utilise the economy's resources fully. Hence government supervision and intervention are necessary.

---

[7]One hundredth of 1 per cent is called a basis point in the context of inflation, economic growth etc.

The position of Marxists is somewhat ambivalent. Their ideological stance is that the edifice of Keynesian economics has the bourgeois agenda of saving capitalism from ultimate doom. Hence they are critical of Keynes' theory and its variants. At the same time, however, Marxist political parties support market intervention. Their stated reason for intervention is strategic. They claim that the market system is an instrument of exploitation, used by capitalists to redistribute income in favour of capital and allied classes. Political parties of the people should use governments to tax capital income as much as possible and use it for transfer to poorer classes. Governments should also establish government-owned businesses to reduce the influence of private capital on the economy. This will also create public sector jobs and curb private capital's ability to exploit workers by dictating wage and work conditions.

Economists outside the Keynesian and Marxist traditions side with the classical view and do not approve of short-run demand intervention. Some take this position on purely economic grounds. They think that short-run intervention does not achieve anything but inflation in the long run. Hence we should try supply-side policy. Others believe in minimal government from their political persuasion or philosophical position. They think that big governments curb individual rights. Systematic intervention in the economy tends to make governments grow in size and power in relation to the civil society. If there is unemployment in the short run, it is better to provide relief rather than creating permanent institutions of intervention.

Though academic opinion is divided, economists involved with policy making are generally prone to using demand-side intervention in the short run, particularly when facing a bad demand shock. This was amply clear in the recession of 2007 and its aftermath. Without exception governments used fiscal and monetary expansion to minimise the impact of the recession. It happened in spite of the fact that some of those administrations were generally against large government spending. The efficacy of spending and cheap money to produce jobs in the short run is not doubted in any quarters. Even if convinced that they cannot be sustained in the long run, policy makers find them the only effective tools when dealing with a recession. Yet, there is also significant circumspection. Many, perhaps most of them, suggest that the policies should be phased out as soon as the economies turn around.

We should end this chapter by noting that the subject matter of macroeconomics is 'activist'; it is seriously concerned with policy. At the same time, economic policies are partisan in nature. That is to say, policies that benefit some groups often harm a few others. Therefore, policy making and its theories are expected to remain subject to significant social and political tension.

---

### Box 6.3: Paul Samuelson

Samuelson (1915–2009) was a prominent supporter of demand intervention by governments in the US. The big recession of 2007 had brought back into attention the simplicity and benefits of demand management through government spending. In an interview in 2009 Samuelson who was then 93, brought this up with some force. He said, 'Today we see how utterly mistaken was the Milton Friedman notion that a market system can regulate itself,' and further ' ... Everyone understands now, on the contrary, that there can be no solution without government. The Keynesian idea is once again accepted that fiscal policy and deficit spending has a major role to play in guiding a market economy. I wish Friedman were still alive so he could witness how his extremism led to the defeat of his own ideas.'[8]

Samuelson received the Nobel Prize in economics in 1970 and was professor emeritus at MIT. He is widely regarded to have given economic theory a uniform theoretical foundation and its present shape. His contribution to economics is too wide and immense to mention here. I will instead mention his classic textbook of introductory economics.

The book was first published in 1948 and has appeared in eighteen different editions with several reprints. It was a best-selling economics textbook for many decades and the source of economics education for generations of students. The book sold more than 300,000 copies of each edition from 1961 through 1976 and was translated into 41 languages. More than four million copies of the book have been sold. William Nordhaus joined Samuelson as co-author after the twelfth edition was published in 1985. Amazingly for a textbook, it has been the subject of academic analysis, criticism, and discussions.

---

[8]Friedman passed away in November 2006. The quote is from an interview by Nathan Gardels published in *New Perspectives Quarterly,* available at *http://www. digitalnpq. org/articles/economic/331/01-16-2009/paul_samuelson.*

# 7 Money, Banks, and Finance

Perhaps the only thing on which J. M. Keynes and V. I. Lenin, the Marxist leader of the Soviet revolution might have agreed is the importance of money in the economic system. This is what Keynes once observed: 'Lenin is said to have declared that the best way to destroy the capitalist system was to debauch the currency .... Lenin was certainly right. There is no subtler, no surer means of overturning the existing basis of society than to debauch the currency. The process engages all the hidden forces of economic law on the side of destruction, and does it in a manner which not one man in a million is able to diagnose.'

As the quote says, malfunctioning money frees up all the sinister economic laws of ruin. Yet, we cannot function without money. In this chapter we will look at this indispensable yet potentially dangerous facilitator of our economic life.

## 7.1 We did not use Money Always

It is surprising to think that there was a time when people did not use money. In the moneyless state, people directly exchanged what they had in surplus, to procure what they wanted. Exchange of goods was an arduous task in this primitive state. It required a reciprocal coincidence of wants of two persons. If Raj had an extra catch of fish that he wanted to exchange for a handful of rice, then he would have to find a person who not only had a handful of rice to spare but was also looking for fish. This sort of double coincidence would be more and more difficult to spot as the number of items used in the society increased.

In the primitive state when communities lived in herds, exchange inside the herd presented little difficulty as they were guided by the ties of the family and the clan. Initially, productivity was low; so there was hardly anything to spare for exchange with another community. Over time as productivity rose with the use of weapons and tools, exchange between communities became frequent. Presumably communities produced or gathered different things because of their habitats in different environments. A highland community that gathered rock salt would look to exchange it with fish and coconuts collected by seaside communities. With increase in productivity and number of items, exchange grew more difficult. A large part of time was spent in spotting the possibility of exchange rather than production and hunting.

It was a great breakthrough to have introduced money to ease that situation. Probably, the communities in different parts of the world started using money independently of one another. The earliest form of money was something that neighbouring communities valued as an object. They were things like bright stones, lumps of metal, feathers and beaks of birds, bones and teeth of animals, piece of silk, shells, and so on. They had value for social and religious rituals or simply as adorable things and hence were acceptable in exchange over a wide neighbourhood. This kind of 'commodity money' is seen to be used even today in special circumstances. Particularly when a country's official money loses credibility, for example, in a hyperinflation, civil war, or when the State is expected to collapse, people switch off from the country's official money and use some form of commodity money.

The introduction of money revolutionised human society. It is one of the greatest inventions comparable to the taming of fire and the use of wheels. Use of money released huge amount of labour time which was previously wasted on searching for exchange possibilities. This labour now turned to production—hunting, fishing, and food gathering, thus creating a surplus of output over need. Further, now that things could be bought and sold, communities had an incentive to produce more than their own needs. As they produced more, they became more skilled and often invented processes and tools to increase productivity. Until fairly recently countries used commodity money in the form of gold, silver, and other metal coins.

The use of gold and silver—and more generally metals—as money continued over a very long period. Archaeologists have found standardised lumps of metal and die-cast metal coins with the seals of kings in very old sites, some older than 3000 years. The seals of kings and monarchs were introduced at an advanced stage of growth of trade and commerce. The main purpose was tamper-proofing and also to keep track of the import of monetary metal from other jurisdictions. It was common to steal a part of the metallic money by filing, cutting, or melting. Rulers started die casting of currency metals to stop these practices. Tampering was made punishable. These efforts facilitated trade and economic development.

---

**Box 7.1: Commodity Money among Nazi Prisoners**

During the Second World War, inmates of POW camps of the Nazis started using their own brand of commodity money. Red Cross used to provide them with canned food, clothing, cigarettes, and medicines. These goods were distributed without assessing personal need or preference. So inmates liked to exchange what they did not want for what they wanted. For this they first started barter but the problem of double matching was serious even with a limited number of goods. Finally cigarettes emerged as the money or currency in the POW camps. Items acquired fairly stable prices in terms of cigarettes. Not only goods, but services could also be bought with cigarettes. Some prisoners were willing to do laundry and similar services for other inmates for payment with the currency. Even those who did not smoke would accept cigarettes as money, because they could readily pay for their purchases with cigarettes.[1] Cigarettes have been seen to be used as currency on many other occasions all across the world.

---

The use of commodity money eventually gave way to 'fiat money', that is, a currency that is declared as money by the fiat of the ruler. Paper currency that we now use is fiat money. The paper used for

[1] R. A. Radford published a paper titled 'The Economic Organisation of a P.O.W. Camp' in *Economica*, New Series, Vol. 12, No. 48, November 1945, pp. 189–201, describing and analysing information about POW camps.

making it has no value for us; it is accepted in exchanges because of the fiat. Governments realised sometime in the past that an item does not have to be valuable to be used as currency. What is necessary is that everyone agrees to accept it for exchange.

This idea was probably around in Europe since the thirteenth century though it was put to practice much later. The Chinese emperor had issued paper money for general use around 650 AD. Marco Polo who travelled to China in the thirteenth century was impressed by it and wrote about it enthusiastically in 1275. It was sporadically tried and found to work by monarchs who were short of gold in times of war and financial stress. They would, of course, back the paper money with the promise to convert it into equivalent amount of gold if anyone demanded.

More generally fiat money was introduced in Europe in the seventeenth century when the Government of Sweden took the lead. Other countries followed over a period of time. Fiat money functioned as well as metallic money with no recorded events of upsets. So it came to stay. Acceptance was ensured by promising that paper money could be converted into gold at a fixed rate. The supply of gold and silver in the world is limited. The growth of business requires increase in money in proportion. If we were still stuck with gold and silver money, economic growth would have been seriously constrained. Fiat money also eased transactions in other ways. Metal money was heavy and carrying it across places and over time was difficult and costly. Paper currency solved these problems. Convertibility of fiat money into gold was necessary as an introductory measure to instil credibility. But that too was abolished a long time ago.

## 7.2 What Constitutes Money?

How much money is in use, say, in India? Is it enough, or should the Reserve Bank of India (RBI) put more into circulation? To answer these questions, we first need a working definition of money. There are alternative measures for different purposes. For our discussion, money is those assets that can be readily used for buying things and settling debts. First note that money is an asset; it is not an income. Though assets and income are both quoted in rupees, they are quite different in nature. Income flows through time and hence is measured by how much one gets per unit of time. It makes no sense to say that my income is Rs 10,000. We would like to know if it is Rs 10,000 in a day, a week, a month, or a year. In this sense, income is a *flow* of rupees. On the other hand an asset is a *stock*, that is, it is measured at a point of time. If I have a house worth Rs 1 million, I will say that my assets include a one-million-rupee house. It will be funny to say that I have a one-million-rupee house per year. Money is like a house in this sense and is measured on a date or a point of time. Only those assets that can be immediately used for payments are money. This is why my house, though an asset for me, is not money. Assets that can be used for payment in India are currency notes and coins issued by the RBI. We can also use those bank deposits that can be immediately transferred to another party's account. A deposit that allows cheque writing is of this kind. So the total amount of this kind of deposits held by the public is also part of money supply. In most countries now money can be transferred from the buyer's bank account to the seller's using an electronic card. The arrangement is called electronic fund transfer at the point of sale (EFTPOS). Bank deposits that allow EFTPOS are money for the same reason as cheque account deposits are. The generic name for deposits that can be transferred with a banking instrument (like a cheque, a debit card) is demand deposits. So, the money supply of a country on a particular day is the amount of currency, coins, and demand deposits held by the public on that day.

The total amount of money in India on 31 March 2009 was Rs 12,53,184 crore.[2] It consisted of Rs 6,66,364 crore of currency and coins, and Rs 5,86,820 crore of transferable bank deposits. The proportion of cash (currency and coins) and demand deposits in money supply differs across countries. The more formal the payments system, less cash and more deposit transfers occur in transactions. In India, as in all other countries, the proportion of cash has fallen steadily as bank transactions have replaced cash transactions.

We noted that a country's money supply is the currency and demand deposits held by the public. The word 'public' means all

---

[2] A crore is an Indian unit equal to 10 million.

persons national as well as foreign. It also includes all institutions and companies, national and foreign, except the central bank of the country and those institutions that provide demand deposits. Institutions that provide demand deposits are called commercial banks. Therefore, currency and demand deposits held by everyone except the central bank and commercial banks of a country make up its money supply. The latter are the suppliers of money. On the other hand, the public wants the money for use; we will say that they demand money.

---

### Box 7.2: Credit Cards and Debit Cards

What is the difference between these two very convenient plastic cards? When I use a credit card I do not pay anyone at all at that time, but only postpone a payment. Hence I do not transfer or use any money at that point. The card is an instrument of credit rather than of payment. It is, therefore, quite appropriately called a credit card. I will pay the credit card company or the bank that issued the card later. I will probably use a cheque to do that or the bank may take it from my demand deposit account. It is only at that time that I would be using any money. The credit card company meanwhile pays the vendor for my purchase. That of course is done by using money—a transfer of deposit from the credit card company's bank account to the vendor's bank account.

When I use a debit card I transfer an amount of deposit from my bank account to that of the vendor right at the time of the purchase. It is like paying the vendor with a cheque but faster, and I cannot bluff by producing a cheque that would bounce. So a debit card payment is a transfer of money at the very time of the purchase.

---

## 7.3 Money Supply: Who Supplies?

The central bank of a country manages the money supply according to objectives laid down by its government. However, it does not supply all the money alone. Demand deposits are supplied by commercial banks. But the central bank takes controlling measures to regulate the amount of demand deposits that commercial banks can supply. So overall it is the central bank that is in control of money supply.

A central bank can alter money supply by buying and selling government securities. Government securities originate when the government takes loans. The securities are evidence of the loan. They can be sold and resold in the securities market. Whoever owns a security is entitled to interest and the principal of the loan. Owners also look to sell securities at higher prices than they bought them for, making a *capital gain*. When the central bank sells securities, banks and other large investors buy them and, therefore, the central bank gets money from the public. This reduces the supply of money in the economy. The opposite happens when the central bank buys these papers. Trading in government securities by the central bank is called 'open market operation'.

When the central bank wants to sell securities, it has to make their price attractive. Therefore, it reduces their price. Recall that securities are loans taken by the government. Making loan papers cheaper means offering higher interest for the loans. Security prices are, therefore, inversely related to interest rate on government loans. So the interest rate on government loans increases when the central bank sells securities to reduce money supply. Because markets for all types of loans are linked, increase of interest rate on one type raises interest rates on others as well. As a result, a cut in money supply raises interest rates in general. On the other hand, interest rate falls when the central bank increases money supply through open market operations.

Just as the central bank lends to the government, it also lends directly to commercial banks. It can vary the interest rate on these loans as it thinks appropriate. When this rate is raised, banks would borrow less and that would, in turn, curb their ability to lend to the public. Loans given to the public are put into their bank accounts as demand deposits. So, when banks are unable to increase lending, the growth of demand deposits is checked. Therefore, the central bank varies the interest rate for lending to commercial banks to alter their ability to create deposits. Like open market operations, this is an important tool for regulating money supply.

We saw that an increase in money supply through open market operations reduces interest rates. Alternatively, if the central bank wants to allow money supply to grow through bank deposits, it lowers the interest rate for lending to commercial banks. In either case, increase in money supply comes with lower interest rates. Conversely, a cut in money supply comes with higher interest rates. Given this, a policy of increasing money supply is called 'cheap money policy'. And its opposite is the 'dear money policy'.

## 7.4 How Commercial Banks create Demand Deposits

Commercial banks earn profits by lending to businesses, households, and the government. When a bank lends, it credits the borrower's demand deposit account with the amount of the loan. This is called deposit creation. The account can be used by the borrower by using cheques or EFTPOS, or withdrawing cash from it. This is how commercial bank lending becomes part of money supply.

Banks, of course, would need money to lend in the first place. They acquire it in a number of ways. The most important source of money to lend is their clients. Clients keep part of their money as demand deposit for use in transactions. Commercial banks use this for lending. Banking laws, however, prohibit them from lending out the entire amount of clients' deposits. They are required to keep a specified fraction of the deposits kept with them in the form of cash and other highly liquid[3] assets. This fraction is called the cash reserve ratio (CRR) and is fixed by the central bank. Cash has to be kept because clients would want to take out a part of their deposits on any given day. However, clients take out only a small fraction of their deposits in a day. That fraction would generally suffice as cash reserve.

If the cash reserve ratio is ten per cent, then a bank with Rs 99 of clients' deposits can lend out up to Rs 90 and keep Rs 9 in reserve. The loan of Rs 90 is credited as deposit into borrowers' accounts. Banks thus create additional deposits using the existing deposits of their clients. In this example, the bank with initial deposits of Rs 99 of its clients can create another Rs 90 of deposits.

However, the story of deposit creation only begins here. What happens after this is fascinating. Borrowers would use the Rs 90 of loan to pay their suppliers, workers, and clients with cheques. Those

[3]An asset is liquid if it is easily convertible into cash or is cash itself. Assets are often arranged in the order of their liquidity, that is, in the order of the cost of converting them to cash. Cash is called liquid because like a liquid it can be given any shape depending on the container.

who get paid will deposit the cheques into their bank accounts. The banking system of the country—that is, all the commercial banks together—now gets Rs 90 as clients' deposit. They can use this amount for further lending. The banks keep 10 per cent as cash reserve and lend out the rest, that is, Rs 81. As they lend this amount, they create Rs 81 of new deposits for borrowers. These borrowers too will use the money to pay out. So Rs 81 will get into various banks again as clients' deposits. This will now enable those banks to create another round of loans. This time they will keep back in reserve Rs 8.10 and lend out the rest. The story continues. Deposits created in successive rounds become smaller and smaller because a part is reserved each time.

Total deposits created with the initial Rs 99 are many times more. The smaller the CRR, more the banks can lend out in each round and total deposits generated from any given amount of clients' deposits would be larger. Therefore, central banks use CRR to regulate money supply.

The system of keeping a fraction of deposits as reserve is called fractional reserve banking. The system evolved through a very interesting financial development (see Box 7.3). In a somewhat recent occurrence, some central banks have stopped setting a mandatory CRR. In their countries commercial banks themselves decide on a cautionary or prudential reserve ratio. Those banks rely on statistical data as guide to determine the proportion of deposits that clients withdraw on a single day.

## 7.5 Role of Central Banks

Central banks create a country's currency and put it into circulation or withdraw it. Hence it is to the central bank that a government looks for money when it does not want to borrow from the market. A central bank's loans to its government are secured by government securities. These securities are documents that acknowledge debt, something like an IOU. The government can repay the loan or carry it on as its ministry of finance thinks suitable. In the second case, of course, it has to keep paying interest.

If, on the other hand, the government borrows from the market, then the central bank works as its agent. It keeps account of loans of the government and advises the government on borrowing and lending. The central bank is thus the government's banker.

Commercial banks also borrow from the central bank when they are short of cash. The central bank charges interest rates according to its reading of the monetary situation. If it thinks that the economic situation demands dear money it will want to discourage commercial banks. In that case it will charge a relatively high interest. On the other hand in a recession the central bank itself may try to induce commercial banks to borrow and create loans. In that case the central bank reduces the interest rate and makes it attractive for commercial banks to borrow.

---

### Box 7.3: Fractional Reserve Banking and Early Paper Money

Before the Industrial Revolution Europeans converted their saving into gold and silver coins and kept these with trusted goldsmiths for safekeeping. The goldsmiths soon found that only a fraction of the gold and silver were withdrawn by depositors on any given day. Therefore, it was quite safe to lend them out if a prudent fraction was kept back as reserve. So they started this practice.

Somewhat later another development occurred. The goldsmiths used to charge a fee and issue receipts for the deposit. They found that depositors started using these receipts, called goldsmiths' notes, to buy valuables and pass them on to the seller. Over time the notes became an established part of money, used alongside gold and silver coins. The coins remained with the goldsmiths while the notes travelled from hand to hand mediating commercial transactions. Goldsmiths' notes were therefore an early form of paper money. Note that they were not created by a decree of the authorities but emerged from commercial practice. They were accepted because the goldsmiths had a trustworthy reputation.

With this development, goldsmiths found that they need not lend gold and silver to borrowers. Instead, they gave them goldsmiths' notes which could be used to pay for purchases and settlement of debts. Lending now generated significant extra income for them—possibly more than safekeeping fees. They started creating more notes than the value of coins they had for safe keeping. There were more notes in circulation than reserves with which to redeem them. This marked the beginning of the fractional reserve banking. It was also the beginning of institutions like today's interest-paying and interest-earning banks.

Besides controlling money supply and being the banker of the government and commercial banks, a central bank is responsible for the working of the country's financial system. In that role, the bank has to support commercial banks in difficulty. The following is an example of a commercial bank in distress. Suppose a bank lent a big amount for a risky venture that collapsed. Unable to recover the loan its liquidity is seriously reduced and the information has seeped into the market. The bank's depositors fear for their deposits and want them back. Naturally this creates a much larger demand for withdrawal than what the bank normally would provide for. The bank is therefore likely to fail to meet the demand. So there will be a run on the bank and it would collapse. This will ruin its depositors and shareholders. The collapse of one bank may lead to a general panic. The public may start doubting the soundness of commercial banks generally and may run on their banks. It is obvious that a central bank has to prevent such possibilities by helping out the distressed bank.

Generally, it would lend the bank adequate short-run funds so that it can meet its depositors' demand. Central banks also come out with public statements declaring that they will provide enough funds to the distressed bank, which generally reduces panic and cuts down the demand for withdrawal of deposits. The central bank is, therefore, called the 'lender of last resort'.

Bank failures were common in the first half of the twentieth century. These failures have provided experience and case studies for central banks and helped them to develop norms for regulation and control. Central banks now advise deposit taking banks on the risk structure of their assets. In most countries central banks set prescriptive and prohibitive rules about commercial banks' asset portfolios. These are designed to prevent situations of crisis or distress. This aspect of central banks' task is called prudential supervision. They can refuse credit and de-register a bank. De-registration means that the institution would not be allowed to accept deposits from the public which means an end to its commercial banking business. These are of course extreme measures; generally central banks operate with soft hands and persuasion.

**Box 7.4: Bank of International Settlement (BIS)**

Prudential supervision has acquired a new dimension with extensive globalisation. Businesses in most countries are now connected to transnational banks through lending and borrowing. Central banks are worried about financial instability coming from outside the country, for example, through the international banking system as highlighted by the 1997 Asian crisis. The Bank of International Settlement (BIS) provides a forum for developing prudential supervision of banks at a global and transnational level.

The BIS has a long history. It was founded in 1930 in Basel, Switzerland to facilitate international transactions. It had the mandate to oversee the settlement of international debts. But for all practical purposes, it was set up to manage the reparation payments imposed on Germany by the Treaty of Versailles after the First World War. Starting from here, the Bank's focus has changed many times as the world financial system has evolved. After the Second World War and until 1970 it focused on the functioning of the Bretton Woods system (see Chapter 8). In the 1970s and 1980s it shifted attention to the management of cross-border capital flows. This change was the result of new developments in international investment in those decades. Oil price rise created a huge amount of oil money. The global financial system of the time was not prepared to absorb this large amount of money as investment. Oil shocks had created another problem. They sent many developing countries into debt creating the debt crisis of the 1980s. This required urgent attention of the international financial system. All this changed the nature of BIS' business.

Regulatory supervision of internationally active banks became an important issue around this time because the amount of international funds had increased so substantially. It was realised that any problem in a bank with multi-country business could lead to a financial catastrophe with worldwide ramifications. That led to what is known as the Basel Capital Accord. The accord produced a set of principles and codes for internationally active banks. The Accord has been revised a number of times as the experience of new financial episodes got absorbed. The Basel Committee on Banking Supervision, which had come up in the 1970s as a committee of central bankers of ten countries is now a forum of a large number of central banks for regular cooperation on prudential matters. Its objective is to improve the understanding of prudential issues as well as the quality of bank supervision globally. Many central banks have adopted the norms of the Basel Committee for prudential supervision of their domestic banking system as well.

Commercial banks are less prone to failure now compared to the period before the Second World War. First, central banks now know more about the weak spots of commercial banking and have developed rules and guidelines for supervision. They have got governments to pass acts that give them greater power of supervision. Second, there is significant research and exchange of information among central banks at the international level. The Basel Committee, for example, provides valuable inputs to central banks on prudential supervision.

---

### Box 7.5: Bank Failures

Bank failures were commonplace in the early twentieth century. More than 600 US banks failed each year on an average in the 1920s. However, these failures did not raise much concern. Too many small banks used to be registered at that time and hence failure was thought to be a normal business process. However, the failures during the Great Depression years were different in nature and attracted a lot of attention. They set in motion the process of institution building for prudential supervision of commercial banks.

**Table 7.1: Commercial Bank Failures in the US, 1921–1933**

| Year | Number of Failures | Deposits Involved ($ thousand) | Depositors' Losses ($ thousand) |
|------|------|------|------|
| 1921 | 506 | 172,806 | 59,967 |
| 1922 | 366 | 91,182 | 38,223 |
| 1923 | 646 | 149,601 | 62,142 |
| 1924 | 775 | 210,150 | 79,381 |
| 1925 | 617 | 166,937 | 60,799 |
| 1926 | 975 | 260,153 | 83,066 |
| 1927 | 669 | 199,332 | 60,681 |
| 1928 | 498 | 142,386 | 43,813 |
| 1929 | 659 | 230,643 | 76,659 |
| 1930 | 1350 | 837,096 | 237,359 |
| 1931 | 2293 | 1,690,232 | 390,476 |
| 1932 | 1453 | 706,187 | 168,302 |
| 1933 | 4000 | 3,596,708 | 540,396 |

*Source*: Federal Deposit Insurance Corporation, US.

*(contd...)*

*Box 7.5 continued.*

An important institution that resulted from US bank failures of the 1930s is deposit insurance. In 1933 Franklin Roosevelt established the Federal Deposit Insurance Corporation (FDIC). The FDIC was empowered to provide deposit insurance to commercial banks. This not only reduced the possible hardship if banks failed, but reduced the likelihood of a run on banks in the first place as the fear of losing one's money was eliminated. This banking act also extended the federal government's power of supervision over all banks.

The act had another useful feature. It separated commercial banking from investment banking and prohibited investment banks from taking public deposits. Investment banking is long-term lending for investment activities. These loans have a much higher risk than short-term business loans and working capital loans. The separation was a useful step in insulating public deposits from the risk of long-term investment. Deposit insurance and the separation of commercial from investment banking have since spread to other countries. Deposit insurance works like a normal insurance business, whereby commercial banks pay for insuring the deposits they hold.

## 7.6 Monetary Policy

When describing the functions of a central bank I mentioned open market operations. These are an essential part of the conduct of monetary policy. The idea that variation of money supply can be used for some effects is relatively new. The two World Wars and the Great Depression produced a variety of experiences for the industrialised countries. These, together with the new macroeconomics of Keynes, led to the awareness that money supply can be used for short-run policy. The developments occurred at a time when central banks were being established throughout the world. Central banks started using monetary variation as an economic tool from their early days.

Monetary policy uses variation in the quantity of money to increase or reduce demand. We have seen earlier that increase of money supply reduces interest rates. Lower interest boosts aggregate demand in many ways. First, it lowers the cost of investment. Even for those who use their own money for investment, lower interest means that they sacrifice less when they use their own money. Second, when the interest rate is low saving is not too attractive and so people spend more on consumption. Big ticket purchases get a boost. Third, lower mortgage rates boost housing demand.

Lower interest rate creates another important effect. It prompts flight of capital from the country to overseas financial markets where the interest rate is higher. To send their funds overseas investors must convert funds from domestic to overseas currency. Thus the demand for overseas currencies increases and that for the local currency falls. This reduces the price of the local currency. That in turn makes the exports of the country cheaper and imported goods more costly. Exports increase and imports fall; both are good for domestic expansion. The foreign currency effect, of course, depends on how open the economy is, that is, whether the government allows free inflow and outflow of funds and foreign exchange. Also, the country needs to have a flexible exchange rate system rather than fixed exchange rates. It is only a flexible exchange rate system that allows the currency price to change freely, reflecting the supply and demand of currencies.

---

### Box 7.6: The Reserve Bank of India

Modern central banks were set up early in the twentieth century. In India, the Reserve Bank of India (RBI) Act was passed in 1934 and the bank was established on 1 April 1935. The Bank's central office was initially in Kolkata and it was moved to Mumbai in 1937. Originally the RBI was privately owned. Following India's independence in 1947, RBI was nationalised in 1949. It has remained fully owned by the Government of India since then. The bank is responsible for regulating the issue of currency notes and it oversees the financial system. It has supervisory powers over commercial banks and other financial institutions.

Apart from the customary responsibilities of a central bank, RBI has handled a very significant aspect of the country's development. It has managed the 'monetisation' of the Indian economy. When the RBI was founded large parts of the Indian economy avoided the banking system. Business was done using cash and informal credit. Even the use of cash

---

*(contd...)*

*Box 7.6 continued.*

was fairly limited in the countryside. Localised barter was common. Local businesses resorted to nearly cashless transactions, where two parties would settle only the balance of accumulated transactions over a period. Over the years, the economy has been steadily integrated with the monetary and banking system. The RBI has played an important role in this monetisation process.

A cheap money policy is pursued when an economy is in the downturn of a business cycle. It lowers interest rate and helps boost the components of aggregate demand. On the other side, when an economy is 'overheated' that is, when demand is running too high for its capacity, the demand raises price more than output and jobs. In this situation central banks apply the dear money policy. This raises interest rate and discourages expenditure.

## 7.7 How Many Things can a Central Bank do?

From what we have discussed, it would appear that central banks can produce a variety of aggregate effects on the economy. They can keep money supply tight and inflation close to zero. Or, if the need arises, they can let money supply increase fast and stimulate aggregate demand, employment, and growth. They can buy or sell foreign currencies to influence the exchange rate against important currencies. This can help exports and improve the balance of payment.[4] Further, central banks can use their power over commercial banks to allocate commercial bank credit to priority sectors. All of these are useful for the economy. Should we then ask a central bank to attend to all of these tasks?

The question arises because central banks that have tried to do all of the above have not generally done any of them well. The failure is not accidental but has a reason. In spite of all its powers, the central bank can fully control only one macroeconomic variable. We may take that variable as either money supply or the average interest rate. These two variables being inter-related, as soon as one

[4]For an explanation of balance of payments see Chapter 8.

is fixed the other is determined as well. So a central bank actually controls only one, whichever of the two it chooses to use. Other macro variables such as income and employment are *influenced* by money supply or interest rate but are not completely *fixed* by them. Interest rate is only one of many factors that influence them. Therefore, a change of money supply can affect a number of macro variables but cannot guide any of them to a desired value. Second, a change of interest rate (or money supply) may create a desirable effect on one thing and an unwanted effect on another. For example, suppose the central bank wants to check inflation and, so, reduces money supply. Interest rate rises as a result. This would now attract overseas financial investment into the country. As this happens, foreign funds are converted into the domestic currency increasing the latter's price. Now this is an unfavourable development for domestic exporters because it reduces the demand for their exports. The central bank cannot really help because it has only one instrument that it can control. Thus, if it has to limit inflation it cannot help exports.

Hence when a central bank is expected to contribute to all good things, short-run monetary policy moves from one temporary target to another, attaining some of them to a degree but abandoning them to pursue another as the situation changes. The general indeterminacy of the effect makes the entire exercise vague. Neither are the goals attained, nor can the bank be blamed.

The long-run relation between money supply and inflation is the least imperfect among the relations between money supply and other macro variables. Hence inflation rate is one thing that money supply can handle best. Therefore, a point of view has emerged that monetary policy should be used to control the price level alone. Many have argued that central banks should be asked to ensure a low inflation rate and not try to influence anything else. The advantage of this is that it eliminates inflation-related uncertainty, which in turn is good for investment and saving. With a single objective the attainment or failure of the central bank becomes transparent. It can be held accountable for failures and that helps. According to this view, output and jobs should be influenced by fiscal policy while the central bank should focus entirely on a stable price level.

## 7.8 A Government and its Central Bank: Should they be Buddies?

After the Second World War when governments used budgets to keep unemployment low, they ran large deficits. These deficits were funded by borrowing from central banks. Government's borrowing from its central bank is equivalent to the creation of so much of new money. This money enters the economy as the government spends it. As discussed in the last chapter, years of deficit financing and the resulting growth of money supply led to high inflation in European countries.

To be able to control money supply, the central bank is expected to be separate from those who use money. The government is an important user and the central bank should be independent of it. But this did not happen because the central banks were hardly separate from their governments. Central bank heads were selected by their governments. So they were persons with significant political allegiance to the government of the day or socially connected to their leaders. As a consequence, central banks were not able to stop the slide into inflationary chaos in the post-war decades.

There was a move in the 1980s to rewrite central bank acts so as to free them from the political establishment. To understand why the idea of reform came up around this time, we need to go back to the context of European inflation. By the early 1970s, it was clear that the policy of sustained public spending had not achieved anything more than inflation. The economy moved back to the natural rate of output and employment after the spending stimulus wore out, and then the government had to provide a round of fresh spending. In each round inflation increased above its previous value. The long-run situation was high and increasing inflation associated with no more than the natural rate of output and employment.

In this context, it was realised that the inflation could be brought down only if the central bank reduced the growth of money supply drastically and held it there. At the same time, of course, the government would have to maintain a reasonable amount of expenditure using tax revenue. This would ensure that employment and output did not shrink too drastically when inflation started coming down. This programme was given the name of 'disinflation'.

It was, however, expected that disinflation would take time to succeed—possibly running into several years. In the meanwhile, it would impose significant hardship. As the central bank curbed the growth of money, the government would have to spend only from tax money. So spending would drop below what the economy was so far accustomed to. This would reduce income and employment even as inflation started dropping a bit. At this point, people would remain unconvinced that the drop in inflation could be really sustained. They would expect that hardship and unemployment would create political pressure on the government to retract, as governments had on other occasions. Hence business and the public would continue to expect high inflation. But with expectation of high inflation rate continuing, actual inflation would not drop much.

Thus how long a disinflation process would drag and how much hardship has to be endured would depend on how soon the inflation expectation gets tuned down. But expectation would not come down unless people believe that the government would persist and succeed. The longer the public remain unimpressed, the longer the hardship would continue. What this means is that disinflation can win only if the public believes that it will win! Only then can lower inflation expectation take over and inflation will come down rapidly. After this happens and the price level falls significantly, the sized-down government spending would become good enough to sustain the natural output. The economy would then be restored to the natural rate with a lower rate of inflation. Hardship would end only at this stage.

It is in this context that the issue of the central bank's autonomy came up. If the central bank was given real autonomy from the political process, then a disinflation programme would be more credible. People would know that even if the government faces serious political pressure it would be unable to increase spending. If a truly independent central bank starts a disinflation programme, expectation of inflation would come down fairly quickly. These considerations led countries with high inflation to consider the issue of central bank independence seriously.

## Box 7.7: New Zealand's Central Bank Reform

With years of large deficit spending since the Second World War, New Zealand faced a serious inflationary situation like a number of European countries. In the 1980s the inflation took menacing proportions. The country had started a series of liberal market reforms in the mid-1980s quite independently of the problem of inflation. The control of inflation became important both for price stability *per se*, and for the success of the reforms. Like Europe, New Zealand also contemplated disinflation around this time. It was, however, realised that the announcement of disinflation would not impress the public given the country's political situation. The Labour Party was in the leadership of the government and of the reforms. Given its populist policies in the past and its constituency of trade unions and workers, people were not ready to believe that it could persist with the political rigour of a disinflation process.

It was evident from the experience of other countries that the close link between the Reserve Bank of New Zealand (RBNZ) and the political establishment had to be snapped. For this the government passed a new act in 1989. The act gave RBNZ complete autonomy from the political system. The governor (head) of the bank was to be employed on a contract through transparent selection from respondents to a public advertisement. He or she would appoint the rest of the bank's staff and the government would play no role in it. The governor and the finance minister would sign a contract. The contract would specify an inflation band (for example, 1 per cent to 3 per cent) of an official price index and the governor's task would be to ensure that the inflation rate remained in this band. This would be the only task given to the bank. The contract would specify what the government could ask from the bank and *vice versa*. The RBNZ might consider requests for loans from the government but would have no obligation to lend. The contract also specified when it might be deemed that the inflation-related task was not properly completed. In case it was not fulfilled the government could terminate the governor's contract.

The provisions of the act were widely publicised to catch public attention. After RBNZ started functioning under the new act it started a well-advertised disinflation campaign. Even though massive de-monetisation brought the inflation down somewhat, inflationary expectation remained high for at least two years in spite of advertising

*(contd...)*

*Box 7.7 continued.*

the provisions of the act. By 1991 it seemed that the public was finally convinced that RBNZ meant business and that the government could not interfere. Inflation expectation started coming down. Inflation rate came down rapidly after this and has remained around 2 per cent on average since 1991.

## 7.9 Financial Institutions

There are two types of assets in a modern economy, real and financial. Real assets are goods held by their owners because they can produce income in the future. Houses, land, mines, forests, orchards, gold, plant and machines, stock of goods etc. are examples. A financial asset is also a source of future income; but it is not a tangible good. It is a claim on someone else. If I have lent money then I have a claim to get back the principal and interest from the party who has taken the loan. This claim is an asset. Similarly, government securities are assets for their owners because they are claims on the government for an amount of money. Share of a company or equity is a claim on part of its profit and is a financial asset as well. Money is a financial asset because it is a claim on a bank. Cash, for example, is a claim on the central bank and demand deposit is a claim on a commercial bank.

Borrowing and lending are immensely important activities. Most of the investment in a modern economy takes place in the business sector. Businesses earn income but turn it over to their owners. So they have little saving of their own. They need to borrow for investment projects. The business sector is thus typically a deficit sector. On the other hand, the household sector is a net saver. Business carries out investment by borrowing from the household sector. If borrowing was not possible, then investment projects would be small as they would rely only on the owners' savings.

Financial institutions connect borrowers with lenders. Hence they are also called financial intermediaries. The scale of borrowing and lending in a modern economy is very large indeed. The total lending and leasing by commercial banks in the US was more than $7 trillion in October 2008. To get it in perspective, note that it is significantly more than the combined GDP of China and India in that year. Second, the financial sector in the US and, with it much of the world, were lying low in 2008 smarting under the financial disarray that had started in 2007. Bank loans are only one kind of financial assets and represent just a part of all financial transactions. The total volume of all financial transactions is mind boggling. This scale of financial activity would not be possible without institutions that specialise in raising and transmitting funds. If investors had to find out by themselves who has some saving to spare, the search cost would be very large and investment would be seriously constrained. Financial institutions reduce the search cost. They mobilise saving and channel it to borrowers. This makes borrowing and lending easier and less costly. It also helps in channelling saving from one part of a country into investment in another part, thus helping the development of backward regions and reducing regional disparity. International investment, similarly, helps reduce international disparity.

Financial institutions help in another important way. They help in risk pooling. Lending has significant risk that the borrower's project might fail and he may not be able to repay the loan. If there were no financial institutions then all lenders would lend to individual businesses and each would face this default risk. This would discourage lending and limit investment. A financial institution pools together the savings of many persons and breaks it into loans to a number of investors. The chance that individual borrowers' projects would fail is not affected by this. But the loss from such failures accrues to the total pool of funds that the financial institution mobilises. Hence, individual depositors bear only a small part of the risk. This encourages saving as well as investment in relatively risky ventures.

There are different types of financial institutions. Each specialises in some kind of lending activity. They also specialise in raising money from particular segments, like saving from urban middle class income, from agricultural areas, saving accumulating in companies' provident funds, and so on. Further, as financing grows in size and complexity new types of financial assets are designed to attract particular segments of saving.

What we ordinarily call banks are technically known as commercial banks. They are the only institutions that are allowed to take deposits from the public for safe-keeping. They are the modern counterparts of the middle age's goldsmiths who used to keep people's gold and valuables in their vaults. Commercial banks' depositors are a vast majority of the saving public. Therefore, commercial bank failures affect the economic life of a country like no other financial disaster. Prudential supervision of banks is extremely important for this obvious reason.

Commercial banks provide short and medium term loans for on-going business, these are called working capital loans. These loans are used to bridge the time between the production of goods and their sale, or sale and getting the payment. They are secured with goods used in the borrower's business or its other tangible assets. There was a time when banks also used to provide long-term loans for investment. But now investment lending is handled by a separate class of banks called investment banks. They raise money at higher interest rates than commercial banks. Saving households thus have a choice. If they like taking risks in order to get a high return, they can lend their money to investment banks. If, on the other hand, they want to avoid risk they can keep their money in commercial banks at lower interest.

## 7.10 Risk and Return

The difference between commercial and investment banks brings out an important feature of financial markets. Risk of a financial asset depends on the activity to which the claim is related. It can be measured by the range of possible returns from the asset.[5] An asset whose return may vary between 0 and 20 per cent is riskier than one with possible variation between 5 and 10 per cent. Activities like the development of new drugs, exploration of minerals etc. are subject to significant amount of chance. Related projects are inherently risky. Return may be very high if the breakthrough comes early, but low if it comes late or never. Lenders face default of payment if the

[5]Standard deviation or variance of the possible returns is also a possible measure of risk. The idea is the same: to measure risk by the spread of possible returns.

projects do not go on schedule or just flop. Sometimes there is no open default but the borrower asks for more loans at a lower rate to be able to pay on schedule and continue the project. Lenders like an investment bank would generally oblige in this situation rather than force default. They lend to these projects only if the expected return is adequately high. This is a general feature of financial deals. If they carry more risk, then they must promise higher expected returns. Projects that have both high risk and low return are not financed; just as in daily life we do not take a risky step unless something great is involved. Therefore, risk and expected return for assets are inversely correlated.

Lenders, however, reduce their exposure to risk as much as possible by diversifying their loan portfolios. Risk is related to chance. Chance factors do not affect different projects, sectors, or countries in the same way at the same time. Thus, a portfolio made of loans to different sectors and countries reduces the average risk per rupee of investment. This strategy is called diversification. Further, it is found that there are activities whose fortunes tend to move in opposite directions quite systematically. For example, a lot of snow fall tends to kill cattle and reduce the return from beef and dairy industry. But the same climate would boost the country's ice sports, tourism, and hospitality activities. A financial firm can reduce its average risk by investing in beef, dairy, and tourism industries of a cold country at the same time. International lenders combine loans in different countries expecting that the phases of their business cycles will not coincide.

## 7.11 Variety of Financial Products

Most of the lendable funds in an economy originate in its households. Households, however, have different attitudes to the risk–return combination. The difference is partly idiosyncratic and partly related to age, wealth, and income. Closer to retirement and after it, people opt for 'conservative' assets, that is, those with secure though lower rate of return. In the middle years of working life, particularly if it is high-earning, a family has some appetite for high-risk, high-growth assets. Financial institutions produce a large variety of investment products to cater to the requirements of various households. These institutions are called investment companies.

Investment companies combine their investments and loans in different proportions to produce a number of separate portfolios. They combine safe and risky assets in different proportions to give different risk and return. They then sell units (that is, parts or shares) of these portfolios to savers. Savers can choose from the different risk–return profiles of the products according to their liking. Investment companies either market them directly or may use commercial banks as their selling window. Commercial banks have a large base among saving households; they use it to sell investment products on behalf of investment companies. Recall that they are not allowed to invest in long-term and risky assets by themselves. Instead they pick up shares of the business by working as retail agents for investment companies.

Some investment company portfolios have more safe assets such as government securities, loans to utility companies and local authorities, fixed deposits in banks, and money market assets.[6] These assets are combined with a sprinkling of relatively higher return assets with some risk. Overall, the return on such a portfolio will not be high but its attraction is its low risk. At the other extreme, there are portfolios with large proportion of risky assets like equity investment.[7] Return from the equity of a company comes as dividend[8] paid by it and from any possible increase in the price of the equity. These returns are variable and risky. Dividend payment is based on the company's profit which depends on uncertain factors. Rest of the risk of equity investment comes from a possible fall in the market price of the equity. Market price falls when the company's profit and performance affect the sentiment of the market. For example, if a company is not doing well, its shareholders start selling off their shares bringing down the equity price. All in all, investment in equities has high expected returns coupled with high risk. Further, equity

[6]Money market assets are very short duration loans to the government and commercial banks and carry very little risk.

[7]It is investment in the share of joint stock companies. The words 'equity', 'share', and 'stock' are used interchangeably.

[8]Dividend is the part of profit of a company that is distributed to shareholders.

investment in emerging markets—that is, in companies registered in China, India, Brazil, Mexico, Russia etc.—has higher expected return than that in the OECD countries; of course, it carries much larger risk. Investment companies use large proportion of shares in general, and emerging market shares in particular, to produce very high growth portfolios.

It is not only households that buy investment companies' packaged assets. There are large institutional buyers too. Foremost are pension funds. A pension fund is set up to support retired employees of a company, the government, or other institutions. Employees, employers, and the government contribute into the fund according to a regular schedule. Pension organisations need these funds to grow fast as they face a number of problems. The first is inflation which constantly erodes the real value of a fund. Second, average longevity has been increasing in all countries. The number of years a person lives after retirement is getting comparable with the number of years of working life. Pension organisations want funds to grow fast enough to beat these problems. On the other hand, they are legally barred from investing in equities and similar risky assets. Therefore, they often invest in the products of investment companies. Investment packages are also bought by insurance companies. They raise money from customers in exchange for promise of compensation in case of an insured event. They invest the collected premium in government securities, banks, and special investment packages. Other funds, like university endowments, local government institutions, charitable trusts etc. also invest in packaged funds.

Unit trusts are quite similar to investment companies. They have expertise in fund management. They raise investment from households, business, governments, pension funds, insurance companies, and so on and invest them in various fields. With these investments they produce different portfolios. An investor buys 'units', that is, a share of a portfolio at the prevailing 'unit price'. The unit price moves up and down reflecting the value of the portfolio. An investor can sell his units to the trust at any time and exit. His gain or loss comes from the difference between the purchase and sale price of the units.

Another very important financial product is the mortgage loan. In this case households turn borrowers. A mortgage loan is taken to buy or build real property. The loan is secured by the property itself which is owned by the lender until the loan is repaid. Commercial banks and a few specialised institutions provide mortgage loans. In industrially advanced countries where financial markets are well developed, mortgage loan is the normal mode of financing a home purchase. Hence markets for mortgage loans and supporting services (like real estate and legal services) are very well developed in those countries. A borrower can choose from a variety of features such as the size of loan, maturity date, schedule for repayment, fixed or flexible interest rates etc. Interest rate on the loan depends on these features. Mortgages are growing all over the world[9] and are poised to become the normal way of financing a home everywhere.

A growing trend in the financial markets is the rise of fund management companies. They do not raise money themselves but manage funds of other institutions according to their requirement. They employ finance professionals who take over the management of the assets of others and convert them into customised portfolios with desired properties.

## 7.12 Lenders and Borrowers

Saving mostly originates in households, governments, and pension funds. Savings of local bodies like municipalities and trusts are also classified as government savings. Let us track where these savings go.

The largest chunk of household saving is invested in fixed term investments in commercial banks. Households also buy units of unit trusts. Depending on the country, they may have to put some saving into compulsory saving instruments such as public and private provident funds. Life insurance is also a popular form of investment in some countries. Life insurance companies now sell a variety of innovative policies which are more attractive than the traditional policies.

Then there are the households that want higher return and do not mind taking some risk. They buy shares of managed funds of

---

[9]with the exception of a handful of countries where they are frowned upon.

investment companies which, as we noted, are retailed by commercial banks. Some of these growth-seeking households lend to a category of institutions called finance companies. These institutions lend to borrowers who cannot provide adequate security demanded by commercial banks and other formal organisations. They also provide consumption loans. Hence they lend at higher rates and can afford to borrow at higher rates too. Investment in a finance company, however, is one of the riskier options. Risk arises because the borrowers of finance companies are more prone to default than borrowers of formal institutions. Because the loans are not secured, the finance company loses money in the event of a default. As a result, the failure rate of finance companies is also significant. Further, unlike commercial bank deposits, investment in a finance company is not insured.

Increasingly, households appear to be willing to bear some risk and are moving out of traditional forms of low-risk investments. They are buying the various products that we have discussed above. It is now relatively easy to buy them as commercial banks retail them and provide advice about their risk and return. Some people, of course, prefer to buy company shares directly from the stock market rather than buying a packaged product.

Next in importance is government saving. It is managed by the central bank as the government's banker. Apart from saving in domestic currency, government's saving may consist of foreign currency deposits, gold, IMF reserve positions, and special drawing rights of the IMF and so on. In some countries, the central bank creates a fund called the sovereign fund with a part of the government's saving and manages it to generate higher returns. Sovereign funds invest globally. Saving of local authorities, municipalities, and public sector companies are not managed by the central bank but are managed locally. Mangers at local levels usually keep part of the saving in commercial banks and the rest in managed funds.

Pension funds invest in relatively safe assets like government bonds and money market assets. Some governments are contemplating a change in laws for pension funds to allow them to invest in wider variety of assets so that they can grow faster. Obviously, this would increase risk and that is why the move has been drawing opposition in many countries.

We may now look at the borrowers' side of the market. Established businesses raise short-run loans from commercial banks. Commercial banks specialise in lending for 'working capital' which is required for bridging the time between various payments and receipts. When an established business needs a relatively longer term loan it may be able to get it from commercial banks if the loan is for a relatively secure purpose. But if it is for riskier operations, the business has to approach investment banks or it can raise it from the share market by selling new stocks. Some investment banks specialise in providing venture capital, that is, funds to be invested in an unproven business. They help the client raise equity by putting their weight behind the venture as underwriters. As underwriters, they buy a part of the equities themselves and thus take the risk of selling them to individual and institutional investors later. The fact that they buy the equity increases the market's interest and trust and helps raise the equity in the end.

## 7.13 Are Financial Markets Efficient?

We have two ways of looking at the efficiency of financial markets. One is as an internal property of the market. The second is to define efficiency in terms of what the financial market does for the economy. The two ways of looking at the question are, of course, related. In financial market theory the question of efficiency is generally posed in the first way and we will look at it first.

Rather than talking in general terms, for concreteness let us focus on the share market. The share market is very competitive in industrialised countries. Regulators try to ensure that competitive trading is not hampered by any structural weakness of the market. In a market without any structural weakness, we would expect a share's price to reflect the market participants' valuation based on information on the company's current and future performance. The internal structure of the market—that is, the way trading takes place and information flows—is what determines if all participants can get and use all the available information. It also determines if the information leads to the best possible assessment of companies.

These considerations can be used as a criteria for the market's efficiency. Accordingly, some economists propose this: a financial market is efficient if participants have full access to all publicly available information and they use it rationally to evaluate companies. This definition focuses on the internal structure of the market. It asks if the market allows unimpeded flow of publicly available information to all participants and if it can absorb and use the information properly.

There is a hypothesis known as the 'Efficient Market Hypothesis' which expects financial markets of industrialised countries to be efficient in this sense. It implies that it would not be possible for anyone to out-perform such a market systematically. The reason is that everyone has all the relevant news and, therefore, no one has better information to beat others, that is, the market.

In such a market, participants would use all available information to decide sale and purchase orders. So the price of the share would embody all this information. To do better than the market, a participant has to predict how price will change from here more accurately than others. For such prediction, the participant has to use new information because the existing information is already known to all. But when any new information comes up, it is quickly disseminated and also becomes available to everybody. No one can get an information advantage over others or over the market. In this situation, no one could do better than others systematically. Participants, of course, mix their hunches with the information to predict price change. Surely, someone's hunches will be better than others' and she or he will do better. But that works by chance. No one can, therefore, beat the market more often than be beaten. Of course, someone can beat the market if he has inside information, that is, information which is not publicly available. But using inside information for trading in shares is a punishable offence and we can ignore that for this discussion.

So we can summarise the efficient market hypothesis this way. The price of a financial asset reflects all relevant information available now, including information that can influence the future course of events. A price change will occur only when any new information comes out in the public domain. Since genuinely new information is not predictable, the future price of the share is not predictable too. (If anything is known about the future course that can help prediction, it would be already absorbed and be reflected in the current price). In efficient markets, share prices are, therefore, unpredictable random quantities. Thus, no strategy can be rationally generated to buy and sell them. Interestingly, an elaborately planned portfolio of shares cannot do any better than the average participant's portfolio. In fact, the hypothesis claims that investors would do better by putting their money in an index fund rather than giving it to any financial expert. An index fund keeps a portfolio made up of the components of a market index such as the Standard & Poor's 500 Index (S&P 500) in the same proportion as in the index or in some other fixed proportions. This means that the fund just follows what the market thinks at any point of time and its value tracks the fortune of the market. If S&P 500 goes up by say X per cent in a period, the value of the fund will increase by X per cent. The point of the efficiency hypothesis is that other clever portfolios may do better than the index fund in some periods, but they will do worse in some other. And, in terms of the long-run average, a clever portfolio would not do any better than the index fund.

Are financial markets really efficient in this sense? There is some obviously contrary evidence though that need not entirely reject the hypothesis. Some fund managers and investors have done systematically better than the market. An often-quoted example is Warren Buffet, who publicly announced a strategy to buy undervalued stocks and sell them when they are properly valued by the market. He is a legendary investor who has not only consistently made wealth for his organisation but has inspired investors all over the world. Note that if markets are efficient then there cannot be any undervalued or overvalued stocks. They would reflect the value consistent with the given public information pool at that point. Warren Buffet's investment criterion would not even make a sense in an efficient market.

Second, there are some well-known patterns in the share market, which can be exploited for profit. If the market was efficient profit would have been made from these patterns so that the opportunities exhausted and the patterns disappeared. The 'January effect' is the known pattern that more than annual-average returns are earned in January. The effect is created by investors selling large amounts in December to create tax losses[10] and then buying in January. December sales lead to a fall in prices which increase with January purchases. Hence, significant capital gains occur in the market in January. In an efficient market, the knowledge of the January effect should lead to countervailing purchases in December and sales in January to derive profit from the effect. This should clean up the possibility of any such profit. There is also a weekly pattern in the share market. It is a statistically seen pattern that prices are higher on Friday afternoon and Monday morning than during week days. This is publicly available information and if the market was efficient, it would have used it until the effect disappeared.

The reasoning that leads to the efficient market hypothesis requires not just good information flow but also rational reasoning by investors. As a result it ignores many behavioural traits widespread in financial markets: cognitive biases like overconfidence, overreaction, belief in luck, faith in only a subset of information, and many other human errors of reasoning and information processing. These issues have been researched by psychologists and established to be repeated behaviour in financial markets. They lead many investors to fail to use available information fully and rationally. At the same time they allow those who reason correctly to be able to profit from the market systematically and persistently.

It is, therefore, obvious that markets are not 100 per cent efficient. However, we should also realise that 100 per cent efficiency is not expected outside of textbook models. The real issue is not the existence of factors such as the January effect and the irrational weaknesses of some investors; but whether they are unacceptably large. We may, therefore, ask if markets closely approximate the idea of the rational use of information. It appears that they do so most of the time but not always. And when they fail to do so, they fail spectacularly. They function well most of the time because there are investors who are on the lookout for smart opportunities. Thus while Warren Buffet's investment strategy implies that markets are not 100 per cent efficient, his investment leads the market closer to efficiency by soaking up the possibility of profit.

[10]that is, business account losses to reduce tax liability more than the amount of the real loss.

The second way of looking at efficiency is to pose the issue from the perspective of the economy. Do financial markets channel savings into the best possible investment projects? There is an obvious difficulty in this question. We can answer it only if we know what the best investment projects are at any given time. But do we? Investment projects yield fruit in the future. At the present we can only judge them with the information available now. That may or may not produce the best outcome in the future. So the only rational way of answering would be to check if we are using all information available as of now in the best possible way. This takes us back to the first approach of looking at efficiency, which asks exactly the same question: do financial markets use all publicly available information rationally? Hence we have to answer along the same lines again that they do so most of the times. It means that the investment projects that are taken up by the working of the financial markets are our best bets most of the time.

## 7.14 But Why must we Agree with the Markets?

Many of you would find this way of judging investment projects seriously disturbing and unacceptable. You may not accept that there are no worthwhile investment projects outside what the fraternity of financial market participants think worthwhile. We saw earlier that the production structure that evolves in a market economy, even when efficient, may not be acceptable to everyone (Chapter 2). Market outputs are determined by the demand of people who have adequate buying power. The resulting production structure may not be agreeable to those who cannot register their demand because they do not have the money. Similar issues arise in investment.

So we can very well disagree with the investment projects that come up through financial intermediation even when financial markets are efficient. These projects promise the highest possible return for the risk that investors are willing to take. The market abandons projects that are too risky for their return. But these returns are narrowly defined as what will accrue to investors, not to the society. A radically different line up of projects will arise if we think of returns in terms of social need. We will then find that the return on investment in R&D in a drug for a poor man's disease is large enough to justify the risk.

But the risk is too high given the insignificant market demand for the poor man's drug and hence the investment will be rejected by the financial market. However, the only way that a dissenting voice on investment can be heard in the market is to say it in the language of the market. If we want investment in research for that drug we need to provide the market with evidence of its commercial return. Somebody has to come up with a promise to buy the drug off the market—the government, an international agency, a philanthropic organisation, etc. But that remains the only solution for getting the investment the nod from the financial market.

## 7.15 Bulls, Bears, and Bubbles

It is no secret that financial markets sometimes fail and when they fail they tend to drag the whole economy down. The recession set off by the financial crisis of 2007 is not yet over even as I revise the draft of this book in early 2012. That recession started with a financial market failure. The Great Depression too was triggered by a financial crisis—a crash of the stock market (Chapter 1).

---

**Box 7.8: Tulip Mania**

Financial market failure is not entirely a problem of modern financial institutions. We have the earliest recorded case, 'Tulip Mania', in 17th century Holland. It was during the period of the Dutch golden age, a period when the Dutch led Europe in technology, production, and trade and, not the least, in art. Tulip Mania occurred in the age of the Dutch masters as Johannes Vermeer, Frans Hals, and other masters were painting their masterpieces. A man named Conrad Guestner is said to have imported the first tulip bulb into Holland in 1593 from Constantinople in today's Turkey. The nobility took fancy to the flower and it became popular. Because it was imported and scarce, it was a pricy flower too; so it also became a status symbol in a few years' time. It became not just an object of collection for the rich and the famous, but a craze. The rage spread to neighbouring Germany. The price of tulip bulbs increased fast. Tulip bulbs soon became an item of speculation and started being traded on local market exchanges.

---

(contd...)

*Box 7.8 continued.*

By 1634, tulip mania caught the middle classes too and everybody was dealing in the bulbs to make quick money. Bulbs were sold in the spot market and in future contracts. Most buyers had no intention of planting tulips at all; they just wanted capital gain and get rich in quick time. Price increased twenty-fold in a month that year. If prices reported by various sources are to be believed,[11] then some contracts sold for more than $75,000 in today's price, and at some point 12 acres of land were being exchanged for a particular variety of the bulb. The market crashed in the very same year.

Major events of financial crises are characterised by speculative bubbles. The price of an asset or a group of assets keeps rising in the course of a bubble. After a while the price ceases to have any relation with the intrinsic value of the asset. The unrealistic value cannot be sustained for long because it is divorced from features that sustain price. For example, the value of shares of business corporations ultimately derives from their performance and profit. In a share market bubble, prices rise to a level not justifiable by the profitability of the business sector. So those prices cannot be sustained beyond a certain time period. Or, consider a bubble in real estate. Price of land in an area may start rising expecting that a lot of commercial space will be in demand. Speculators wrestle with one another to corner the land and set off a bubble. Price will eventually rise to a level where firms looking for commercial space would think it too costly given the productivity of their business. They would then decide to move to other areas. The price of land will now crash. Commercial land price derives from the expected profit of business that would use the land and is intrinsically related to it. When a price bubble snaps that tie, it is certain that the price will crash.

In more normal times, however, a financial market continuously corrects its own tendency to overshoot or fall below the right price. The 'right price' is what can be justified by 'market

[11]*Extraordinary Popular Delusions and the Madness of Crowds*, written by Charles Mackay in 1841 provides most of the information about the Tulip Mania, and subsequent historical research has tried to fill in the gaps.

fundamentals'—a phrase describing the real economic factors that should determine the price. At any point of time, a group of participants may think that the price is too high and so is due for a fall. They would, therefore, sell off their stocks at the current price. Thereafter they would wait for the price to fall when they can buy back the assets at a lower price. Financial markets have a colourful term for these participants: they are called 'bears'. As opposed to them, the market also has 'bulls' who expect price to rise further and hence they continue to buy, with the hope of selling shares at higher prices. In a normal situation, some players would want to sell and others would want to buy depending on their reading of the price situation. The change in market price is the result of the bears' sales and the bulls' purchases. If the balance is net sales, the price falls; if it is the opposite, then price rises.

A bubble builds up when the majority of players develop bullish expectations. They expect price to rise and keep buying. So there are more purchase orders and fewer sales. Because the assets are fixed in supply, their prices would increase continuously and a bubble builds up. Sooner or later prices would snap ties with the fundamentals and the market will crash.

Obviously, investments made in the bubble asset lose a large amount of value when a crash occurs. Further, the profits or windfall gains made during the bubble are generally invested in other activities and drive up prices in those areas too. Those prices also crash following the burst of the main bubble. Banks and financial institutions that provided money to the speculators might fail or get into distress. The word 'bubble' is quite appropriate because it captures the idea of quick swelling along with the inevitability of a burst.

## 7.16 Once Again: Are Financial Markets Efficient?

If markets are efficient, the market participants are expected to use all publicly available information in the best possible manner. Why would two market participants with the same set of information harbour different expectations about price change? If they are not able to process the available information adequately, they are free to hire the services of analysts and consultants. So the ability to process information is not a bottleneck in today's markets. Should not everyone, therefore, be either a bull or a bear in any given moment in an efficient market?

The answer is that people have different tolerance for risk. For the same assessed risk some would like to go for an asset while others would abandon it. On the basis of available information the market works out various probabilities. The information about the probability that price will increase or fall by certain amounts is either freely available or can be bought from analyst firms. This information provides an idea about risk. Given the expected value of the asset some think that the risk is worth taking and others do not. Hence some do buy while others sell at a given point.

What happens when a bubble starts forming? Almost everyone then wants to buy. The general assessment of risk at that point is low or the expected return is very high or both. As a result even those who are generally shy of risk would want to buy the asset. Almost all participants thus turn bullish. Initially, this could be the result of extraordinarily good circumstances, for example, very fast economic growth, some new products doing unusually well, and so on. But as the bubble grows, the price of the asset increases beyond these fundamentals and yet most players continue to remain bullish.

There could be two possible explanations of the persistence of bullish expectations even when the bubble has grown for some time. The first is that the market's ability to process information is after all poor in spite of the available techniques and the impressive volume of quantitative data. This is the belief of a section of economists. The information on factors that influence the fundamentals is publicly available as it is mandatory for corporations to publish this sort of information. If the ability to process this information was reasonably good, then the expected value of an asset could not be very different from that supported by its fundamentals. The second possibility is that market participants behave irrationally when a bubble gets going. This is the belief of market psychologists. The idea of an investor taking a rational decision with objectively available probabilities seems to be terribly off the mark in times of a bubble.

We may conclude that either the market is unable to process information, or that players get into an irrational frame of mind and ignore the information. Why markets that work reasonably well in normal times get into an irrational mode in a bubble time is a question of social psychology. Keynes had observed some of the fundamental features of the financial market which are very insightful in this context. He wrote that participants want to keep their financial investment as liquid as possible all the time. That is, they want to be able to sell off and get their money back whenever they want. This is a sort of paranoia resulting from the financial uncertainties of a modern economy. Because of this it is more important for investors to follow the opinion of the market than study its fundamentals. They would buy an asset if the market values it highly, because that is the best way to keep one's assets highly sellable. It does not matter if the asset is even hugely over-valued above its realistic value as long as others in the market are willing to buy it.

*The General Theory* used a telling metaphor for this: financial investment '.. may be likened to those newspaper competitions in which the competitors have to pick out the six prettiest faces from a hundred photographs, the prize being awarded to the competitor whose choice most nearly corresponds to the average preferences of the competitors as a whole; ... '.[12] The idea is that investors want to keep close to what the rest of the market thinks. This 'herd behaviour' governs how expectations and valuations are formed. Objective calculations using hard data on fundamentals slip out of attention and herd behaviour takes over. Because everyone wants to follow everyone else, the valuation of the market is based on collective frenzy. When the stock value is going up everyone follows the next investor in pushing up the price further. When the sudden downturn takes place, as a few players start selling, everyone else follows, making sales difficult and only taking the price down to the bottom.

Major financial market meltdowns have resulted from speculative bubbles. The crash that started the Great Depression was preceded by a long bull run of the US stock market. After a run of unprecedented prosperity for years, the stock market got into a bubble possibly from around 1924. Starting in 1924 average stock prices increased

---

[12]*General Theory*, The Royal Economic Society edition, 1973, p. 156.

three-fold just before the crash in 1929.[13] The depression started when the bubble burst.[14]

The recession that started in 2007–08 was preceded by the US housing bubble which had peaked in 2006. Low interest rates had initially started the boom in house purchases. This led to an increase in house prices. Because banks hold the house as security for mortgage loans, increasing house prices allowed them to be lenient on the selection of loan applicants. This gave rise to a category of loans that would be later called 'sub-prime mortgages'. To have earned that name, obviously they had compromised the normal creditworthiness criteria for mortgage lending. Sub-prime mortgages originated from borrowers whose credit and income history would not have qualified them under ordinary circumstances. The reason for issuing sub-prime mortgages was that banks had the loan secured by property and the price of property was rising. Banks thought they would not lose if the borrower defaulted and might even gain by selling off the property in the rising market.

Sub-prime loans made mortgage loans easy to get. More mortgages led to higher house prices. Inevitably house prices increased beyond what average Americans could afford. Then the bubble burst. Property prices crashed. With the value of the underlying asset falling, banks became strict about instalment payment and repayment by borrowers and a sizeable number of mortgagees defaulted. People lost homes, got broke and that affected consumption goods market to begin with. At the same time banks too ran into a problem. They had a huge number of defaulters' houses to sell, and that sent house prices down further. They could not sell many properties and incurred significant cost in protecting them from illegal occupation and vandalisation. Just as banks were in serious trouble so were the construction and ancillary industries. Large builders lost money and the usual recessionary sequence of one industry affecting another started.

[13]Standard & Poor Composite index of stock prices. Based on the data provided by Robert Shiller on the Yale university website: *http://www.econ.yale.edu/~shiller/data.htm.*

[14]While this is the sequence of events, there are several views about the cause of the Depression. Not all of them agree that the crash was the basic cause.

The effect on the financial system was not confined to banks alone. Mortgage loan is an asset for a bank secured by the house for which the loan is made. Hence it is a good asset to own. But it does not earn income or 'perform' until the mortgage matures. In the 1970s banks found a way of making this sort of asset-based loans perform. They classified mortgages by maturity and other characteristics and packed them into lots. These lots or mortgage pools were offered for sale as an investment product. An investor who bought a lot was entitled to the earnings on the loans from that lot. Banks would price them so as to retain a margin for themselves. But their real advantage was the early recovery of the funds they lent for mortgages. Proceeds of selling the mortgage pools could be used again for mortgage lending and deposit creation. The process was named securitisation, that is, making securities or financial instruments out of something else.

When house prices crashed, it affected not just banks but all those who had bought the mortgage based securities sold by the banks. These assets had meanwhile developed secondary markets, that is, they were being resold. As a result they were held by a wide community of investors. Naturally that extended the reach of the crisis. Like the mortgages, sub-prime mortgages too were pooled into lots and securitised. When house prices started falling banks stopped allowing borrowers any re-scheduling of instalment payment. They feared that the houses held as security would lose more value if the loan period was extended by rescheduling. When rescheduling was not allowed, sub-prime loans defaulted simply because the borrowers were not sufficiently creditworthy. Later estimates suggested that about 20 per cent of US mortgages were sub-prime during that episode and they were held by a large community of investors. So the crisis in the house loan market became a system-wide financial crisis fairly quickly. During all this development, investors were not acting rationally that is, not basing investment on the fundamentals. They laid more faith on the herd, that is, what others were doing.

## 7.17 When Money is 'Debauched'

In classical thinking money was a mere facilitator of transactions—a means of payment, and nothing more. It was necessary of course, but the amount did not matter. More or less of it would increase or reduce prices as described by the quantity theory of money. But the price of one thing in terms of another, the relative price, was a technical property of production and that would not be affected by the quantity of money. Resource allocation is guided by relative prices; so it is not affected by the quantity of money. Hence output would not be affected either. We have seen that this neutrality of money towards things that really matter is true only in the long run. But in the short run, change of money supply alters the interest rate and affects aggregate demand and hence output and jobs. This possibility was not seen by classical theorists because they thought that production would always generate its own demand.

Generally, we take money for granted and fail to appreciate its role fully. We can have better appreciation by looking at situations where it becomes dysfunctional—a state that has been described in the opening quotation of this chapter as money getting debauched. One such instance is a state of hyperinflation. It is inflation of more than 1 per cent a day. That would cumulate to 50 per cent inflation in a month. Prices would rise more than 100 times in a year and more than 2 million times in three years! You may wonder if such a state is just a theoretical possibility. Unfortunately, such states are real; many countries have had the misfortune of being visited by hyperinflation.

After losing in the First World War, Germany was forced to pay an unmanageable amount of compensation to the victorious countries. The government had to use unsustainable deficit financing to generate the compensation to be paid at regular intervals. This started an inflation which eventually turned into a monstrous hyperinflation. Between 1922 and 1924 the price level increased $10^{12}$ times (that is, 12 zeroes after 1). Shops and business establishments had to announce new prices every 15 minutes. Wages were revised every day and more frequently afterwards. Relative prices lost any logic as different prices were revised at different times. Tax money collected by the government at the end of the fiscal year was next to nothing in real terms, and so it had to print more money. People spent a lot of time and effort to buy early and store the stuff. So did businesses and factories. Saving stopped as everyone wanted to spend money as soon as it was earned. To carry money to the stores for purchase became a weight-lifter's feat. The government tried to help by often printing higher denomination currency with more and more zeroes. Economic life virtually came to a standstill.

Greece and Hungary faced hyperinflation during the Second World War. China had a taste of it in 1948–49 and then it continued with varying severity in different parts of the country for a few more years. Several Latin American countries have been through it. In some cases people abandoned their national currency and took to using US dollars or barter or some form of commodity money. Most recently Zimbabwe went through a prolonged period of hyperinflation.

These instances alert us that while money is an invention of human genius like fire, we need to take care of it as much as we are careful with fire. John Adams[15] succinctly cautioned about this in 1787 in a letter to Thomas Jefferson, 'All the perplexities, confusions, and distress in America arise, not from defects in their constitution or confederation, not from want of honor or virtue, so much as from the downright ignorance of the nature of coin, credit, and circulation.'

---

[15]John Adams (1735–1826) was the US president for the period 1797–1801.

# 8 Trade, Foreign Investment and Migration

We have been occupied so far with the operation of national economies—a scenario where markets are contained within one country and a single currency works as means of payment. We should now turn to international transactions. There are three important types of transactions across national borders. They are trade in goods and services, cross-border investment in real and financial assets, and migration across countries. The first one refers to the movement of goods and services, and the last two refer to the cross-border movement of factors of production. Together they make up the subject matter of international economics.

Recall that it was the gold from South America and then the trade with Asian countries that unleashed the revolutionary industrialisation of Europe. Therefore, even in the earliest discussions of economics—in Hume, Smith, and Ricardo—the nature of international trade was an important question. Early economists wanted to settle the question of whether trade with other countries was good or whether it was to be avoided as the mercantilists advised.

## 8.1 Is International Trade a Good Thing?

Recall the mercantilists who held that a country grows wealthy by tucking in more gold. In their time cross-country trade used to be settled with gold and silver. If gold and silver were wealth, the surest way to wealth was to increase exports and minimise imports. An implication was that countries should restrict imports by stiff custom duties or simply ban them. Trade was thought to be a zero-sum game; a country could gain only at the expense of others.

But if all countries were bent on minimising import, then export could not get very far either. Therefore, international trade was severely restricted during those days. Interestingly, that was the time when European ships were getting bigger and more powerful. Mercantilist instincts would propose that they bring in as much gold as possible, but not goods, from other countries. European explorers discovered more gold and silver in South America than they could legitimately procure by exporting their goods. So Europe got shiploads of gold and silver from America procured not through trade but through violence and deceit.

However, as trade and enterprise grew in Europe the emerging traders, bankers, and industrialists found the mercantilist philosophy a hurdle. The reasoning against mercantilism gathered momentum. In David Hume's (1711–76) writings, arguments against mercantilism took a fully developed and coherent form. Writing in 1752, he reasoned that it is not gold but goods bought with gold that are the source of human satisfaction. Hence standard of life or satisfaction cannot be improved if gold is acquired but not used to increase production or import of goods. Second, he pointed out a serious flaw in the programme of gold accumulation. He first established that when there is more gold in circulation it increases the demand for goods and raises the general price level. This was possibly the earliest statement of the quantity theory of money and prices. Then he argued that when a country gets more gold through exports, that gold would, therefore, drive up the price of its goods. This would then reduce the country's exports. Over a long enough period, accumulation of gold would, therefore, reduce exports to a trickle or choke them off. Thus even if the accumulation of gold was a desirable objective, it could not be done through exports. To increase exports to amass gold defeats the goal of accumulating it in the long run!

The intellectual battle against the mercantilist anti-trade ideas continued in the classical economic theory. Like Hume, Adam Smith too argued that wealth and prosperity come from the production of goods and services. But production cannot increase much if it is to be sold strictly within the country. Exports are useful not because they get gold, but because they provide larger markets, which generate income and prosperity through increased production, employment, and investment. Hence international trade is essential for prosperity. That obviously meant that international trade is not a zero-sum game. It increases production and prosperity of all participants. Second, production for bigger markets allows producers to specialise. Specialisation reduces cost. This is a further advantage for the participating countries.

## 8.2 Trade and Comparative Advantage

Smith, however, did not discuss a very significant feature of trade which David Ricardo would moot a few decades later. Ricardo argued[1] that trade between two countries increases the output and

---

### Box 8.1: Ricardo Again

We encountered Ricardo in Chapter 2. Here I talk about him once again just to convey the amazement he creates among today's economists.

He amazes because it is not possible to get through the most elementary economics without learning some of his ideas. He also amazes because even at the highest level of economics education we have to encounter him. This is most impressive for contributions that are now nearly 200 years old. Further, Ricardo was not educated in European universities under famous mentors as used to be the case for noted scholars of that time. He was a self-made economist and his economics was entirely home-grown.

His brilliant insights aside, Ricardo amazes by his awesome ability to derive complex conclusions without using the mathematical gizmos that are now considered indispensable for economics. Use of mathematics for economics had not started in any significant way in his time. David Friedman put this amazement very aptly: 'The modern economist reading Ricardo's Principles feels rather as a member of one of the Mount Everest expeditions would feel if, arriving at the top of the mountain, he encountered a hiker clad in T-shirt and tennis shoes.'[2]

---

[1]Ricardo, David, *On the Principles of Political Economy and Taxation*, London: John Murray, 1817.

[2]Friedman, David D. , *Price Theory: An Intermediate Text*, 2nd edn, Cincinnati: South-Western Publishing, 1990, p. 618.

consumption of both as compared to the pre-trade situation. He produced a very compelling reasoning with a two-country example which has provided the foundation of modern trade theory. His little example is also the template for modern trade theory models. Think of two countries A and B. Both produce only two goods: food and cloth. Initially, there is no trade between them—we may call that the state of 'autarky'. Food and cloth are produced with labour alone. A produces one unit food with 1 day's labour and one unit cloth with 2 days' labour. B needs 3 and 4 days' labour to produce them, respectively. To produce more of one good, labour has to be withdrawn from the production of the other, that is, less of the other will be produced. So to produce a unit of food in A, they have to give up ½ a unit of cloth. In B, they have to give up more, ¾ units of cloth. Recall from Chapter 2 that the sacrifice of one good to produce another is called its opportunity cost. Using that jargon, the opportunity cost of food is half a cloth in A and ¾ of a cloth in B. Ricardo described this by saying that A has 'comparative advantage' in food production. So to have comparative advantage in something means to have lower opportunity cost for its production. Note that if A has comparative advantage in food production, it automatically means that B has comparative advantage in producing cloth.

If the two countries do not trade with each other, they will settle into their domestic equilibrium. In this autarky, the relative price of food and cloth in A or B will reflect the opportunity costs. So in A, a unit of food will sell for half a cloth. In B food will sell for ¾ of a cloth. Now suppose the two countries open their borders or ports for free trade. Producers in A will then find that they can sell food to country B at a profit. They can sell it at a higher price than at home but cheaper than the autarky price of B. Similarly, producers in B will find that they can sell their cloth to A at a profit. When the two countries start trading, the common relative price of food and cloth will settle down somewhere between ½ and ¾. That allows food producers of A and cloth producers of B to make profit by selling in each other's country. At any price between these limits, food producers of A would do better than at its autarky price of ½. Similarly, cloth producers of B will fare better than they did with the autarky price of ¾. We cannot work out the equilibrium price exactly without more information. But that is not necessary for the purpose at hand.

Given this, producers in A would like to use all their labour resource to produce only food because this gives them more profit. Similarly, producers in B will completely specialise in cloth. Each country would import from the other what it stops producing. Consumers in both countries would get food and cloth cheaper than before trade. Further, all the food produced in this 'two-country world' would be produced by A, the country that has an advantage in food. Similarly, all the cloth is produced by B with advantage in cloth. So, more of both food and cloth will be produced in the two countries together than before.

This was Ricardo's defence for international trade. He constructed an example similar to the one above to make his point. It is more accurate to say, I have used an example similar to his. Ricardo thus established that if trade is voluntary then it increases prosperity in both countries as well as the total output. It is not correct to say that one country has to gain at the cost of the other. This was theory-making at its best; using the barest essential of a complex phenomenon to see into all its essential properties. This is why Ricardo is still remembered as one of the great theorists of economics.

Ricardo's framework has been extended by trade theorists of the twentieth century bit by bit. They have asked what if: (i) production requires not just labour but several inputs as in a real situation, and (ii) if there is diminishing returns in production, that is, on average more input is needed when production increases. The conclusions remain valid in these cases as well. The analysis has also been extended to trade involving many goods and many countries. Ricardo's insight survives: voluntary trade should increase the output and consumption of all trading countries.

## 8.3 Free Trade and Protection: Early History

Ricardo's writing came in the context of an important issue in England of his time. The British Government had blockaded the continent of Europe during the Napoleonic war in order to create hardship in France. A further result of the blockade was that goods produced in England were protected against competition from imports. As a fall out, grain prices soared in England, farming became extremely lucrative, and the price of farm land increased giving large windfall to landowners.

When the war ended in 1815, England's landowners were threatened by cheap imports. They managed to get the British Parliament to pass an act imposing significant tariffs on the import of food grains. The right to vote was not universal at that time; it depended on land ownership. So there was no opposition to the act in the parliament. This law and the successive amendments to it were known as the Corn Laws. The 1815 act stated that no foreign corn would be allowed into Britain unless domestic corn reached a stated (and very high) price. Corn Laws imposed tariff not only on corn, but on other food grains too.

---

**Box 8.2: Comparative Advantage—Not Absolute**

What if country A can produce both food and cloth by using less resource than B? In this case one country, A, has absolute advantage in both goods. Would A then gain anything by trading with B? If the US can produce everything more cheaply than Mexico, is there any reason for it to import anything from Mexico? Paul Samuelson had put this question quite nicely in an edition of his introductory textbook. He wrote that he could type faster than his secretary and also did better research. Given this, should he take over the typing from his secretary even as he continued with his research?

Ricardo's answer would be, no. Though Samuelson might have absolute advantage in both typing and research, his secretary had a comparative advantage in typing. One country may produce both goods with less resource; but that is not important. We should look at the opportunity cost, not absolute cost. To produce a unit of food how much cloth do the two countries have to sacrifice? Whichever country gives up less cloth to produce a unit of food, should produce more food and sell it to the other country. And, the other country should produce more cloth. To type out a few pages in a day, Samuelson would have to sacrifice time for some valuable research, while the secretary would

---

*(contd...)*

*Box 8.2 continued.*

sacrifice hardly any. With 24 hours a day for both, Samuelson should produce research and his secretary, typing.

In a two good situation, it is obvious that if A has lower opportunity cost of food, then B will have lower opportunity cost of cloth. With many goods, many countries, and many inputs for production, the reasoning becomes difficult to keep track of without mathematics, but the basic insight about gains from trade can be established.

Because of the Corn Laws, British manufactured products found their markets closed in France and other parts of Europe. Also, high grain prices due to tariffs meant that workers had to spend most of their income on food grains, leaving little to spend on manufactured goods. So the demand for manufactures suffered further and industries had to lay off workers. Ricardo realised that the Corn Laws were benefitting landowners at the expense of industry and workers. He understood that this was hampering industrial development. He was of the opinion that the Corn Laws needed to be abolished. It was to reason against the Corn Laws that he developed the idea of comparative advantage and the gains from trade that I have outlined above. He was emphatic that unrestricted trade benefits both the exporting and the importing countries.

The economic theory of the twentieth century has endorsed Ricardo's position. It is definitional that in any voluntary exchange both sides would make some gain. If an exchange is not imposed by force but is voluntary in nature, it would simply not take place if both sides did not gain. That international trade produces gains for both countries is an illustration of this idea. Of course, the trade has to be voluntary. That excludes forced imports or exports that imperialist countries used to impose on their colonies.

The idea that trade should not be restricted and trade barriers should be eliminated comes from this understanding. The contrary viewpoint, that domestic producers should be protected from imports, has not however disappeared. This idea is called *protectionism*. Ideas of free trade and protectionism are both alive in today's world as they have always been. Official policies have veered to one or the other on different occasions and neither has been able to banish the other so far.

Protection was the favoured policy in mercantilist times. During those days, manufacturing industry was still primitive and landowners were the dominant economic group. For landowners, protection meant higher agricultural price, larger profits, and hence high level of rent and land prices. As manufacturing took hold, England made great strides in the production of coal, iron and steel, and textiles. Relentless technological push and investment gave it the ability to serve bigger markets by the early nineteenth century. Falling cost of shipping and inland transport made large volume of external trade, unimaginable in the past, now feasible and profitable. Industry realised that protection harmed it because other countries retaliated. British industrial exports to Europe and America were blocked because Britain did not import their agricultural goods. Protection was also limiting the growth of domestic market for industry. By keeping food prices high, domestic spending on manufactures was reduced. The debate around the Corn Laws in the parliament represented a fight between the landowning aristocracy and the growing brotherhood of industrialists. Finally, the industrialists won and the Corn Laws were repealed. Ricardo, however, did not see it happen. The Corn Laws were repealed in 1845—two decades after Ricardo's death. The repeal signalled the arrival of industry as the bigger political force. It would dominate the society and politics from this point onward.

---

**Box 8.3: The Corn Laws**

By the end of 1830s, the common people of England became keenly aware of the Corn Laws and started identifying them as the source of their misery. Socialists saw them as a tax on the poor because they kept food prices higher than otherwise. It was plain that the Corn Laws were making landowners richer and workers poorer. In 1830 a violent protest movement, named the Swing Riots, rocked the countryside in England. It was a general protest against the condition of farm labour which had particularly deteriorated since the Corn Laws were passed in 1815. It

---

*(contd...)*

*Box 8.3 continued.*

---

became violent and spread across England's agricultural counties. The riots, however, were not directly pointed against the Corn Laws but asked for a rise in wages, a cut in tithe[3] payments, and the destruction of the hated threshing machines.

Britain was ahead of the rest of Europe in industrialisation. But British industry found that other countries refused to buy their products because Britain did not buy their food. They naturally identified the Corn Laws as a hurdle to export and profit. Two factory owners from Manchester, Richard Cobden and John Bright, set up the Anti-Corn Law League in 1838. Soon it was joined by many other factory owners.

The League organised its campaign very well both inside and outside the parliament. It was perhaps the first funded political campaign with many modern traits. Campaign leaders ran a membership drive among factory owners and well-to-do people. Membership cost was £500. In 2008 this would have amounted to £38,000 using the retail price index, and as much as £416,000 if blown up in proportion to the average income. Clearly it was a movement of the 'nouveau riche' industrialists. But the campaign also tried to mobilise industrial and farm workers. It printed leaflets and distributed them widely. It also organised street-side lectures at important places. The repeal of the Corn Laws in 1845 was a signal that industry was finally developing political clout and the influence of the land-owning nobility was on the decline. Prime Minister Robert Peel who signed the repeal was himself the son of a factory owner.

---

With the repeal of the Corn Laws Britain entered into an era of freer trade. It reduced protection and persuaded other countries to do the same. The period of free trade, however, would not continue for very long. Germany and France were industrialising throughout the nineteenth century and the technological gap with Britain was closing down fast. By the 1870s Britain found these countries were strong competitors in its own domestic market. The view that free trade is good for both sides was given short shrift now, and up went tariff walls to protect British industry. Germany and France retaliated

---

[3] Tithe was the tax paid on virtually all production activities of rural life in England of that time. Initially, by Common Law, this was required to be paid to the parish. After the dissolution of monasteries, rectories etc. it was paid to the government.

and Europe went back to the protectionist mode once again. Further, European countries introduced protection in their colonies too making it difficult for a country to export to another's colonies. Though industry itself lobbied for protection, it no doubt felt the negative effects on sales. By the early twentieth century it was widely recognised that protection was hampering growth and prosperity. Lifting of protection, however, had to be done in all countries together. A country that opened up while others did not, would obviously be a sore loser. But international political relations at the time were far from conducive for any concerted action. The First World War started in 1914 before any action could be put in place. Protection inevitably increases during wars because it is used as a strategic measure. So protection deepened. Interestingly, this does not mean that warring countries automatically go back to free trade after the war. Domestic business enjoys the protection it gets during a war and hence opposes liberalisation when the war ends. Trade liberalisation after the war has to overcome this hurdle, which may or may not happen, depending on the politics within the country.

---

### Box 8.4: What was happening in America All This While?

Most of the white settlements of North America were British colonies until they declared independence in 1776. These colonies had stiff import tariffs. But that was not to protect local American industries. British law prevented the colonies from manufacturing the goods that were imported from Britain. Hence, there was not much local industry to protect. Tariffs were used to get money for the colonial governments. When Americans fought the Revolutionary War in 1775–83, they blockaded British imports and domestic manufacturing grew to replace them. This led to steady industrialisation in some parts of today's USA. These industries enjoyed complete protection through the blockade during the Revolutionary War. They demanded the continuation of protection even when the war was over. The United States passed its first comprehensive legislation on trade in 1789. It was driven by the theme of protection and concern for government revenue.

---

*(contd...)*

*Box 8.4 continued.*

New-born US, however, remained split over trade policy. Northern states were steadily industrialising but the South was primarily agricultural. The South exported cotton and tobacco to Europe and imported manufactured goods from them. They objected to import tariffs because it made their imports costly. But the North needed the tariffs to protect their industries. Not only that, they further wanted export taxes, because that would generate more government revenue. But export tax would seriously hamper the export of cotton and tobacco from the South. The South had prevented the northern states' attempt of levying export tax in the 1789 Trade Act. But they could not prevent tariff on imports.

Protection made life costly in the South and they wanted none of it. The problem was not resolved and tensions continued. This was an important reason behind the Civil War in the 1860s. The North used its tariff revenue to fund the war against the South. The South was defeated in the end. Tariffs were continued after the Civil War as a source of revenue as also for protection. When the Civil War ended, Britain and other European countries had already turned protective as I have mentioned earlier. Now USA joined this league as well.

After the end of the First World War, the political situation did not allow any liberalisation of trade. International tensions kept trade restrictions in place. However, industry was growing fast and in Europe and the US they were pressing their governments to ensure more liberal trade. But before this could be achieved came the Great Depression of 1929. During it, industrial countries raced with one another to protect their shrinking markets by restricting imports. The US set a bad example with the Smoot–Hawley Tariff Bill of 1930. The bill increased tariffs across the board and the average tariff rose to a historical high. Other countries retaliated. The war of tariffs only accentuated the Depression. World trade came down spiralling. It fell by two-thirds in the four years between 1929 and 1933!

Many within the US administration had, however, realised soon after the Smoot–Hawley bill that liberalisation, not protection, would help fight the Depression. In 1934, the US passed the Reciprocal Trade Agreement Act, which authorised the president to negotiate tariffs with other countries on a reciprocating basis. This act helped increase trade with other countries on a bilateral basis. But the gains were to last only for a short while as the Second World War started in 1939.

The US was the only industrialised country whose production system was unaffected by the Second World War. Its production capacity increased through those years as it supplied the major part of the allied countries' civilian and military demand. By the end of the war, the US was clearly the biggest and the most dynamic economy with a huge technological advantage over the rest. It was now in its interest to have a liberal international trade environment. The US was also interested in the quick recovery of Europe from the devastation of the war to limit the spread of Soviet influence. General intellectual opinion in the US too favoured trade liberalisation. In Europe, where Keynesian influence was growing, trade liberalisation was favoured as well.

## 8.4 End of the Second World War

All warring countries as well as the US faced a huge fall in demand as the war ended. Further, many European countries were devastated with their infrastructure and factories partly destroyed. The fall of demand and the disarray in supply made for a grim picture. Fear of another depression loomed large on the horizon.

There was a consensus now that governments would have to play a significant part in the recovery and reconstruction process. Keynesian ideas, which were well established by now, prescribed large government spending and other forms of autonomous demand. Export, an important part of demand had to be restored on an urgent basis. But countries had developed a protectionist state apparatus during the war. Though that had to be changed, they were reluctant to open up on individual basis. They wanted assured reciprocation. The need for an international mechanism to coordinate trade, currency flow, and cross-country investment was, therefore, seriously felt at this juncture.

There was another reason for international co-ordination. During the Great Depression countries tried to raise exports and reduce imports to minimise the effect of the depression. For that purpose high tariff walls alone were not sufficient. Tariffs can restrict imports but do not increase exports. To increase exports the countries had individually resorted to devaluation of their currencies. Cheaper currency makes a country's exports attractive. But in the paranoid environment of the depression, devaluation by one country was promptly matched by another and thus there was 'competitive' devaluation of currencies. It is easy to see that this course of action does not bring net gain to any country. Exports do not increase if all countries devalue their currency. Rather, fall of exports shrinks the income of all. That, in turn, reduces their demand for imports. And to compensate for this, they may devalue again. The only way to stop the race to the bottom was to bind countries to an agreement to keep currency values fixed. However, it could not be done without certain radical changes in the international payments system. I will clarify this by first explaining the international payments system used till then.

## 8.5 The Gold Standard

Until the First World War the monetary system followed in industrial countries was the so-called 'Gold Standard'. They used paper money, but it was convertible into gold at a fixed rate. The value of money was, therefore, fixed in terms of gold. Banks were obliged to pay the amount of gold if it was demanded by anyone holding a currency note. Accordingly, money-issuing banks[4] were required to keep gold reserves in proportion with the amount of currency issued by them. The Gold Standard ensured a fixed value of money inside the country which also meant fairly stable prices for goods. The system also had a feature extremely valuable for international trade and payments.

Think of trade between countries A and B that are both on the gold standard. Their banks buy and sell their currencies for gold at fixed rates. So the mutual exchange rate[5] between their currencies is also fixed. There is an open market for currencies where vendors

[4]Countries did not yet have central banks in today's sense; however, certain banks issued currency notes.

[5]Exchange rate is the price of one country's currency in terms of the other country's currency.

buy and sell the two country's currencies at this rate plus a handling commission. Now, for trade between the countries, importers of A need the currency of B and *vice versa*. Suppose that this year A exports less to B than it imports from B. In economic jargon, A has a trade deficit or negative trade balance with B. Importers of A need more of B's currency than they can get through exports. As they buy the balance amount from the currency market, the price of the currency will rise. But recall that the banks of B are committed to sell the currency at a previously fixed rate. The increase in its price in the currency market means that it will now be higher than the price fixed by the banks.

When this happens, currency traders will take advantage of the situation. They will buy the currency from the banks of B and sell it in the foreign exchange market to make some profit. As the banks sell currency to these traders they will get some gold in exchange. So B will now have more gold than earlier. Money supply will increase in B because of this extra gold.[6] Remembering the quantity theory, it will raise the price of goods in B. So B's exports cannot remain as attractive as earlier. At the same time, A's imports would now look somewhat cheaper to B's buyers. So B's exports will fall and imports will increase. This will reduce the trade deficit of A. This process would continue as long as the trade deficit is not eliminated. In the end, trade between A and B will be balanced with neither having deficit or surplus.

This was quite a remarkable mechanism. It used to correct unfavourable trade balances automatically. However, the gold standard became difficult to operate because the amount of gold a country had or could get was limited. As an economy grows it requires more money to work. But increase in money supply would require a proportional increase in gold reserve. Thus, the gold standard was not tenable beyond a point in the growing world economy.

The difficulty had surfaced occasionally during the long era of gold standard. Governments needed to provide for large expenditures

---

[6]Money-issuing banks were private, for-profit businesses. If they got extra gold they would issue more money rather than keep it idle.

during wars. Tax revenue could not be easily increased and governments looked for big loans. When loans were not adequate, they would sometimes suspend the convertibility of money into gold and increase money supply for government use. This happened on a number of occasions. The US, for example, had suspended convertibility during the Civil War and England during the war against Napoleon. Convertibility was restored in both cases after the wars. But the episodes showed the constraints of the gold standard, that it could not be used in a world with increasing expenditure.

After the First World War and again during the Great Depression the system of inter-country trade and currency exchange had become seriously disorderly. First, some countries had left the gold standard during the war and tried to restore it after the war ended. They found the task difficult in the post-war environment. Second, some countries facing trade deficit devalued their currency. We have just seen that trade deficit is expected to be wiped out in equilibrium under the gold standard. But that requires all trade partners to work with the gold standard, which was not the case in the post-war scenario. The disorderly state continued and was carried into the Second World War. During the latter war allied countries used to settle trading accounts bilaterally and with *ad hoc* means. Quite naturally, the system required attention when the war ended.

## 8.6 Bretton Woods

Thus, an orderly international currency system was the cry of the day as the war came to an end. As I have mentioned earlier, a serious boost to trade was required for post-war recovery and reconstruction. Co-ordination among countries was needed to dismantle the war-time trade barriers. At the same time, an organisation was required to handle temporary trade imbalances of deficit countries. It was clear that the gold standard could not be revived and so imbalances would not be corrected automatically. Unless there was a way of funding temporary trade deficits, deficit countries would use trade barriers and devalue their currencies. So an international bank was required that could give short-term loans to a deficit country in a currency acceptable to other countries to tide over the deficit.

With these two goals delegates from all the forty-four allied countries met at Bretton Woods in New Hampshire in the United States for the United Nations Monetary and Financial Conference. At the time the war had not ended yet but an allied victory was in sight. The participants signed a number of agreements together known as the Bretton Woods Agreement. It established a set of rules for trade and financial interaction among member countries. It was the first example of a voluntary international system to govern economic relations among sovereign countries. Apart from setting the rules, the conference established three important institutions: the International Monetary Fund (IMF), the International Bank for Reconstruction and Development (IBRD), and the General Agreement on Tariffs and Trade (GATT). The IMF and IBRD were created in 1945 and GATT in 1947. The IBRD now belongs to the World Bank Group and GATT was absorbed into a new organisation called the World Trade Organisation (WTO) in 1994. These institutions and the overarching agreement are together known as the Bretton Woods system. They have been at the centre of economic news; they have been hailed as often as criticised. We will take a brief look at what they were expected to achieve.

## 8.7 The IMF

The IMF was conceived to help the settlement of claim among countries arising from trade deficits. It established a clearing system for these transactions. The idea was that the IMF member countries would have a fixed exchange rate system of a special kind. The value of their currencies would be fixed not in gold but in US dollars. At the same time, the US dollar itself would be convertible into gold at a fixed rate. Member countries would maintain deposits at the IMF. When a country had a trade deficit, it would use the deposits to pay for it. If the deposits were not sufficient, then IMF would provide it with a loan to be repaid with interest. The loan would be in the form of a deposit in the country's account at the IMF. The country would transfer its deposits to other countries' accounts to settle deficits. For these activities, an initial fund was created (hence the name Fund). Member countries initially contributed to building the fund as shareholders. The fund then started functioning as a bank. Its size would grow from banking profit as well as later contributions from member countries. The US was to peg the value of its dollar to gold. It was decided to fix the official price of gold at US $35 per ounce. The dollar was officially convertible into gold on demand at this rate. All other countries were required to peg their currencies to the US dollar as mentioned. One per cent variation of exchange rate on both sides of the peg was allowed for their currencies. They had an obligation to maintain the exchange rate within this band. That could be done by selling and buying overseas currencies when required. But they were not required to provide gold in exchange for their currencies. A member could revise the exchange rate of its currency against the dollar with the consent of the IMF. Since the dollar had a fixed gold value and other currencies had fixed dollar values, the world got a fixed exchange rate system. The US dollar became the 'reserve currency' for all members as it was convertible into gold. This meant that they would accept US dollars as payment for all external transactions and their central banks would hold US dollars as an asset like they earlier used to keep gold.

The fixed exchange rate and the IMF formed the architecture of the post-war international finance outside the Soviet bloc. The IMF was seen as a fund to help members bridge temporary external deficits. The system was expected to handle balance of payment problems without being constrained by the fixed supply of gold as in the gold standard. On the other hand, members would not slip into competitive devaluation as their exchange rates were pegged to the dollar.

This system served for some time in clearing international loans and deficits. But fixed exchange rates have some inherent problems which built up stress within the system. After working for about a quarter century the system came to an end in 1971. For some time, the US was finding it difficult to maintain dollar–gold convertibility as it had to sacrifice other economic policy goals for its sake. In 1971 it unilaterally ended the convertibility.

It will be useful to check out the weak points of the system that led to its breakdown. Fixed exchange rate means that the central bank is obliged to buy and sell its currency at the specified rate. When there is a trade surplus, the country's currency is in high demand and its price starts rising. The central bank then has to sell its currency to bring down the price to the stipulated rate. Note that this will automatically increase the country's money supply. In the opposite case, when a country has a trade deficit, its currency price starts to fall. The central bank then has to buy its currency from the market to keep its price steady. This reduces the country's money supply. What is inconvenient in all this is that the country's money supply has to follow the state of its external trade. The country loses its freedom to operate a monetary policy, that is, vary money supply to influence aggregate demand. Thus, a fixed exchange rate costs a country one of its most important economic policy instruments. Internal economic policy in the member countries was handicapped by this difficulty.

Another problem arose for those countries that repeatedly got into trade deficit. The IMF provided loans for deficit countries to tide over the deficit. This is useful if a country gets into deficit occasionally, or if deficits and surpluses occur randomly. In that case the country would borrow in a deficit year and pay off in surplus years. But if a country has a trade deficit year after year then loans pile up. After a few years the country will exhaust its quota of loans. If it then turns to commercial borrowing, its loans will be rated poorly and it would pay relatively high interest. Obviously, these loans too and also the interest will keep accumulating and the country will soon be unable to borrow anything from anywhere.

This scenario occurred quite often in fact. At the time of the Bretton Woods conference in the 1940s, the focus was on industrialised countries whose trade deficits and surpluses were expected to be random. But after the war, many of Europe's colonies became independent. Most of these newly liberated countries—the developing economies—became members of the IMF. These countries inherited an economic structure that would lead to trade deficits almost every year.

They required large amount of industrial imports because they had not adequately industrialised during their colonial past. They could pay for imports by exporting only agricultural and primary products. Income elasticity of demand for these goods is small. This means that if the world's income grows by one per cent, the demand for these goods increases by a rather small fraction of one per cent. On the other hand, the income elasticity of imports of developing economies is large. Typically, imports would include machines and tools, steel products, cars and commercial vehicles, railway equipment, chemicals, and so on. These are mostly needed as inputs for production. When income increases, the requirement of these imports increases almost in proportion. Consumption imports are to be added on top of this. The overall result is that when a developing economy grows, its imports increase much faster than the demand for its exports. This leads to a trade deficit. Once it gets into a deficit, it recurs every year and becomes larger as income grows. This sort of deficit is not a random event. It follows from the structure of developing economies and is called a structural deficit.

The arrangement of fixed exchange rates and IMF loans did not have an answer to the problem of structural deficit. Countries with structural deficit needed loans every year. But they lacked any means of repaying them. Devaluation of their currency could increase exports to some extent and reduce inessential imports. But as members of the IMF they could not alter exchange rates without protracted consultations.

## 8.8 How the Bretton Woods Arrangement broke down

Though the above problem is serious, it did not bring down the Bretton Woods system by itself. The breakdown came with the US leaving it. There was what we may call a design fault in the system from the beginning. It required the US to peg the dollar to gold at $35 per ounce. But there was also an open international gold market. The price of $35 per ounce was approximately the price of gold in the open market at the time of the Bretton Woods agreement. But the open market price was bound to increase over time because the amount of gold in the world was almost fixed. Whenever the open market price was higher than $35, countries with US dollars could buy gold from the US and sell it in the open market for profit. So there was a serious temptation for central banks or governments to do this and use the profit for the country's internal use. This had the potential of draining out the gold reserve of the US.

The problem would not have arisen if the agreement had a provision for changing the price of gold in terms of dollar from time to time. But that was not the case. Trying to do this at a later time would change the system significantly. It would need many related changes—of rules, laws, and procedures—both at the international and national level. Further, it would require an agreement about when and by how much the price revision could be effected. Overall, the exchange system would become rule-bound and bureaucratic. Fortunately, it was not required to take these steps. Central banks of a number of countries collectively decided to intervene in the gold market whenever necessary and formed a consortium for this purpose. They decided to sell gold when its price increased above $35 to bring it back to par, and then buy gold back from the market at a suitable time to replenish the stock.

Even though this solved the difficulty initially, it remained a source of potential problems. Because of the dollar-to-gold convertibility at a fixed price, the dollar became as good as gold. Central banks would be happy to hold dollars as reserve rather than gold. Prior to Bretton Woods, central banks used to acquire gold because it was the only globally accepted means of payment. But after the Bretton Woods agreement, the dollar became more convenient than gold. It was accepted for payments everywhere (outside the Soviet bloc). Second, central banks could lend their dollars and earn interest. To transfer dollars around the world was less costly than gold. For one reason or another—for example, the Korean War and the Vietnam War—the US had a trade deficit more or less continuously since the 1950s. This meant that there was net payment of US dollars to other countries. This kept the world supplied with enough dollars for international transactions. Countries that had trade surplus built up a large reserve of dollars.

Given this, it seemed for some time that the system was working very well. US trade deficit supplied other countries with an adequate flow of US dollars to facilitate international trade and growth. Just as it was smooth for other countries, it also looked as if it was fun for the US as well. The US could buy from the rest of the world more than what it could sell. And pay for the difference with its own currency which it could print. The US could, therefore, buy from others without any constraints and the world would actually welcome it! In fact if the US failed to run deficits, the world would be short of world money and would have no liquidity to buy and sell one another's products. International trade and the world's economic growth would falter.

However, this scenario could not, and did not, last. The pile of dollars held by other countries increased rapidly. And at that point it was realised that they were not really very good as an asset. Dollars did not produce any capital gains because the value was fixed in gold. So the only way of earning something from dollars was to lend them out. But as the years went by, many countries accumulated a large stock of dollars. So the interest rate on dollar loans was falling. Therefore, barely a couple of decades after Bretton Woods, the world started complaining. Large industrialised countries such as Japan, Germany, France, and the UK were particularly worried. The US imported mostly from these countries. If the Bretton Woods system continued, their central banks would acquire more dollars indefinitely. But the stock would become less and less of an asset. They also worried that the overhang of dollars would undermine the confidence in it as a reserve currency sooner or later. And if the US was to ever back out of the system, then the dollar price would drop and their assets would crumble overnight.

After the recovery of Japan and the European countries, other countries started keeping a part of their assets in European currencies or the Yen rather than dollar. In academic journals and the financial press concern grew that the international exchange system was in a sort of impasse. But there was a major dilemma. Big-country central banks which themselves worried about the problem, would not quite like the idea of abandoning the system. They were afraid that their portfolio of dollars would collapse.

For the US on the other hand, continuing with the system meant a commitment to work up trade deficits forever which was an absurd proposition. If the exchange rate was flexible, then it would have fallen because of the trade deficit. That would reduce, if not eliminate, the deficit. The fixed exchange rate was preventing that. In effect it meant that the prices at which Americans, both consumers and producers, bought and sold goods were completely out of line with their resource costs. You may recall that when prices are out of line in this way, economic efficiency is affected and resources are wasted. Further, the fixed exchange rate was constraining US monetary policy. So finally came the inevitable end of the Bretton Woods arrangement in 1971. The US withdrew its commitment to keep the price of dollars fixed in gold.

The US adopted a flexible exchange rate after this, which meant that the exchange rate would be determined in the currency market by demand and supply. The government, of course, reserved its right to change the exchange rate from time to time if needed. After the US, many other countries moved over to flexible exchange system. Some countries adopted a hybrid arrangement. They pegged their currency to the US dollar keeping the option of changing the pegging rate if necessary. Pegging to the US dollar means to have a fixed exchange rate with the dollar, while the exchange rate against other currencies might change depending on the state of the market. The end of the fixed exchange rates system, however, did not mean an end of the Bretton Woods organisations—the IMF, the World Bank, and the WTO. They adapted to the new world situation.

## 8.9 GATT and WTO

General Agreement on Tariffs and Trade (GATT) was planned to promote international trade by reducing protection and trade barriers. The nations at the Bretton Woods Conference felt that free trade was necessary to increase global production and welfare. But if one country restricted imports, others' strategy was to restrict their imports as well. For unrestricted trade across the world, it was necessary that all parties were assured that others would play fair. The conference wanted to secure this commitment from members and then work out the modalities through a permanent institution. GATT was the institution it created. It served the purpose for quite some time. But its terms of reference and organisation were failing to cope with the increase in trade and trade-related issues that arose in the 1970s and 1980s. Between 1948 and 1990, the volume of world merchandise trade increased more than eleven times.[7] Trade in services and cross-country investments also increased in proportion. With this were associated new kinds of difficulties and disputes not thought of in the 1940s.

The nature of international trade has changed since the end of the Second World War. First of all, new countries were born after the inception of GATT. Europe's colonies became sovereign countries in the 1950s and 1960s. A second group of new states were formed after the fall of the Soviet bloc. All these new countries have joined the world market. Second, the trade between industrialised and developing countries involves new and contentious issues. Third, the product structure of trade has changed immensely. There is now a large volume of trade in services and goods involving intellectual property which raises complicated disputes. Cross-country investment has also grown enormously. This needs suitable laws and institutions. All in all, an overhaul of GATT's terms of reference became necessary by the end of the 1980s. After the member countries agreed, the World Trade Organisation (WTO) was formed in 1994 replacing GATT.

The WTO, like GATT before it, tries to establish rules and codes of conduct for member countries. It has 157[8] member countries representing more than 95 per cent of world trade. It provides a framework for negotiation of trade agreements and a process of dispute resolution. The framework and principles are produced by discussion among members. When members agree on a principle, WTO/GATT produces procedures based on them. Member countries then take a second look, and if they accept them, they are placed in their parliaments for ratification. The procedures then become laws at the national level in the member countries thus producing a uniform cross-national procedure for the relevant trading activity.

Most issues that the WTO works on have originated from earlier negotiations, particularly from the Uruguay Round (1986–94) started when GATT was in existence. The WTO is currently focusing on a set of issues called the Doha Development Agenda (or Doha Round). It

[7]Measured in terms of 1990 US dollar, global merchandise trade was 304 billion in 1948 and 3338 billion in 1990 (WTO data).

[8]Subject to ratification of three newest members, as I write this chapter.

began in 2001 to address a number of standing issues. An important agenda is to enable smoother participation of developing countries in world trade. It also wants to address the complaint that GATT rules have created unfair benefit for the rich countries. The negotiation has not been smooth. It has broken off a number of times to resume after background diplomatic work. The most difficult problem facing this Round is in the trade of agricultural commodities. The largest exporters of agricultural commodities are the US, European Union, and Australia. These commodities are also produced by developing countries. During the Uruguay Round, GATT wanted to persuade developing countries to reduce and eventually eliminate tariff protection of these commodities. The developing economies pointed out that there were large farming subsidies in the US and Europe, which make their agricultural products artificially cheaper. They have reasoned that farm subsidy is a veiled form of protection. They demand that subsidies should be abolished as a pre-condition for eliminating tariff on these products by developing countries. On the other hand, the subsidies are important in the domestic politics of US and Europe. The issue has been, therefore, dragging on for a long time without any resolution.

## 8.10 The many Faces of Protection

As an institution WTO believes that freer trading would benefit all participants and hence the world as a whole. Therefore, one of its main tasks is to persuade members to reduce and eliminate import protection. It is interesting to take a look at the many forms that import protection takes.

The most obvious, of course, is import duty or tariff. In many markets, importers sell foreign products in competition with domestic producers. The latter are forced to sell at the price at which importers sell. If an import item has to pay Rs 100 per unit as duty, then it becomes Rs 100 costlier for the importer. This gives an advantage to domestic producers. The government can fix the duty so as to increase the domestic price of an imported item to any level it thinks appropriate. This is how an import duty protects domestic producers. Obviously, the extent of protection can be increased by increasing the tariff rate. If the rate is set very high, import of the good stops altogether and domestic producers get full protection.

When there is an import duty, consumers are the losers as they are forced to buy at higher price and reduce consumption. On the other hand, domestic producers gain because they get a higher price and sell more than they would have without protection. The loss of consumers, however, is always more than the gain for domestic producers and hence there is a net loss to the country. The country could have done better if the good was imported freely at the world price and domestic producers sold whatever they could at that price. They would, of course, produce less than they would with a tariff. This reduced production would save resources which would be used to produce what the country can produce cheaper than in the world market. By producing and exporting things in which it is globally competitive and importing things which are cheaper elsewhere, the country clearly gains. This is the argument put forth by those in favour of trade liberalisation. Trade liberalisation is a general term for the policy of reducing tariff and non-tariff barriers to trade.

Advocates of protection, however, point out that the first effect of any liberalisation is that workers lose jobs to imports, and machines and material become under-used. Eventually they may be employed again when businesses start producing things in which they are globally competitive. But it is of little comfort because the adjustment takes time. During the period—which may extend into several years—workers who lose jobs have to put up with hardship. Many of them, whose skills do not match those required for the new sectors, may never be employed again. Some others may get discouraged by the continued failure to get a job and may drop out of the workforce. Pro-trade theorists do not disagree with these observations. Rather than using protection they suggest the following course: (i) providing income support to workers who suffer because of imports; (ii) providing help in quickly channelling the unemployed resources to sectors that are globally competitive; and (iii) retraining of workers by the government so that they can acquire skills for new sectors. It should be clear that the success of these measures depends on the country's governance culture. Where governments are poorly run, these measures are likely to get stuck. Import duty obviously appears to these governments as a handy tool to avoid the rigours altogether.

Another common form of protection is an import quota. The government fixes the maximum permissible annual import of an item called the quota. When a quota is in place, total supply of the good within the country consists of the quota (which will be imported) and the amount locally produced. A smaller quota would mean smaller total supply and hence higher domestic price. The amount of the quota can be fixed in such a way as to produce a desired price of the product inside the country. Thus a quota can produce the same effect as a tariff and governments can use it as an alternative. Like in the case of tariffs, consumers lose and domestic producers gain. There is, however, one important difference. The government gets some customs revenue in case of tariff protection, while there is no such revenue in case of a quota.

Note, however, that though the government gets no money for a quota, it is potentially there for any enterprising party to pick up. Because the domestic price will be higher than the world price, all importer firms will want to import the good. The difference between the domestic price and the world price is the profit per unit of import. So importer firms will compete to get import permits for as large a part of the quota as possible. They would not mind spending an amount less than the potential profit to get the permits. In a corrupt administration, administrators can manoeuvre to get this as their cut. Where this does not occur, the entire amount will be the importers' profit. In the case of tariff, the government gets precisely this amount as revenue. Since a tariff and a quota can produce otherwise equivalent economic effects, it is better to use the tariff as it gets the government some money rather than corrupting the system or swelling importers' profits.

Export subsidy is another widely used form of protection. It makes the country's exports artificially cheaper. The most obvious form is to give exporters some money per unit of export. Often exporting firms have to import intermediate goods and machinery to be able to produce at the world quality level. If the imported material carries any import duty, an exporting firm may be reimbursed the duty paid at the time of import. Hence this is also a form of export subsidy.

Sometimes subsidy is paid on the production of an exportable item, no matter whether it is actually exported or sold at home. US and European farm subsidies are of this kind. There farmers get tax waivers and cheaper inputs etc. based on their entire annual production rather than the amount of export. As mentioned before, developing countries hold that as long as these subsidies stay, they would be justified in setting tariffs on agricultural imports from the US and Europe. However, export subsidies rarely take the form of direct and transparent payment of money. These subsidies were disallowed for industrial products in the GATT guidelines even before the Uruguay Round. To avoid detection, subsidies are disguised and difficult to establish. Cheap loans, differential tax treatment, subsidised inputs, allocation of land etc. are common forms of providing subsidies. The WTO negotiations spend a significant effort in defining what constitutes an export subsidy.

A simple and ancient form of protection is to ban an import item. Under the WTO system, a member country cannot normally ban an item which is not an international contraband. But like all rules, there are exceptions. The most important exception is for sanitary and phyto-sanitary (SPS) reasons. A country is allowed to ban items harmful to the health of its nationals, to its flora and fauna, or its ecology. For example, the import of specific fruits and farm products can be banned alleging that they contain alien insects or their larva which might proliferate in the host country's ecosystem. The WTO requires that SPS restrictions be based on scientific evidence verifiable by the international scientific community. A country can also ban products for cultural and religious reasons. Developing countries have often complained of abuse of SPS restrictions by rich countries against their agricultural and horticultural products.

Another important form of protection comes through government purchases. National governments have their own purchase policy which need not be in consonance with any international law. Domestic businesses lobby with their governments for purchase policies in their favour. A government can pass an act prohibiting the purchase of certain items from international vendors if they are available domestically. In defence related purchases governments have strategic reasons to buy only from a group of countries or vendors and this obviously discriminates against other international sellers. There are also subtler ways. A government may publish its purchase intent only in local newspapers and media or in its national language and so on. In case of services, a government can specify certain language and cultural requirements for the service and effectively push out some firms.

As should be evident by now, there are many ways in which imports are restricted and exports helped and some of them are difficult to detect and prove. These tendencies are helped by many factors: nationalism, dislike of neighbours and alien countries, misunderstanding about the effects of trade, and also because it is not ensured that all countries practise fair trade.

I will end this section with a discussion of 'dumping'—an unfair trade practice about which heaps of complaints appear from time to time. Economists use the word 'dumping' to describe the sale of a product below cost in overseas markets presumably to capture market share. Dumping can be sporadic or persistent. Sporadic dumping takes the form of a large overseas producer selling its goods cheaper for a brief period. It does not damage the market in a permanent way. It is also difficult to fault it as an unfair trade as it is similar to a discount sale. On the other hand, persistent dumping is, as the term suggests, the sale below cost by an overseas firm for longer periods. Complaints of persistent dumping are heard quite often, though they are generally difficult to prove. It is also difficult to see how an overseas firm would at all gain by persistent dumping. In the 1970s and 1980s Japanese companies were often accused of dumping. There are similar complaints about Chinese companies in the twenty first century. But it is difficult to think of a convincing commercial reason why a firm would persistently sell below cost. Firms selling in several countries are expected to sell at different prices in different countries. This happens because markets for the same product in different countries have different price elasticities of demand. A commercial formula for profit maximisation in this situation is to fix the price higher in the market with relatively inelastic demand (see Chapter 3). It is very likely that the world market for a Chinese product is more price elastic than the Chinese domestic market. In that case a Chinese producer will sell it at a lower price overseas than in China. But this does not constitute dumping unless the overseas price happens to be below the cost of production. Generally it is not possible to get data on the cost of production of a foreign firm, and complaints of dumping are always impressionistic. It is quite possible that the complaints are used to lobby for protection or get a subsidy from the government. If persistent dumping occurs at all, would it be considered a form of unfair trade? It is not clear because as I have said the commercial motive for such behaviour is not obvious.

## 8.11 Why do Countries go for Protection?

Trade between two countries is expected to improve things for both of them in terms of income, production, and consumption. But there is always a redistributive effect of trade, that is, income increases more for some and less for others. There may be also fall of income for some groups. Therefore, even though overall gain from trade is positive, typically there would be losers and gainers in each country. Trade improves welfare in the aggregate, which means that the gainers' gain exceeds the losers' loss. As an example, think of countries A and B that have been producing both steel and clothing. If B has comparative advantage in clothing, trade theory would prescribe that A should import it from B and pay for it by export of steel. It would increase overall income in both countries. But when this happens, clothing workers lose jobs in A and steel workers in B. The owners of clothing factories in A and steel factories in B would also lose some profit income. Because A would now produce more steel than earlier, it is expected that workers and other factors of production that lose employment in clothing will find it back in the expanded steel sector.

---

### Box 8.5: Effective Rate of Protection

When a tariff is imposed, protection is not only obvious but also quantifiable. The rate of protection enjoyed by an industry is calculated using a concept called the 'effective rate of protection'. It depends on the rate of tariff on the import of the product and the import of any

---

*(contd...)*

*Box 8.5 continued.*

inputs used by the industry. A higher tariff on the product increases the effective rate of protection, while higher tariff on inputs reduces it. Import duty on an input makes it costlier and thus reduces the competitive position of the producers using it. Hence it reduces the effective rate of protection.

Many developing countries adopted an 'import substitution strategy' for development after their independence. The strategy was to reduce imports from rich countries by producing them at home. For this they used stiff import duty believing that it would provide protection for domestic producers from overseas competition. It was not understood that all import duties are not actually protective. There was tariff protection on the product of domestic industry and also tariff on their inputs. As a result domestic industries were not getting much protection, even though the countries had set up elaborate and costly customs establishments. Note that if tariff on inputs is larger than that on the product, and the industry uses the input in substantial amount, then the effective rate of protection can be even negative. This is not just a theoretical possibility. The three biggest developing countries with pervasive tariff protection were, in fact, doing a dis-service to their industries in the 1980s. Many of their producers were actually getting a negative effective protection from their governments. See the figures for 1986 in Table 8.1.

Table 8.1: Effective Rates of Protection (in per cent)[9]

|  | Brazil | | China | | India | |
|---|---|---|---|---|---|---|
|  | 1986 | 1997 | 1986 | 1997 | 1986 | 1997 |
| Agriculture | −43 | −5 | −28 | −15 | −14 | −5 |
| Labour-intensive manufacturing | −72 | −17 | −54 | −35 | −45 | −23 |
| Capital-intensive manufacturing | −79 | −22 | −46 | −28 | −60 | −35 |
| Services | −31 | −3 | −26 | −14 | −16 | −6 |

[9]*Source*: World Bank, *Global Economic Prospects 2004*, Washington, DC, 2004, p. 77.

As these countries were persuaded to reduce their tariffs and simplify them, the effective rate of protection actually increased as shown by the 1997 figures.

It takes time for displaced workers and resources to find their feet in a new sector. Allowing time for all this, we may like to say that in the long run everyone will be better off. But that is not helpful unless there is a support arrangement that looks after the losers in the meantime. In particular, if the country has significant unemployment, imports will aggravate it. The promise of export sector jobs is too distant in time. Second, workers skilled in one industry may not find jobs in another unless they learn new skills. Similarly, machines and land used for one industry may not easily find application in others. These complications mean further wait and loss for the losers. Generally most of the demand for protection arises from groups that would lose in the short run.

Developing economies have often opted for protection of what are known as infant or baby industries. Baby industry protection arises for industries with pronounced economy of scale. A developing economy may have the resources and skills for a certain industry, but initially it cannot produce at the competitive world prices. To compete with established overseas producers, it is necessary to produce a fairly large amount of the good to get the scale economy. Further, some industries have a kind of economy called 'learning by doing'. Production skills and productivity increase in these industries as they go through real time experience. In all these cases, a country may want to protect a baby industry that is expected to become competitive in the future.

Presented this way the baby industry argument appears to be quite convincing. But many economists are sceptical. They point out that it is improbable that a country would be able to spot an industry *ex ante* in which it will be able to develop comparative advantage later on. There is no doubt that there are many industries with economy of scale and learning by doing. That only means that if production is carried on large scale and for long, the average cost of the industry will fall. But that does not mean that it will become competitive in the global market. These industries in other countries also enjoy the scale and learning economies. Becoming competitive, therefore, depends on other factors. They point to large industries with economy of scale set up in the past in India, Mexico, Brazil, and China with import protection. They have been in operation for decades, but have remained globally uncompetitive in terms of cost and quality. Protection allows them to remain alive even though they use more resources than similar industries overseas. If there were no protection, consumers would have benefited from lower global prices and the resources locked up in these protected industries would be released for other uses.

---

### Box 8.6: Brazil's Infant Computer Industry

To protect its nascent computer industry, Brazil passed a law in 1984 banning the import and use of foreign computers. Brazil was serious about developing a world class computer industry and the law was enforced zealously. The government set up 'computer police' who would search business premises, offices, and universities to hunt out foreign computers and mete out appropriate punishment to offenders.

After a few years the result was this: Brazil-made computers were technologically several years behind those on the world market and Brazil's buyers had to pay more than two and a half times for these computers. Because their products were costly and out-of-date, Brazilian companies could not sell them in the world market and so could not avail much economy of scale. Because they were unable to utilise economy of scale, it was clear that the baby industry would never be able to reduce its average cost significantly. High computer prices and their outdated functionality affected other domestic industries that were forced to use them and so they also lost global competitiveness.

Brazil dropped the law in 1992 under pressure from its business and consumers and with the insistence of US negotiators for open market. Brazilians now got access to world class computers, laptops, and printers at world prices. This restored the competitiveness of computer-using industries. Many of these were the industries that used to export to the world market before the computer debacle, that is, those in which Brazil has comparative advantage.

---

Trade barriers are often defended by a country on the ground that other countries use similar restrictions. Governments are not sure that others would reciprocate if they offer to trade without restrictions. If a country removes tariffs, its trade partners need not reciprocate. They would be better off in the short run by exporting more to this country and at the same time keeping their own trade protected. But if that is expected of trade partners, then the first country's government would not remove restrictions unilaterally. This, though, is not the best move from a long-run perspective. Even when a partner country has protection, a country may be better off by eliminating its own tariff and letting in goods at lower international prices. But generally countries think in terms of reciprocation and retaliation.

So it should be clear that global trade is beset with the problem of international co-ordination. International trade, as it were, can settle down into one of the two possible states: a 'good equilibrium' or 'a bad equilibrium'. In the bad equilibrium all countries protect their economies with tariffs. If this prevails, given what other countries are doing, each country's best move is what it is doing, namely, protection. Hence it is a stable arrangement and once world trade gets into this groove no country has the incentive to break it. In the 'good equilibrium' all countries practise free trade. In this case also each country finds that given the other country's move, their best move is what they are doing, namely unrestricted trade.

Though the so-called good state is better for all countries, if a single country practises free trade, it will be a loser. This is why the world system cannot transform itself from the 'bad equilibrium' to the 'good equilibrium'. It requires an agency to bind all countries to the commitment of free trading. If all countries commit and believe that the commitments will be respected, less restricted trading can be established. The GATT and now WTO have the task of working out suitable commitments from member countries to keep trade free of restrictions.

Political opposition to trade liberalisation arises mostly from concern about unemployment and income loss. As we saw above, though overall income is expected to increase, some groups lose jobs or other forms of income in the short run. These groups justifiably oppose liberalisation. Even when governments are convinced that liberalisation is worthwhile, it is likely to be blocked by domestic groups whose income will be adversely affected. The countries that started with import substitution and turned to some degree of trade liberalisation in the 1980s and 1990s have faced serious political opposition against the removal of protection.

The dilemma is that liberalisation is desirable for aggregate advancement but at the same time many will be hit hard in the short run. The notion of the short run and long run in this context is also somewhat misleading. When it is said that the hardship is only a thing of the short run and things will be better in the long run, an important aspect is missed out. The short-run loss and the long-run gain may not be incident on the same persons. Those who lose jobs and suffer hardships through liberalisation may continue to suffer for the rest of their lives. Meanwhile new jobs may be created in the export sector, others get these jobs, and the country as a whole does better. To get the benefit of liberalisation it is, therefore, necessary that governments are sensitive to the problem from the beginning and develop an adequate support system even before steps are taken for liberalisation.

## 8.12 Cross-country Input Flow

We have seen that countries have comparative advantage in different goods and hence are expected to gain when they trade in these goods. But why do they have comparative advantage in different goods? This can be tracked down to a country's resources and technology. A country that has abundant labour has comparative advantage in labour-intensive production. This, for example, is the reason why Bangladesh has advantage in the production of ready-made clothing. Countries that have plenty of good land relative to their population have a comparative advantage in land-intensive production. This is the reason behind the advantage of the US in farm production and New Zealand in dairy products and wool. Resources such as land, capital, unskilled labour, and labour with particular type of skills explain the pattern of trading specialisation in today's world quite well. A second source of comparative advantage is technology. If a country develops better technology for a particular product, naturally it will enjoy comparative advantage in it.

Quite interestingly, when trade takes place in products, it sets up a tendency for the price of resources that produce them to get more equal across countries. Suppose country A is labour-abundant and hence wage is low there as compared to B which is short of labour.

In that case, A will be able to produce labour-intensive goods[10] at lower opportunity cost than country B. If now A starts exporting the labour-intensive product to B, wage rate in A will start increasing, reducing the wage gap between A and B.

We can look at this process a bit more closely. Bangladesh, as we noted, is a labour-abundant country. Its average wage rate is much lower than that in Australia where labour is less abundant. Bangladesh can produce readymade garments at lower cost than Australia, because garment production is labour-intensive. If there is no trade between the two countries then garments will be cheaper in Bangladesh than in Australia. If now Bangladesh exports garments to Australia, it will sell them at a higher price than it was selling at home prior to the trade. It will also produce more than otherwise. This will create important effects in the Bangladesh labour market. Demand for labour will increase. Because garments sell at a higher price now and sell more, producers will be willing to pay higher wage to ensure more labour supply. The wage rate will, therefore, increase. This is how income would increase for a labour-abundant country when it starts exporting labour-intensive products. If a country is capital-abundant and starts exporting capital-intensive goods, the income of capital owners will also increase in the same way. This is the general process of income increase through cross-country trading.

We will now ask an interesting question. Is this not a roundabout way of increasing income? Why can we not buy and sell the resources directly? A labour-abundant country can export labour rather than garments and similarly a capital-abundant country can export capital directly. That would also increase the income of workers and capital owners from the pre-trade situation. If Bangladeshi workers are employed in Australia, their income will increase directly. In this case Bangladesh would be exporting its abundant factor to Australia. Alternatively, Australian business can set up garment factories in Bangladesh, which will be an export of capital. We might ask, which is better, the movement of labour and capital across countries or trade of the products produced by them?

---

[10]Loosely speaking, a product that requires more labour per unit of other inputs, for example, machines, is more labour-intensive.

The question cannot be answered in general terms. Even if the effects on income were equal, the answer would depend on the relative cost of moving inputs and products across countries. These costs are not just economic costs but a range of social costs that depend on the tolerance of the people of the two countries and their cultural, ethnic, and linguistic differences. As a matter of fact, international trade in labour and capital is subjected to more protection and restriction than trade in products. Their movement attracts a number of objections and hence additional barriers that goods and service do not face.

## 8.13 Migration

Migration is the direct movement of labour from one country to another. It has shaped the demography of the world as it is today. There have been several great waves of migration in the distant past in response to changes in the earth's temperature, food availability, and so on. They led to migration across continents and between areas with varied climate and vegetation. In the more recent past, large scale migration has taken place from Europe to North America, Australia, and New Zealand. In the twentieth century too we saw migration from Europe and Russia to these countries. More recently after the fall of the Soviet Bloc countries, large-scale migration has taken place from these countries to west Europe and other places.

Here we will focus on one kind of migration, that in response to the possibility of earning higher income. This can be thought of as trade in labour between a labour-abundant country and one abundant in some other factor. This kind of migration requires immigration formalities which is partly a protectionist restriction on the import of labour. Most countries use a quota system to regulate the import of labour, setting an annual upper limit to immigration. Yet, if we think in terms of economic gain, immigration from a cheaper labour market increases income in the source country as well as in the host country. The host country gains because of relatively cheaper labour and the source country because of higher income of emigrants. Emigrants save a significant part of their income and remit it back home. These remittances are large for the first generation of emigrants and in many cases continue beyond the first generation. They are an important source of income for many third world countries. For example, remittance to India in 2007 represented more than 3 per cent of the GDP in that year.[11] This is an enormous amount given the size of India's economy. There are many small countries where annual remittance varies from 20 per cent to 25 per cent of their GDP, reaching close to 30 per cent for some![12]

Generally immigration is opposed, quite bitterly in many cases, by the workers of the host country. This follows from the fear of income loss. Another reason is that many governments, particularly in rich countries, ensure a minimum level of income, housing, health care, and education to all their residents. Governments and tax payers often regard the cost of welfare support to immigrants as an avoidable burden.

Migration of labour does not take place only in the unskilled labour market. A country can be short of specific skills and immigration can occur in response. The US workforce grew in number, skills, and talent through the flow of people from Europe at the end of the nineteenth century and again in the inter-war years. The US and Europe, particularly UK, import a large amount of skilled manpower from South Asia and Africa. Urban centres in the United Arab Emirates have developed entirely with migrant workforce of skilled and semi-skilled labour and professionals.

Cross-border migration has grown with the worldwide tendency for urbanisation and globalisation. Demand for a number of semi-skilled services has rapidly increased in developed countries as life has shifted to urban centres: construction and road works; town cleaning; garbage, sewerage, and recycling; supermarkets; restaurant and hospitality; nursing of the aged; security; house-keeping and so on. These are low paying jobs and generally there is a shortage of workers for them. The shortage is not accidental but a structural feature of rich country labour markets. As these services cannot be

[11]Source: World Bank (2008, *Migration and Remittances Factbook* 2008, Ratha, Dilip and Xu, Zhimei). Provisional estimate for 2008 was initially $45 billion and was later set at $ 43.5 billion. This is more than 4 per cent of GDP.

[12]Lesotho got remittances close to 30 per cent of GDP in 2001. *Source:* World Bank, *Global Economic Prospects 2004.*

imported, rich countries need migrant workers for them. Many of the services such as town keeping, garbage, sewerage and recycling, old age care, babysitting etc. are paid for publicly. They are either produced by public agencies or contracted out. The remaining services that are privately bought are relatively price inelastic. As a result, the demand for all these services is rising with urbanisation and rising average age. This development produces a pull for immigration given the shortage of low-skill and low-wage labour in these countries. Second, the construction of urban centres has got a boost as more developing countries graduate to decent income levels. Growth of new cities and infrastructure causes significant labour inflow.

---

**Box 8.7: The Brain Drain**

While emigration of unskilled workers is looked upon as helpful for the source country, there are complaints of brain drain when professionals from a poor country migrate to a rich country. There is then a conflict between the emigrant professional's personal interests of earning a higher income overseas with the loss of human capital of the country that spent resources on it. The complaints can be quite bitter in countries where higher education is heavily subsidised by the government.

The grievance loses some force as emigrant professionals—particularly the first generation—remit a significant part of their income home. Further, the tendency of professional emigrants to settle in the host country is reportedly weakening. More recently, a sizeable fraction are returning to their countries of birth at the end of their overseas career. Their return brings back not only savings but also experience and business practices which tend to be useful. Returnees typically set up businesses or engage in social activities. These enterprises and activities tend to disseminate business and management practices picked up in their overseas working life. The return migration has visibly weakened the criticism of professional emigration from poorer countries significantly.

---

Added to all these are the effects of globalisation. Large companies now produce in several countries as they look for tax advantage and nearness to markets and raw materials. They require workers and professionals not available on location. From their point of view, labour is the only input that can be transported, while location parameters like tax rate, government concessions, or distance from markets cannot. This has given rise to a significant flow of labour and skills criss-crossing the world.

Until very recently the process of migration was looked upon as a bilateral political issue between the host and the source country where the two sides make reciprocal gestures and concessions. This is changing as the importance of cross-border labour flow and its contribution to global production are getting understood. Labour flow is gradually acquiring the status of what it indeed is: the supply of an input across the border and thus, is being treated accordingly. The pattern of migration has changed in the last couple of decades. Previously, the vast majority of emigrants used to settle down in the host country. But now there is a fair amount of in-and-out migration and movement of migrant workforce from country to country. These changes have helped the development of more professional and less political handling of cross-country labour flow.

Migration, however, is not an inert flow of input. It is people in transit. It involves separation from families and reunion, interaction with different cultures, and issues of human interest and rights. These issues are a little better understood now than earlier. Human, political, and economic rights of migrants should be considered to be one hundred per cent portable as they move across countries. Institutions and legislation at the global level fall far short of this requirement. But as the importance of migration in a globalised production order is appreciated more fully, we may hope that the deficit will narrow down.

## 8.14 Movement of Capital

There was a time when the flow of capital from one country to another would be related with only wars and conquests. Later, during the era of imperialism, capital from European countries flowed into their colonies. It was guided as much by political as economic considerations. Here I want to discuss the cross-country flow of capital in more recent times. Any flow of capital is an investment. So we will use investment and capital flow interchangeably. Two types of capital flow take place across countries: portfolio and direct investment. Portfolio investment means acquiring financial assets. In a cross-country context it means buying financial assets in another country. An example is buying bonds issued by a foreign government or company. Portfolio investment involves very little transaction cost and time. It can be completed online through the websites of one's bank or other financial companies. As a result it is very volatile. It flows in and out in large amounts depending on the state of expectations and investment prospects. Developing countries look at this source of funds with some caution. Though it boosts resources substantially, it is prone to sudden flight and that remains a source of worry. Some Asian countries especially Malaysia and Thailand experienced massive flight of portfolio capital just before and around the time of the financial meltdown in 1997.

The second type of investment is in real assets and is called direct investment. It takes many legal and institutional forms but all of them provide funds for buying real assets. A company may set up a joint venture with a private or a government company in another country; or it can set up a subsidiary company. Direct investment may also take the form of buying shares of an existing company. All these investments help increase production and income in the host country. Wage and rent incomes are directly created by these activities. When there are local partners, some profit income is created as well. Indirectly, they may lead to the growth of ancillary industries and markets that generate more income. The host country expects further benefits from diffusion of technology and business practices, training, and skill formation. Foreign direct investment (FDI) has grown very rapidly in the last three decades. To get a perspective, total world exports grew three times between 1982 and 2001. During the same period, FDI increased by more than sixteen times. A notable feature of recent FDI is the increase in the number of source and host countries. There is a clear break from the past when mostly US, Japan, and some European countries used to directly invest in one another or in the ex-colonies of Europe. Companies from many more countries are now investing overseas. They are also investing in many more countries than earlier.

However, FDI still remains large among rich countries and much less from rich to developing economies. Differences in wages and input prices are not significant across the rich countries. Therefore, investment from one such country to another is a way of taking production closer to the market or closer to material input sources, and in some cases, to escape regulatory issues. Generally rich countries have similar property and investment laws and investment across them is relatively easy.

On the other hand, investment by rich countries in developing economies faces hurdles from both sides. Property and investment laws may be different and, further, they may be poorly enforced in developing countries. That introduces an element of extra risk for overseas investors. Risk perception is compounded if the politics of the host country appears volatile. On the host country side sometimes there is an element of distrust and fear. It is often feared that foreign investors will evade tax revenue, subvert workers' welfare, and take advantage of the country's relatively lax environmental supervision. On some occasions political campaigns based on these fears have led potential FDI projects to be abandoned. However, these fears seem to be lifting as FDI in developing economies like China, India, Brazil, Russia etc. is seen to be making significant contributions to the economies.

## 8.15 Multinational Enterprises (MNEs)

Industrial production and services at the global level are dominated by multinational enterprises (MNEs). They are firms that manage and control production in at least two countries and typically operate in all the major markets—North America, the European Union, and South and South East Asia including Australasia. Some very familiar examples in consumer products are Coca-Cola, McDonalds, Kellogg's, Cadbury Schweppes etc. An important feature of MNEs, particularly in consumer goods and durable consumer goods, is that they have recognised brands. According to some global surveys, Coca-Cola is the second best known expression in the world after 'OK'! Multinationals not only use their brands across the world but also use similar marketing models across the world, for example, with similar distribution and retailing techniques, advertising, and promotions. Some MNEs produce the same or similar goods in different countries and are called 'horizontally integrated'. The examples of MNEs that I have given above are of this variety. Another type of MNEs produces parts of a product in different countries and assembles the final product at several other places. For example, the Tonawanda (New York) plant of General Motors (GM) produces engines that are supplied to GM plants all over the world to be assembled with car bodies. These firms are known as 'vertically integrated'. They may sell not only the final product but also some of the intermediates they produce. There is yet another type of MNEs that produces different and even unrelated products in different places and countries. They are called conglomerates. Tata is a conglomerate that produces a range of consumer and producer goods as well as services. Japanese electronics firms like Sony and Toshiba are electronic conglomerates.

Why do companies go multinational in the first place? Economic theory suggests that capital would flow from a country with low return to one with higher return. Rich countries are capital-abundant; hence return on capital is low. So, rich country capital is expected to go where capital is in short supply and the return is high. But this bookish explanation does not fit the MNEs. Most of the MNE investment represents flow of capital from one capital-abundant country to another. A vast majority of MNEs are North American, European, and Japanese companies and their multinational investment is also confined to the same group of countries. If we take out China and Mexico from the list of the 10 leading host countries, then those that remain also belong to the top 10 source countries for MNEs. Further, MNEs raise a large part of the required capital from the financial market of the country where they invest. Hence the explanation that capital flows from abundant to poor areas does not explain the formation of MNEs.

The basic puzzle is this. MNEs want to sell in more countries. But that does not really require them to produce their goods in all those countries. If it is cheaper to produce in a particular country, say China or India or Mexico than in the US, then an MNE from

US can locate all its production there. It is possible, of course, that when the goods are produced in Mexico, transporting them for sale to Europe may be costly. Hence the part to be sold in Europe can be produced in Europe. But this too can be avoided if the US firm could license the production technology to a European firm for a fee with the provision that its output should be sold within Europe. Hence it does not really make sense to own and manage a production facility in Europe. We should reckon that owning and managing operations in multiple locations has significant cost. The company has to move goods, employees, information, and resources across the world; and has to invest in learning the laws, customs, politics, language, and business environment in a number of countries. Further, the parent company at its headquarters has to monitor the state of affairs in all the locations continuously. So becoming a multinational is not really explained by the difference in production cost in different countries.

Preference for producing in a country rather than exporting to it is often the result of trade barriers in that country. If the market is large and the tariff is high then producing inside the country makes full business sense. Tariff and quota jumping, as the move is called, is a common motive for MNEs to produce in more than one country. It is not a new phenomenon. In the 1930s when the US passed the Smoot–Hawley Act, Europe retaliated with stiff tariffs. A number of US firms set up production in Europe for the first time as a result. Similarly, Japanese investment in auto production in the US in the 1980s was a response to the US' protection of its own auto industry. The more the US tried to protect it with import restrictions, the keener the Japanese auto makers became to invest in the US. Statistically speaking there is a significant correlation between the level of protection of a market and MNE investment into it. In fact it has prompted some countries to use tariff barriers as a way of attracting MNE investment!

Whether the company would produce in a foreign country or license out the production there depends on the nature of the product. In branded consumer products like Coca Cola the MNE would not want to license as a matter of policy to keep its recipes and processes secret. Products based on intellectual property and innovations present another problem. They use innovation in electronic, chemical, bio-medical, digital, and other applications. MNEs find licensing them difficult because they cannot easily establish their price with potential licensees. To convince them of the worth of a technology typically requires exposing its secrets which risks copying and stealing. This problem is particularly severe in developing economies and emerging markets where intellectual property rights are not well-protected.

There is a lot of controversy about the effects of MNEs on their source countries as well as hosts. Most of it relates to how the costs and gains get shared by the source and host countries. A common complaint in developing countries is that investment by MNEs leads to exploitation of the host country. The companies bargain for tax breaks, cheap land, and other subsidies from the host country. Environmental groups claim that MNEs take advantage of the lax regulatory administration of developing countries. Another common grievance is that MNEs deliberately prevent the diffusion of technology and business practices into local business. On the side of source countries, the most important complaint comes from labour organisations. They claim that MNEs 'export' jobs to low wage countries while those jobs rightfully belong to them.

## 8.16 Summing Up

International trade is necessary because countries cannot produce all they need. But trade theory pushes the question further. If it was possible to produce all we need, would we still go for cross-country trade? We have explored the answer to this question. Like the question of market *vs* government, here too the answer cannot be a plain 'yes' or 'no'. Trade gives rise to many benefits because the opportunity cost of producing things differs across countries. If a country produces goods in which it has relatively low opportunity cost and trades it for other goods, it is plain that it will benefit. The problem, however, is that the benefits depend on whether all parties play to the rules of free trade or not. Hence international co-ordination is necessary if we wish to get as much from international trade as possible.

In spite of all the obstacles to global trade the world has been steadily going through a process termed 'globalisation'. National markets have become more connected to the international market through this process. It is the result of a push partly by MNCs to reach markets and resources in different countries and partly by governments trying to open up their economies. The effort of the governments is led by the belief that more open economies attract FDI and this promotes growth. International trade in goods and services; migration of workers and professionals; and cross-border investment have all been boosted in course of the process. Similar movement of goods and factors of production across countries took place for a period in the nineteenth century. But the subsequent political developments—two world wars, the rise of the Soviet bloc, and the Cold War had dampened the process. It started again in the 1980s almost unnoticed and has sped up after the fall of the Soviet bloc. However, much we dislike clichés, the best way to describe the development is to say that the world is getting smaller every day. W.H. Auden (1907–73) a British-American poet had penned the following romantic lines:

'I'll love you, dear,
I'll love you Till China and Africa meet,
And the river jumps over the mountain
And the salmon sing in the street.'

Obviously he thought a meeting of China and Africa was as improbable as the river jumping over the mountain. Well, globalisation in recent years has flooded Africa with Chinese products and a massive quantity of FDI by Chinese companies in that continent.

There are, however, serious issues of income distribution that cannot be glossed over even when trade and globalisation enrich all participating countries. Loss of jobs and income in the short run is a substantive problem; it cannot be waved away by suggesting that it will be sorted out in the long run. International trade and other aspects of globalisation have to be accompanied by a rigorous support mechanism for all who lose in the short run. International co-ordination and code of conduct are also required for the flow of capital, technology, and labour across countries to benefit all participants more evenly.

# 9 Economic Growth and Development

In the early nineteenth century many wondered if their economic system could provide livelihoods and necessary goods in the future as the previous regimes had done in the past. In today's idioms, the question was about economic growth. Is sustained growth of income possible? We will first look at the doubts raised by the early scholars. I will start this chapter with Thomas Malthus who set the ball rolling by claiming that long-run growth was not sustainable. And, that started the theory of economic growth and development.

## 9.1 Thomas Robert Malthus (1766–1834)

Malthus, born in England, was twenty-three at the time of the French Revolution. He must have known about the goings on in Paris as his father was a Jacobin.[1] He studied mathematics, theology, and philosophy and became a professor of political economy at the college at Haileybury, England. This college was run by the East India Company for the education of civil servants. In 1798, Malthus wrote a tiny book, more a pamphlet than a book, titled *An Essay on the Principle of Population.*[2] Before talking further about Malthus, I

---

[1] Jacobins were a moving influence behind the French Revolution. They have been described as believers in 'extreme democracy' and 'absolute equality'. The founding group had meetings in Paris at the old convent of the Jacobins, and hence the name Jacobins.

[2] The first edition was written under a pen name. Most probably a very small number of copies were printed, judging by the rarity of that edition. Malthus later

must apologise that I have taken the liberty of abridging the title of his book. If you are one of those who must always have the whole truth, please take a look at the title of the book in the footnote here.[3]

It would be an understatement to say that the book created a stir. It is quite remarkable that it continues to stir the imagination even today. Malthus developed the argument that population would necessarily increase faster than the means of sustenance and thus human society was inevitably heading for doom. He used a simple but compelling mathematical analogy. Economic prosperity raises a population's natural growth rate. Now, the number of new-borns depends on the current adult population. So the growth of population is proportional to the current population. Thus population multiplies itself not just figuratively, but in a mathematical sense. It grows by multiplying last year's value by a growth rate. A growth of this type is called a geometrical growth. On the other hand, the country's ability to produce food and daily requirements does not grow geometrically. It grows by adding so much more to its current production every year, a process called an arithmetic growth. This means that sooner or later production will fall short of the requirements. Even if there is prosperity today, as it would have been in England at the time of Malthus, it will dwindle over time. With certainty, there will come a time when there will not be enough to live on.

Let us rephrase Malthus using the economic terms that we have used in this book. When GDP exceeds that needed for subsistence, population tends to increase. This happens for two reasons. One, better living and nutrition reduce the death rate, that is, fewer persons die in a given time. Second, better eating and living increases the number of births, because couples can spend more time together and are less tired. These two factors trigger off an increase in population. This increase is multiplicative or geometrical in nature. Now, more people will, of course, produce more food and other things needed.

---

published further editions and the book grew from 50,000 words to 250,000 words in its fifth edition. Interestingly, J.M. Keynes commented that the first edition of 50,000 was better and more focused.

[3]Here is the title of Malthus' book: *An Essay on the Principle of Population as it affects the Future Improvement on Society, with Remarks on the Speculation of Mr Godwin, M. Condorcet and other Writers.*

But unfortunately output does not grow like population. It grows additively. So in the race population would always grow faster than output. Hence, GDP per person will start to fall. Thus GDP per person cannot stay above the subsistence level for long. If population growth still continues then GDP per person will fall below subsistence level. This will lead to malnutrition, starvation, and social disruptions that will reduce the population. The numbers will fall until income reaches the subsistence level again. In sum, per person income can increase only for a brief time and not forever. In the long run, GDP will hover around the subsistence level that is, the level that keeps population static.

The following lines from Malthus' book are often quoted: 'Population, when unchecked, increases in a geometrical ratio. Subsistence only increases in an arithmetical ratio. A slight acquaintance with numbers will show the immensity of the first power in comparison of the second.' He further added that when population increases to a level unsustainable by the economy's ability to support it, 'crime, disease, war, and vice', will necessarily result and will pull down the population. These rather unsavoury instruments that would appear on the scene to moderate the population, have been given the name of 'Malthusian checks' on population.

Malthus' formulation was very 'modern' in a number of ways. It is the one of the earliest 'feedback' systems described in the Anglo-Saxon political economy literature. A feedback system describes a dynamic interaction where the change in one variable leads to a change in a second, which in turn reshapes the first, and the process goes on. Quite apart from that claim, Malthus is possibly the first person to have stated the problem of sustainable growth in the same language as the environmentalists of today. As a result he has always remained at the centre of the debate, as much in his own days as today.

A few years after his death, Malthus attracted the derision of no less a person than Karl Marx. Karl Marx, who viewed the future of humanity with the greatest of optimism, was naturally annoyed by Malthus' bleak pronouncements. He called Malthus' little pamphlet 'a libel on the human race'. He paused to add that a man is born not just with a mouth to feed but also two hands to work with. Hence, as population grows, so does the output of things to sustain that population. If population grows geometrically, so should food and other things, because in Marx's vision it is labour that produces things, not land as Malthus implied. On the other hand, Malthus is still a crowd-puller and attracts followers from 21st century environmental workers and activists. We will discuss these issues later again. For the time being, note that Malthus started the ball of growth theory rolling by asking the most relevant of all questions: is growth sustainable?

## 9.2 David Ricardo (1772–1823)

I have referred to Ricardo earlier on two occasions, in Chapters 2 and 8. He and Robert Malthus were almost exact contemporaries. They had serious differences on economic issues and wrote critical pieces on each other's ideas. But they also got to know and like each other and became very good friends. Ricardo, a phenomenally successful investor, used to pass on investment tips to Malthus; what else would you demand as proof of friendship? A famous instance that has been written about is when Ricardo egged on Malthus to invest in the bond market. Ricardo was expecting a British victory at the Battle of Waterloo[4] and hence significant gains from investment in British government bonds. Malthus with a conservative and risk-shy temperament was not persuaded. Ricardo, of course, made a killing from this investment as always.

Ricardo's father was a stockbroker who migrated to Britain shortly before Ricardo's birth. Ricardo did extremely well at his father's trade at a fairly early age. But he had to get separated from his father, an orthodox Jew, when he wanted to marry a Quaker. He set up as a dealer of government securities and became enormously rich in no time. At the age of 41 he gave up his business because, as he wrote to his good friend James Mill, he had got enough wealth to satisfy all his needs and desires, and set himself up as a country gentleman. He became an independent member of the British Parliament in 1819 and served till his death in 1823. In the parliament he remained actively interested in all questions related to commerce, currency, and trade.

[4]June 1815. Napoleon was fighting the Anglo-Allied army under the command of the Duke of Wellington and a Prussian army under the command of Gebhard von Blücher. Napoleon lost.

Though Ricardo disagreed with Malthus on many issues, he agreed with him on the question of economic growth. He noted that workers spend their share of GDP on consumption. In his time, workers did not earn more than the bare subsistence level and it was realistic to assume that all wages were spent on consumption. The remaining part of GDP went to land-owners. That was spent partly on consumption and the rest was saved. This saving allowed land-owners to employ more workers next year. Now recall Ricardo's law of diminishing returns discussed in Chapter 2. When more labour is used, the output of land does increase, but the marginal product is less than the previous year's. So, although GDP grows from year to year, its growth rate falls from one year to the next. This process goes on until marginal product falls so low that it just manages to pay off the workers' wages. Employing any more workers now would cost more than it would produce. So, employment and GDP cannot grow any further from now on. Ricardo concluded with this analysis that economic growth cannot go on forever; it is a transient process. How long the phase of growth lasts depends on how fast marginal product falls. In turn that depends on the quality of land and technology of production. Malthus and Ricardo both, therefore, believed that economies would reach a 'stationary state' sooner or later.

In Malthus' account economic growth spurs population increase which requires a corresponding increase in food production. However, food production cannot grow as fast. In the long run, GDP would equal the minimum amount needed for human survival and no more. Any more only raises population for a short while and then brings it back to the subsistence level through Malthusian checks. Ricardo's view was not very different from this. Growth necessarily ends because the output of land falls down to the amount required to feed an extra worker. In Malthus' model, the whole population was taken as workers and all would live at the level of subsistence in the end. In Ricardo's model, workers would earn the subsistence level of wage, while landlords would have a better but stagnant living standard.

Thus these earliest theorists of growth did not think that the future of capitalism was too encouraging. Also note that Malthus' and Ricardo's predictions were not based on the nature of industrial capitalism, its relation with workers, or the possible inadequacies of the market mechanism. Their predictions were more elemental: the limited ability of land to provide for indefinite economic growth. In Ricardo's views, the ability in fact diminished via diminishing returns and thus sped up the approach of stagnation. Their gloomy outlook would be soon seconded by Karl Marx, but for a different reason altogether.

## 9.3 Karl Marx (1818–73)

Karl Marx, one of the most influential social thinkers of the 19th century, also had a bleak prognosis about economic growth. He was one of the first scholars to examine economic growth in the specific institutional context of industrial capitalism. So his model of growth is more complex, with more cogs and wheels compared with the simplicity of Malthus or Ricardo. In his analysis, growth under industrial capitalism would falter again and again—episodes that he called 'crises'. Each crisis will reduce the ability to recover from a future crisis, until the system comes to a state of permanent crisis or stagnation.

But in Marx' scheme the permanent crisis of capitalism was not a permanent crisis of human society, because civilisation was to traverse beyond capitalism. The series of crises would continue to weaken the ability of capitalists to rule as a class. If the working class could organise itself suitably, it would be able to take over the reins of the economy and the political system, and establish a different organisation of production and living. The new organisation, socialism, would be free from many of the weaknesses of industrial capitalism and would provide a better life. In turn, socialism would be transformed through time by the logic of its own organising principles into an arrangement that Marx called 'communism'.

Why was capitalism expected to face repeated crises? Malthus and Ricardo provided a single compelling reason why growth must end in stagnation. In Marx's model there are a number of reasons. One important reason is known as 'under-consumption'. Like we assume in modern economics, Marx noted that capitalists engage in enterprise for the sake of profit. But he looked at profit quite differently. He held that profit as we understand and count in rupees or dollars is not something that arises from market transactions. When workers work, they produce profit for the employer and it remains in the product. It is only converted into money when the product is sold; but that is only a change of form. Marx termed the profit produced by workers 'surplus value', which remains in the product until converted into monetary form. The latter is what we are accustomed to calling profit. Thus, the origin of profit is in production itself and to understand capitalism we need to understand its production system, and not so much its markets.

Surplus value is created because workers work longer than is required to produce what they can buy with their wages. Of course, a worker who works in an auto factory does not buy a part of the car with his wage but buys food. But if we look at the working class as a whole, we can see the sense in which Marx made this observation. Suppose workers work for eight hours a day and earn Rs 200. All that a worker can buy with Rs 200 can be produced by the workers who produce those things, say, in 2 hours altogether. If that is so, a worker's eight-hour working day has two parts. In two hours he produces what he earns as the day's wage. In the other six hours he adds value entirely for his employer—this is what Marx called surplus value. Marx focused on this quantity. The sale of a good merely converts it into profit. Conversion of surplus value into profit by sale was called the 'realisation' of surplus value.

Capitalists, of course, are not happy until they realise their profit. This is how market events acquire importance. To realise all the surplus value that has been produced, all the output has to be sold. And that sale is a perennial problem in capitalism. What workers can buy from the GDP is only one part of what they produce, corresponding to two hours of work of the average worker. Who is going to buy the product made by the other six hours of work? That is a substantial amount of goods, whatever the composition. Capitalists obviously cannot buy all that stuff just for consumption however lavishly they may live. They of course buy plants, machines, tools, and factories for investment. Hence, all of an economy's output can be sold only if capitalists buy those six hours of product partly for consumption and the rest for investment. As capitalism grows, the gap between what workers produce and what they can buy grows bigger, and hence more investment in plants and machinery would be needed to buy all the output.

This remains a potential problem. What would sustain more and more investment over the years? To put it differently, what would sustain an increasing demand for machines? A machine is expected to produce consumption goods in future years, or produce another machine that would produce consumption goods. So ultimately the demand for machines is tied to the production of consumption goods. If consumption good sales are falling as a proportion of GDP, why would businessmen buy more and more machines to produce consumption goods? Surely, then, investment cannot be expected to increase faster than the demand for consumption goods. Therefore, as a capitalist economy grows the problem of selling its output becomes more difficult. But surplus value cannot be realised into profit if goods are not sold. Therefore, capitalism has a problem built into its very structure.

To increase the share of profit, capitalists must try to reduce the part of the value to be paid to workers. This only deepens the realisation problem. It reduces the purchasing power of workers who constitute the overwhelming majority of buyers. The problem may not show up all the time because of various extra sources of demand. For example, in some periods investment is driven by long-run expectations or by speculative activities. Also business can sell its products overseas. Further, a country may go to war and that may demand large quantity of output. But the mismatch between the enormous growth of productivity and stymied growth of purchasing power remains and grows. It shows up from time to time as a 'realisation crisis'. What Marx described as a realisation crisis is what we have earlier described as recessions triggered off by a shortage of aggregate demand. Vast amounts of goods remain unsold in such a crisis; and so production and employment take a downward turn.

Marx further elaborated on a problem closely related to the above syndrome and called it 'disproportionality'. We have seen that the part of GDP that is not bought for consumption must be sold off for investment. But investment goods are distinct from consumption goods. Machines are not edible nor can a loaf of bread be used to produce something else in the future. So the production of consumer goods and investment goods has to be in the required ratio. One cannot be converted into the other *ex post* after finding out the market situation. But there is no mechanism that would lead an economy to produce consumption and investment goods in the right ratio. Businesses produce as they sense opportunities and there is no co-ordination among them—a situation described as 'the anarchy of capitalism' by Marx and Marxists. So the production of consumption goods and investment goods is expected to occur in arbitrary proportions. If it is too much out of line with what is needed, there is a 'disproportionality crisis'. In that situation consumption goods or machines are significantly over-produced. This would push the businesses which overproduced into problems. Unable to sell, they may be unable to repay their banks, become bankrupt, and so on. The crisis would work itself out only after the overproduced goods are either wasted or sold at dirt-cheap prices, and capital owned by some of those who had produced in excess is written off. The system starts again with the right proportions from then on.

Marx also drew attention to a number of other possibilities that lead to, or aggravate, crises. All in all, he looked at capitalism as a contradiction-ridden system driven by profit motive. The contradictions would lead to more and more frequent crises till the end of the system.

---

### Box 9.1: Karl Marx

Marx wrote extensively on the economy, politics, society, history, and philosophy. But he is best known as a revolutionary who wanted to transform society and to provide a theory of this change. His 'analytical package' on capitalism was unique. It provided an analysis of the inevitability of the end of capitalism and also an analysis of the strategy and tactics, almost a recipe, of the transformation. His economic analysis of capitalism was published in the well-known book *Das Kapital*, known to the English-speaking world as *Capital*. The first volume in German was published in 1867. Marx died before he could publish the second and

---

*(contd...)*

*Box 9.1 continued.*

third volumes of *Capital*, which had been already drafted. The volumes were edited by his co-author and friend Friedrich Engels and published in 1885 and 1894, respectively.

The first non-German edition of *Capital* was published in Russian in 1872. In spite of censorship by the Czarist government, the book made it to the book shops. Russian censorship of the time was quite determined to prohibit 'the harmful doctrines of socialism and communism'. But, the Czar's censors found Marx's book as a 'strictly scientific work' and its analysis not applicable to a country like Russia where 'capitalist exploitation had never been experienced'. One of the members of the censor board was quite complacent about a man called Karl Marx. He is recorded to have said that 'very few people in Russia will read it, and even fewer will understand it'. *Capital*'s first print run sold out within the year with Marx himself acknowledging that it was in Russia that the book 'was read and valued more than anywhere'.

Karl Marx is the most prominent of those economists who are known outside the charmed circles of academic scholarship. His writings influenced history for a whole century starting from the third quarter of the nineteenth century in a manner that no non-religious work has ever done. His influence on political and intellectual movements is still very much perceptible in the twenty first century.

## 9.4 Being Judgmental about the Classics

Malthus, Ricardo, and Marx were pessimistic about the future of the economic system they lived in. But their views were fundamentally different. Malthus and Ricardo saw the problem as an insurmountable constraint posed by nature. In Malthus' view, the requirement of a growing population would outstrip the system's ability to provide. In Ricardo's view, capital accumulation would increase output at a diminishing rate. They were thus talking about the limits coming from nature and natural laws.

But Marx's pessimism was based on the social arrangement: the relationship among the actors—workers and capitalists. He was living in the middle of technology and social institutions unimaginable by Ricardo and Malthus. The rate of population growth was coming down in industrial countries in spite of prosperity and new supplies of food, minerals, and material were opening up around the world. So Marx did not think much of Malthus and Ricardo's views about the limits of resource and diminishing return. He did not think there would be any problem with economic growth once human society progressed beyond the contradiction-ridden capitalism. He believed that when workers became free from exploitation and worked for the fulfilment of their productive urge, there would be a magnificent increase in productivity and ingenuity. Work would become fun—a liberating experience, applying labour and mind. In short, the contradiction between parts of the society, workers and capitalists, was the problem for sustained growth. About the fight between the society as a whole and nature as an inert force, he thought that the former would always come up victorious. Malthus and Ricardo instead looked at the opposition between society and nature as one where the latter would win.

Was Marx right or did Malthus and Ricardo have a better vision? In hindsight, we know that capitalism has not stagnated, nor has the system fallen through under repeated crises. In fact, it is a vibrant system which has brought about stupendous technological changes that could not have even been dreamt of in the nineteenth century. Standards of living in advanced capitalist countries, including those of the poorest households, have increased continuously. Hence, all three authors were very much off the mark. On the other hand, the history of the last two centuries also shows that they had profound intuition about the economic process.

We need to first realise that the future of society is not predictable in the same manner that the future of a physical system is. The society consists of wilful actors—workers, capitalists, buyers, sellers, politicians, and what have you—who learn from the events that they themselves precipitate and change their course if they think necessary. Now, the method of any rational prediction would be to analyse how actors behaved in the past, and then extrapolate that (or a theoretically inferred related behaviour) into the future. But if the actors change their behaviour pattern in response to the result of their own actions, then these predictions cannot hold. Therefore, all long-run forecasts about human society that predict stagnation or retrogression have inevitably failed. This simply shows that human beings are intelligent creatures who do change course when they see peril approaching. Marx, Ricardo, and Malthus were among the smartest of scholars, but humankind is clever too. If Marx, Ricardo, and Malthus had seen danger coming, so would the society see it in due course and would act in order to avoid it.

For example, Ricardo's intuition of diminishing returns has been verified to be true in real world production conditions in various contexts. But the prediction of stagnation derived from it has not materialised because of human intervention. Businesses understand diminishing returns when they face it in course of business. Having seen it, they beat it with inventions and innovations. Patent rights were developed as incentive for inventors; academic research was funded by business and drawn into the commercial arena. All these events were happening in the nineteenth century even as Malthus and Ricardo were writing and they gathered unprecedented momentum towards the end of that century. This produced the spectacular process of technical progress seen in capitalism. And, collectively they have beaten the diminishing returns that Ricardo was so concerned about. Diminishing returns tend to lower marginal product for a given production process. Technical progress has intervened every now and then replacing the entire production process with a more advanced one. The process of technical progress under capitalism makes Ricardo's predictions wrong, and yet proves his intuition right!

---

**Box 9.2: Predictions in Economics**

Successful predictions in economics are generally of two types. The first are short-run forecasts, where the time horizon is too short for any change of actors' behaviour on which the forecast has been based. If the model is good, the forecasts are expected to be good as well. The second are forecasts that trigger off actions favouring the forecasted event itself. An example: a forecast that the price of rice is going to rise substantially in the next three months. If the forecast is believed, then traders will stockpile rice to sell it later at higher price. This will reduce current supply of rice and raise its price automatically. The process will be helped further if households start over-buying due to panic. Similarly,

*(contd...)*

*Box 9.2 continued.*

---

a forecast of a fall or rise of the exchange rate of the rupee can trigger off self-fulfilling behaviour.

Robert Lucas Jr (born 1937), who received the Nobel Prize in economics in 1995, produced what was later called 'The Lucas Critique' of macroeconomic policy. He drew attention to the fact that economic behaviour is heavily governed by expectations. Consumer spending depends on expected future income and business investment depends on the expectation of future prices. This makes policy making tricky and sometimes outright ineffective. When a policy is announced, it influences the expectation of households and business in ways we do not fully understand and are unable to quantify. The effect of the policy depends on these new expectations, while the policy has been designed on the basis of past behaviour. Past behaviour was based on expectations which will now be irrelevant.

---

So we would very much expect to find Malthus, Ricardo, and Marx wrong simply because they had predicted peril. The right way to evaluate their work is not to check if their predictions came true, but to judge the factors and reasoning that led to their predictions. Do we find in subsequent events a large impact of those factors? Is there evidence that conscious human behaviour led to the avoidance of the perils predicted?

In that test all the three scholars score very high. Take Malthus, whose gloomy forecast generally attracts the most derision. He had predicted an impending famine in his book of 1798. It is often pointed out with ridicule that starting from then the world population doubled in the 1920s and became four-fold in 1973, while the world lives on and people eat better. Paul Ehrlich, an American entomologist known for his Malthusian ideas, argued in a 1968 book[5] that India would fail to feed the two hundred million more people who were to appear on the scene by 1980.[6] He predicted that millions would starve to death in India. It is pointed out with scorn that the predictions were proved

---

[5] *The Population Bomb.* New York: Buccaneer Books.

[6] Ehrlich is a leading proponent of birth control. Many advocates of population control in Europe and the US in the 1960s and 1970s used his reasoning to make a case for population control.

wrong only six years later, when India announced self-sufficiency in food grains in 1974. Obviously, Malthusian predictions about famines and depopulation have proved wrong. But they failed because of conscious action against those dire possibilities. Many countries have been quite close to the unpleasant Malthusian catastrophe and then have taken corrective steps at the brink. India's Green Revolution launched in 1965 was a conscious effort of a very large population standing at the edge of a Malthusian disaster. It both prevented the disaster and vindicated the theory!

In Ricardo's model, diminishing returns eat into the economy's ability to generate investible surplus. His prediction of a stationary state where per capita income stops growing has of course not come true. But that does not make his observations on diminishing returns incorrect. Even though diminishing returns work all the time, major technological breakthroughs have pulled up the returns ever so often. We have won the race against diminishing returns with technical progress, a conscious action against diminishing returns in the real world.

What about Marx? Capitalism is alive and kicking and people in capitalist countries, including workers, live far better lives than was imaginable by even pro-capitalist visionaries of Marx's time. These are held as obvious proof that he was completely wrong. But if we use the yardstick mentioned above, we would have quite a different opinion. Under-consumption that Marx pointed out as a basic problem has not disappeared in spite of the onward march of capitalism. It is recognised to be so by today's macroeconomics though the latter uses a different set of jargon.

Marx reasoned that the part of GDP that workers do not buy for consumption creates a difficulty. This part is large and would get larger. This is the crux of the under-consumption problem. Classical and neo-classical theorists both before and after Marx, did not think that this was a problem at all. They argued that the part of GDP which is not consumed will be used for investment in the end. The financial mechanism looks after this while it equates saving and investment. But we can recall from Chapter 5 that this is not true. The central concern of modern macroeconomics is that consumption and investment together may not be able to buy the economy's potential output. That is exactly what Marx had claimed.

Marx predicted that this problem would appear repeatedly until capitalism becomes dysfunctional. However, this has not happened. But the vulnerability of the system has been shown up again and again until it was brought into sharp focus by the Great Depression. During the Great Depression, the issues were understood and then determined human action changed the scenario. Capitalist economies emerged from the Great Depression stronger, not weaker. Macroeconomics that was born during the period shows the ability of the human society to understand and avoid social disasters. Paul Samuelson had put this with insightful wit: 'Funeral by funeral, theory advances'. The experience of the Great Depression made it clear that the government has to spend whenever private investment is too little. So a calculated amount of government purchase became routine. Governments introduced unemployment benefits and a number of other measures; they became regular features of capitalism. These are designed precisely to prevent under-consumption. Therefore, while capitalism has not broken down, the causes that Marx presented for its possible breakdown are verifiably true.

We may sum up the discussion so far. The classical economists like Malthus and Ricardo actually theorised about stagnation rather than growth. So did Marx. However, we now know that growth has been sustained since the time of these authors. Their fear of stagnation was based on issues which are real and important. But they have been taken care of by economic and social development. Those issues now inform the action of governments as well as private actors so much that the prospect of permanent stagnation seems improbable.

With the hindsight that economic growth has been sustained it seems unfortunate that so much intellectual effort revolved around the question, 'Is economic growth possible?' We should have instead asked how we can raise the rate of economic growth. This question was asked surprisingly late in the day, only in the early 1950s!

## 9.5 Modern Growth Theory

The modern phase in the study of economic growth started after the Second World War. Macroeconomic data was now available and standardised. With that the big picture of a country's economy was clearer than ever in the past. It was found that GDP and a number of aggregate variables move through time with some common patterns. For example, a plot of GDP for any country showed a series of ups and downs of sizeable amounts. On analysis, it appeared that a part of the variation is just seasonal, that is, every year they would be up at specific times and down at others. Agricultural countries may have a higher quarterly GDP around harvest time. Christian countries may have it around Christmas and the New Year. As opposed to seasonality which is a regular variation, there is an irregular variation caused by business cycles. Buoyant activities inevitably slow down and then give way to a decline, a tendency which in turn is inevitably reversed. These ups and downs are a universal feature but their periods are irregular and severity uneven. Finally, in spite of the ups and downs, GDP generally shows increase when seen over a long period.

Business cycles were known since the nineteenth century and statistical studies were undertaken. I mentioned earlier that long recessions were seen by Marxists as episodes of crisis. By contrast, others concluded that cycles simply characterise the way an economy grows. Economies neither stagnate forever nor breakdown in spite of occasional downward movements. All this emerged more convincingly as better statistical data became available. Hence, this was a good time to ask questions about aggregate economic performance and look for answers. Conjectures about cycles and long-run growth could now be developed and tested. Questions about comparative economic growth could also be asked. That is, we could explore why some countries grow faster and others lag behind. The Cold War had brought comparative growth very much to the fore: can socialist countries grow faster than capitalist market economies? The mother of all growth questions of the time was: would the USSR grow faster than USA and overtake it as the premier global power?

During the early post-war days, Roy Harrod (1900–78) and Evsey Domar (1914–97) developed a theoretical model of economic growth independently of each other. Harrod used to teach at Oxford and belonged to the close circle of J.M. Keynes. He later wrote the biography of Keynes[7]. Evsey Domar, on the other hand, was born in Russia and raised in Manchuria. He migrated to the US in 1936 and pursued university education. He taught at several universities and finally held a chair at the Massachusetts Institute of Technology (MIT). Harrod's and Domar's ideas and models were very similar and later came to be known together as the Harrod–Domar model. This model was based on Keynesian ideas of income determination. Investment in one period leads to more production capacity in the next period. If that capacity is used, then there is an increase in GDP. Economic growth essentially is just the sequence of these increases through the years. Harrod and Domar used this minimal vision to explore what factors facilitate and hinder this process.

Harrod pointed towards two potential difficulties for a growing economy. The first is that if investors correctly anticipate the growth and invest accordingly, the economy next year will be free of strains. But if they overestimate demand and invest in line with it, then the extra investment would create even more demand through the multiplier process. So they will think that they had underestimated (rather than overestimated) demand. They will then invest further in the next period and the economy would thus go off on a path of ever-growing investment and demand. The opposite would happen if they once underestimate the demand. The economy would then proceed on a path of shrinking investment and demand year after year.

The second problem is that the economy's capacity to employ may not grow at the same rate as the increase in workforce. The capacity to employ depends on the production capacity of the economy which increases through investment. Investment depends on saving habits. On the other hand, the size of the workforce increases through the demographic process. So the workforce and the capacity to employ depend on different factors. Obviously, they need not grow at the same rate. Therefore, an economy would either face growing labour shortage or growing unemployment after a few years of economic growth!

The upshot was that growth in a modern economy is a seriously unstable process. First, unless business expectation is just right, the

[7]Harrod, Roy, *The Life of John Maynard Keynes*. London: Macmillan, 1951. The preface of the book mentions that Keynes's younger brother Geoffrey Keynes requested Harrod to write the biography.

economy takes off on a path of either explosive growth or implosion. We should note that explosive growth is not something good. In practical terms, it means that output will grow to the limit allowed by workforce and infrastructure. Thereafter, it cannot grow but demand continues to increase. Hence, the economy would face run-away inflation. The second instability comes from the mismatch of the growth of workforce and production capacity. So even when expectations are right, the economy will either face increasing unemployment or it will soon employ all its workforce and then growth will stop. The path of growth, therefore, is like a tight rope walk where perils result from the slightest imbalance.

Later economists, however, did not think that these problems were so serious. They pointed out that the problems came from artificial assumptions in Harrod's model. Harrod followed Keynes and assumed fixed prices. But prices are sticky only in the short run; in a growth model it is appropriate to consider them as flexible. With flexible prices, Harrod's mismatches disappear. Suppose the workforce grows more slowly than production capacity. If wage is flexible, the shortage of labour will push up the wage and dampen its demand. That would alleviate the problem to an extent. At the same time, as fewer workers are employed, output will be less than what it would be if wages were not flexible. So the growth rate of production capacity would also be moderated. These two effects will bring the growth of production capacity and workforce in line. They would also work if the workforce grows faster. Harrod had ignored another important source of adjustment. Labour and capital (that is, machines) are substitutable to an extent. If the workforce grows too slowly, then wage rise would encourage employers to substitute some labour with capital. Some tasks will be taken over by machines, tools, and computers. In the opposite case, labour would substitute capital. This also helps in the adjustment process. Third, Harrod had assumed a fixed saving rate. But the saving rate changes with the interest rate on offer. This flexibility would further help adjustment. Thus flexible price, wage, and interest rate and labour–capital substitution help adjustment in the growth process and eliminate the mismatches that Harrod worried about.

Both of Harrod's problems arose because his model did not allow the adjustments characteristic of a market economy and modern production process. It carried through the features of a short-run macro model into the discussion of long-run growth. But the Harrod–Domar model is valued nevertheless because it described the basic mechanism of growth in the starkest possible manner, paving the way for later development in growth theory.

## 9.6 The Solow Model

Contemporary growth theory is based on the insight developed by Robert Solow. Solow, like Harrod and Domar, abstracted from unnecessary aspects to focus on the essentials. But unlike them, he set his model in a context where price, wage, and the interest rate are flexible and they help markets to adjust. Second, labour and capital are taken as substitutable to the extent permitted by technology. The resulting model focuses on how saving is converted into investment and then investment leads to increased output and growth. Throughout, price, wage, and the interest rate change to keep markets in equilibrium and keep up the growth process. Solow analysed the effect of various parameters on the growth process and explored questions about policy actions that might help growth. He was awarded the Nobel prize in economics in 1987 which prominently cited his contributions to the theory of growth.

Solow was born in 1924 in NewYork in a family of immigrants. In his family, he and his sisters were the first generation to get university education! Solow did extremely well in his education, earned many distinctions, and chose an academic career. He made major contributions in a number of areas of economics. His studies of the labour market and of the importance of technology resulted in a serious change in the focus of policy in the US and elsewhere.

Solow's growth analysis describes the course of a market economy through time. Each year the economy saves a part of GDP. The financial market lends this to business to buy capital goods, that is, machines and tools. A competitive financial market and flexible interest rates ensure that all the saving is invested. New machines installed in a year make up the gross investment. Some of them will replace plants and machines that wear out. This part of investment is called depreciation. The rest represents net investment. Thanks to net investment last year, workers will work with more or better machines and produce more output this year. This process repeated through time is the growth process. All available labour is expected to be employed because prices and wage are flexible. There is no tight rope walking as in Harrod's model because flexible prices and substitution between labour and capital make adjustment possible.

When the process is described in the form of a mathematical model, we can explore the effects on the growth rate and per capita income of changes in the rate of saving, growth rate of the workforce, the degree of substitutability between labour and capital, and so on. We can also explore the effects of tax, government spending, exports, and imports.

What is the model's answer to the basic question raised by Malthus, Ricardo, and Marx? Can the growth process go on indefinitely or would it come up against some inevitable constraint? You might wonder why there should be any problems or issues at all. Given that growth is simply the result of yearly investments, all that is needed is to keep investment going. There is, however, a factor that works unnoticed to choke off the process. A race goes on between the wearing out of machines and infrastructure and our ability to replace them.

Suppose machines have an average life of twenty years. Then, on average, one in twenty will need replacement in any particular year. As the stock of machines increases over the years, the number of machines wearing out each year would also increase at the same rate. On the other hand, investment or new machines will increase output a little less than a similar amount of investment did last year. This is due to diminishing returns. And, as output increases at a diminishing rate so will saving and investment. This means that investment increases at a falling rate over the years even though depreciation increases at an undiminished proportional pace. A time must, therefore, come when the economy would be unable to produce more machines than are wearing out! The stock of machines cannot increase anymore after this point, because as many of them are scrapped as are produced. Output cannot increase either and growth would come to a standstill.

What all this means is quite astounding. Investment and capital accumulation, the common recipe for economic growth, cannot give an economy sustained economic growth! Investment increases capital stock and per capita income only for so many years but the growth rate gets smaller and smaller till it stops. The ability of capital to gift us higher per capita income is only transient. Its ability is constrained by the iron law of diminishing returns. At the same time, more machines create the need to replace more machines too. So the need for replacement will inescapably catch up with the production of machines. And, thereby ends the process of economic growth! Note that this is not very different from what Ricardo had claimed would happen to the growth process. It is the curse of diminishing returns.

## 9.7 Technical Progress

I wonder how you would react to this claim of inevitable end of economic growth. This surely cannot be for real? If it were true how would we explain the sustained growth of the US economy over such a long period? America declared independence from England in 1776. The colony had started on a path of growth much before the declaration and has been growing since. There have of course been halts—many recessions on the way—but the economy has resumed growth after each halt. England has had an even longer run. Germany, France, and other countries in West and North Europe have had similar runs as well. These countries should have been in a permanent state of stagnation long time ago.

Well, diminishing return and depreciation are undeniable facts of economic life. What sustains economic growth in spite of them is technical progress. Marginal product of capital does fall with capital accumulation as long as we operate with the same technology. But then it is lifted from time to time, sometimes quite dramatically, as new technology appears on the scene. Output of the new vintage of machines with new technology spikes up, and with it GDP, saving, and investment as well. This saves net investment from dropping to zero and thus output keeps moving. Looked at this way, the history of economic growth is the history of technical progress. Net investment is necessary to transfer one year's surplus production to the next year in the form of machines. But it is just that, a vehicle of inter-period transfer. What it can transfer from one year to the next decreases relentlessly and would fall to zero if there was no technical progress.

I will now sum up the insights of the Solow model. A modern economy can produce more than its current consumption needs. It uses the surplus or savings to build up capacity for future production in the form of machines and infrastructure. This enables increase of production, even though at a diminishing rate through time. At the same time, more and more machines and infrastructure are required just to replace the wear and tear. Eventually, the wear and tear would grow to a size when it needs all of the current investment to make it good. Growth should come to a standstill at this point. However, this has not happened yet because continuous technical progress has accompanied the process of growth. It takes the form of not just improvement of tools and machines but also better organisation, transport, management, and so on. Apart from such continuous improvement, we have the periodic appearance of major inventions and discoveries like the steam engine, railways, electricity, telegraph, computers, the internet, and so on.

A significant amount of statistical work has been done to verify the status of Solow's model. The story we outlined above is not directly verifiable. We do see sustained long-run growth in developed economies together with technical progress. But that does not mean that growth has been sustained by those technical changes or that it would have stopped without them. To test Solow's model we need to focus on some conclusions that are verifiable. When formally written out Solow's model produces a number of verifiable corollaries. The most important among them is that the shares of GDP going to capital and labour would remain constant in the long run. This proposition appears quite counter-intuitive. We hear so often that workers are becoming poorer and capitalists richer. Hence, we would like to bet that capital's share of GDP has been continuously increasing. Econometric verification using long period time series data from the US, UK, and other European economies, however, upholds Solow's conclusion that the share is statistically speaking, constant.

With the same statistical data researchers have tried to explore what part of growth of real output, say, in the last one hundred years can be attributed to the increase of only factors of production, that is, to the increase of capital and labour. It turns out that no more than 15 to 20 per cent of the increase of output can be statistically explained by the increase of these factors. Thus, no less than 80 per cent of economic growth has come from the improvement of production technology and organisation.

Solow's model would suggest that the history of economic growth over the last two hundred and fifty years is a contribution of successive technological breakthroughs. We may rephrase this to say that the story of capitalism in an important sense is the story of the development of technology. One person who put forward this view in a most emphatic way is Joseph Schumpeter. Though Schumpeter's major writings precede Solow's growth model by quite some time, it is good to discuss him in this context and hence after Solow's model.

## 9.8 Joseph Schumpeter (1883–1950)

Schumpeter was a theorist of capitalism rather than of economic growth. He did not develop a mathematical model, and, like Marx, analysed capitalism without abstracting from its social and political context. The so-called 'Schumpeterian' view of capitalism appears mostly in two of his books *Theory of Economic Development* (1911), and *Capitalism, Socialism and Democracy* (1942). In the 1911 book he first reasoned that a capitalist economy without innovations and technical advances would stagnate to a stationary state in the long run. He then went on to argue that it was the capitalist entrepreneur who breaks the tendency of stagnation every now and then with wide-ranging innovations. Hence, there is no long-run equilibrium in capitalism as it is ever evolving.

Schumpeter was not referring to scientific discoveries and technical inventions. He was talking about commercial innovations and applications which come from envisioning new products and markets, creating and supplying new needs, and inventing new processes and management methods. In his analysis, the central character of capitalism is the entrepreneur who, prodded by competition, is ever exploring ideas to outsmart his competitors. It is competition that lends dynamism to the system.

This aspect of competition and the entrepreneurial side of the capitalist were alien to economic thinking before Schumpeter. Mathematical formulations had abstracted from all features of a business except its profit seeking so that a firm/capitalist was a one-dimensional economic agent looking to maximise profit. Similarly, social and entrepreneurial dimensions of competition were assumed as inessential. Competition was taken to mean atomistic markets: an individual producer cannot influence prices and acts as a price taker. Marx, of course, did not use the narrowly focused method of neo-classical economics. But he also did not find anything more in a capitalist than a person who tries to squeeze out the most surplus value from workers.

Schumpeter's view of the entrepreneur as a dynamic agent of innovation rather than a mean and exploiting person was certainly not liked by Marxists and socialists. Neo-classical theorists also did not make much of his ideas. They abstract from all the institutional aspects of business and focus on price as the only variable for two confronting firms to battle it out. And in perfect competition they cannot even do that. Hence, firms in a competitive market are entirely passive agents in the neo-classical theory. Clearly such faceless actors cannot be the agent of anything like social change.

Schumpeter saw that competition plays a very different role. It provides incentive to stand out from competitors by transforming products and processes. Markets provide a field for a battle of innovations. Capitalism is thus a dynamic and vibrant system of progress. His method of analysis is to portray wide-ranging economic and social interactions and their feedback on one another. In the course of this analysis he provides interesting insights.

Though his method was different, Schumpeter's *analytical* conclusion is not too different from those of Ricardo, Marx, and Solow that the long-run equilibrium of the bare production system is stagnation. Malthus and Ricardo left their analysis at this point. Marx too left it here as far as capitalism was concerned suggesting that things would be different in societies that would succeed capitalism.

---

### Box 9.3: Joseph Schumpeter

Schumpeter was a native of Triesch in Moravia. He studied law at the University of Vienna and was a student of a famous Austrian economist Eugen von Böhm-Bawerk. Later he worked as a professor of economics at a number of European universities. He became the finance minister of the Austrian Government at the end of the First World War. His tenure as minister was short-lived and not very successful. Inflation in Germany, uncertainty about the future of Austria, and the redrawing of national borders had brought the economies of that area almost to a standstill. After leaving the minister's job, Schumpeter served as the president of a private bank during 1920–24. That bank, however, collapsed in 1924 as did many other Austrian banks of the time. The failure made Schumpeter bankrupt. He then took up a professorship of economics at the University of Bonn.

Schumpeter moved to the United States during to the rise of Nazism in Germany. He was close to fifty when he arrived in the US in 1932. He taught at Harvard from 1932 until his death. He had a most remarkable following among his students at Harvard. There were budding economists of all shades including Marxists, Keynesians, and Neo-classicals. Three of his students, Paul Samuelson, James Tobin, and Robert Solow, would later get Nobel prizes and there were other no less illustrious economists among them. As students, many of them were promising mathematical economists and Schumpeter encouraged them. He also served as the president of the Econometric Society (1940–41) but was not a practising mathematical economist in any sense. He tried to develop a theoretical view of the capitalist system and business cycles integrating sociological and economic forces and their mutual interaction. Though his model of the economy was intrinsically mathematical in nature, he presented it verbally.

---

Schumpeter also held that the capitalist system has a tendency for the rate of profit to fall and that this is a perennial source of worry for capital. This would lead to stagnation if nothing intervened. And it is here that the entrepreneurs acquire a crucial role. They break the tendency for stagnation. This is very much like Solow's model that shows that investment without technical change must lead to stagnation; but technology breaks this tendency and enables sustained growth. Solow did not discuss the mechanics of technical progress, that is, how it takes place and if it would always take place. Schumpeter, on the other hand, looked at the process of entrepreneurship closely. He reasoned that innovations are a part and parcel of capitalism rather than accidental events.

Very much like in Marx's *Capital*, in Schumpeter's theory changes occur discontinuously, in spurts. When entrepreneurial activity is not significant, the system takes a downward trajectory—a typical downturn of the business cycle. However, Schumpeter did not think they represented crises. To the contrary, he reasoned that they destroy the inefficient and the uncompetitive, and scrap old technology and business practices. They call entrepreneurs to either innovate or perish. Capital that gets written off during a downturn is, in his famous phrase, 'creative destruction of capital'. At the bottom of a recession the incentive to invest is huge for those who dare to pick up the things from there. It beckons the more spirited of the entrepreneurs to conquer new territories. Schumpeter would thus look at capitalism as the triumph of enterprise and innovation against the diminishing returns and falling profits. It is the sporadic feats of spirited activity that generate the irregular path of economic growth.

---

**Box 9.4: Economics: Anglo-Saxon and Continental**

The majority English tradition of economics had eventually converged to the neo-classical theory by the end of the nineteenth century. Though economists from all parts of Europe contributed to it, it was solidly owned by the English and the North American academia. In England the tradition was led by Alfred Marshall (1842–1924) and in North America by J.B. Clark (1847–1938). Hence, we might call this tradition the majority Anglo-Saxon view of economics of that period. It looked at economic actors in their barest role as utility and profit maximisers. This abstraction spread through the academic circles and became the dominant mode of thinking about the economy.

But some traditions, notably the Austrian and the Swedish, kept alive other ways of regarding economic actors and processes. Their ways of

*(contd...)*

*Box 9.4 continued.*

---

looking at a problem often produced significantly different insights. The Swedish school formulated economic dynamics very differently from the Anglo-Saxons. The Anglo-Saxon theory of economic dynamics was heavily influenced by Newtonian particle dynamics—its elegance and power persuaded theorists to adopt a similar methodology. As a result, dynamic models in mainstream economics resemble the dynamics of inert natural quantities. An unfortunate result is that there is little appreciation that economic dynamics is affected by conscious actors through their expectations and learning. Swedish economists were not impressed by these dynamic models. They developed a methodology for dynamics where expectations play a major role. Equilibrium of an actor was defined as an outcome that corroborates his/her expectations. And, an aggregate equilibrium is a state where the expectations of all relevant parties are fulfilled. The tradition has been continued by prominent Swedish economists.

Austrians differed from the Anglo-Saxon tradition in terms of how they viewed economic actors. Rather than regarding them as maximising robots not interested in anything else, they presented them as human beings with personality and spirit. This led to very different conclusions in many situations. Schumpeter's view of the capitalist entrepreneur as a person is an example of his Austrian grounding, notably under Böhm-Bawerk. His view of competition as facing a challenge rather than conforming also derives from the Austrian tradition.

---

## 9.9 Endogenous Growth Theory

Growth theory took a useful turn following Solow's work. As discussed, his theoretical work attributes sustained economic growth to the development of technology. His and others' empirical work found the contribution of technical progress overwhelming. However, when we take stock of this research, we find that it is not at all clear what is meant by technology in the first place. It is presumed that the part of growth that cannot be explained as the contribution of capital and labour must have been the contribution of technology. For example, the statistical works show that around 85 per cent of the growth of USA in the last hundred years cannot be explained by capital and labour. This is then used to claim that 85 per cent of the growth came from technology. The claim is true because by definition technology is what increases productivity. But it does not tell us what exactly helped growth. Is it innovations, new discoveries, better education, or other factors that are known to promote productivity? It is necessary to know which factors are more important than others. That would not only help understanding but also assist governments to prioritise their support for these things.

This problem was appreciated as more and more empirical research produced similar conclusions for other countries. The studies reported large amount of unexplained residue of growth after accounting for the effects of capital and labour. Rather than claiming the residue to be due to technology, research now tried to identify factors that would explain the residue. It was soon found that they are not merely inventions such as personal computers, mobile phones, and the internet; a significant contributor is human capital. Physical capital (what we have called capital so far) may have become less important in the new circumstances where human capital, intellectual property, skills, and talent have come to the fore. Factors that influence GDP also include literacy, tertiary education, health status, governance, financial intermediation, and many others. Researchers have used measurable quantities for these influences and explored how much of the unexplained part of growth they can explain. This line of research has produced a better understanding of growth factors.

When Solow initially concluded that technology is the most important contributor, it was thought of as an external influence on the economic process coming from an independent world of science and technology. If such a large contribution as 85 per cent comes from external sources, then it would be difficult for an economy to influence its own growth. But later research shows that parts of this so-called technology are endogenous to the economic, social, and political system. They are, to repeat, things like nutrition, health care, literacy and education, law and order, governance, and so on. Thus we now know that economic growth can be influenced by policy and by effective handling of these factors. This work called 'endogenous growth' research is essentially econometric work. It uses time series data to explore the contribution of plausible factors to the growth process.

## 9.10 Need for 'Development Economics'

The number of ex-colonies of Europe that became free in Asia and Africa after the Second World War increased rapidly through the 1950s and 1960s. Most of them presented a similar picture of dual economies with small modern sectors co-existing with tradition-bound agricultural economies. The fast growing population pressed hard on limited land, water, and other resources. Poverty, malnutrition, disease, unemployment, extreme inequality of income and wealth, corruption, and illiteracy were common features. The issue of economic development of these countries acquired global importance.

There was another group of countries with the problem of limited development, the South American countries. They had become free much earlier; they were independent in the nineteenth century. Since then evolution had taken different courses for different countries of that region. Some became republics in late nineteenth or the early twentieth century. Some remained under dictators and faced intermittent civil wars. The latter group became republics much later. Bigger countries in Latin America had significant industrial production base, good infrastructure, and banking. Their per capita incomes were much higher than the newly freed ex-colonies of Africa and Asia. But there were also many countries in the region with lower incomes. At the end of the Second World War, Latin American countries, both big and small, were generally in a state of stagnation. Newly independent colonies of Europe and the stagnating Latin American countries had many common economic problems.

The classification of countries by their state of development became customary in the early 1950s. Industrialised countries of the West came to be known as the First World. The Second World was the USSR and the communist bloc while the Third World comprised all the other countries. They were the countries of Asia, Africa, and the Pacific that had gained independence by now, and those of South America. These titles did not come up all at the same time. After the war ended, countries of the West and the communist bloc were members of either the NATO or the Warsaw Pact and were referred to as the Western and the Eastern blocs, respectively. A great many countries, however, were in neither bloc. Though global issues could be discussed without reference to these countries in the pre-war era, they started drawing more reference after the war. The French demographer Alfred Sauvy used the term 'Third World' in 1952, for this group of countries. Once that caught on, the first two groups came to be known as the 'First World' and the 'Second World'. Later the term 'developing economies' came to be used for describing the Third World. Particularly when the context of discussion is economic rather than political, it is customary to describe countries as developing or developed countries.

At that point, examples of successful development were the European economies, North America, Japan, and the USSR. Europe had industrialised and grown rich through the Industrial Revolution and USA had a very similar path. They had industrialised without any guidance of their governments. But their development had taken more than a hundred years. Even assuming that similar growth could be replicated in the newly liberated countries, the time horizon of a century was impractical. Ex-colonies were in urgent need of food, income, housing, health care, education, and infrastructure. Was there a method with which they could start on a path of rapid economic growth?

USSR and Japan provided examples different from those of Europe and North America. In the USSR all means of production, for example, land and factories, were taken over by the government which also held the reins of the economy. It planned economic development and achieved spectacular growth of income and standard of living. In Japan also the government played a very active role in directing the economy though land, property, and capital remained in private ownership. The government guided private business through magnificent industrial achievements.

Developing economies had to decide about their strategy. Abolition of private property was not thought feasible or politically attractive; but planning by the government as practised in the Soviet bloc appealed to many countries. It was the period of the Cold War. The Soviet Union was keen to advise the new states about economic policy. So was the USA, which had taken over the leadership of the First World from England by then. It was determined to stop the spread of communism and communist ideas to newly liberated countries. It is against this backdrop that 'development economics', a new area of economics started taking shape. The challenge was to find ways that could deliver income growth quickly in developing economies.

## 9.11 Simon Kuznets and Statistical Data

As I have mentioned elsewhere, we were in a better position to see the big picture of an economy in the 1950s than any time before. In the decades of the 1940s and 1950s, a lot of effort went into collecting statistical data of aggregate variables. Remember that macroeconomics was shaping up as a separate subject area at this time. Verification of macro propositions and their application required statistical information. Uniform international standards were necessary for multi-country studies and to test the generality of theories. Hence, economists tried to standardise the definitions and measurement of aggregate variables. Institutions and methods for data collection were also put in place. All these came handy in understanding economic development.

A number of very able economists dedicated themselves to collecting information on the world's economies. The most notable was Simon Kuznets (1901–85), a Russian-born American who would later get the Nobel Prize in 1971. He collected and analysed a large amount of macro data, developed historical series from fragmented information, and tested many aggregate hypotheses using his data. He extended national accounting statistics for the US back to 1869. He also analysed the composition of income by sectors and type of use such as consumption, investment etc. Further, he tried to establish the facts and patterns of business cycles, and helped the US Department of Commerce to standardise the measurement of national income. All this gave a huge boost to the development of econometrics and Keynesian demand management. Interestingly, Kuznets was neither an econometrician nor a Keynesian. The best way to describe him would be to say that he had a passion for economic data and fact finding. All in all, by the early 1950s it was possible to visualise the macro picture of many countries around the world, and make comparisons across countries as well as a particular country's past and present. This was a significant step for development economics.

To understand an economy better, economic activities were now classified into three groups: primary, secondary, and tertiary. The primary sector includes agriculture and allied activities; fishing; mining and forestry; that is, activities most directly connected with land and nature. The secondary sector is what we normally understand by manufacturing. It includes construction and power generation as well. The tertiary sector is the production of services. Services are items such as banking, insurance, transport, health care, education, hotel and restaurant services, and so on.

Data revealed a common pattern among the countries that were already industrialised. They had started as heavily dependent on the primary sector with a very large chunk of income and jobs coming from this sector. As they industrialised, the share of the secondary sector in GDP and employment increased and that of the primary sector fell. The tertiary sector, though relatively small at that stage, kept growing. At a fairly advanced stage of industrialisation, the tertiary sector grew rapidly and became the largest sector. So for the developed countries of that time, the tertiary sector was the largest, followed by the secondary and then the primary. Theories were soon woven around this pattern to suggest that this is how all countries would develop. However, Kuznets argued against this idea quite strongly. He reasoned with data that the economies of under-developed[8] countries of his time were very different from those of the industrialised countries prior to their industrialisation. This helped to dispel the simplistic view that all countries must go through the same path of economic evolution. In some sense, the acceptance of this view led to the study of development economics as a separate field. The new field could be described as the analysis of the special experiences of evolution of modern underdeveloped countries.

## 9.12 Development is different from Growth

The kind of growth theory that we have surveyed would be of little help to developing economies. Growth theory analyses an already

---

[8]Developing economies were described as 'under-developed economies' until the phrase was abandoned in favour of 'developing economies'.

industrialised economy. It assumes well-developed markets for goods, labour, capital, and finance. It also takes for granted that the economy has individualistic property rights and contracts are enforced by an established legal system. These contextual assumptions did not hold for the newly independent countries. Markets for labour, capital, and finance were underdeveloped. Markets for goods were relatively better organised but their reach was limited. They functioned in cities, towns, and ports, and were linked to the markets of their ex-colonisers. But a large number of transactions in the interior of the countries were done informally. Economic actors were more conscious of their group identity than individual rights. So standard economic analysis based on individualist behaviour would be off the mark. Property rights were not clearly defined in many cases or were community-oriented which made private investment difficult. Therefore, the theory of economic development had a different task: it had to analyse income growth in countries that did not have most of the modern institutions. Second, growth theory focuses on GDP or per capita GDP alone. But a third world country would require development in many dimensions.

Hence, the term 'economic development' came to acquire a meaning distinct from economic growth. It became understood as a process that combines growth of income with a transformation of the society. The transformation was expected to establish markets and market institutions; contractual law and legal infrastructure; adequate governance etc. Development was understood as the process of this transformation accompanied by a steady growth of per capita income.

Later, a further dimension was added to the idea of development. It was realised that the ultimate goal of development is to advance human capability for living and doing things. In practical terms it means the advancement in health, education, and cultural attributes that give individuals the capability of freely participating in the society and utilising economic and social opportunities. Hence the process of income growth of the Third World must not lose focus of human development and capability. Amartya Sen, an Indian economist who received the Nobel award in 1998, spearheaded the intellectual movement to free economic development from the narrow agenda of income growth. Sen was also active in persuading international development agencies like the World Bank to refocus development funding and counsel to broader issues of human development and capability.

---

### Box 9.5: Amartya Sen

Amartya Sen was born in 1933 in Santiniketan, on the campus of *Visva-Bharati*, a university established on universal and liberal principles by India's eminent poet Rabindranath Tagore. He studied at Santiniketan and then at Presidency College, Kolkata and Trinity College, Cambridge. He taught at eminent institutions in many countries and devoted his time to theoretical and policy research.

Amartya Sen has worked in a number of areas of economic theory. The hallmark of his work has been to expose the philosophical weakness of existing paradigms. But rather than stopping there, he has tried to provide constructive structures to harness the criticism for use and application. His most important contributions are in the theory of welfare economics, understanding and measuring inequality and poverty, and the theory of economic development. His research into famines and their causes has led to a change of focus in the management of food shortages around the world.

Sen spearheaded the intellectual movement for regarding economic development in broader terms than just the growth of per person income. This produced a very rich literature on practical and philosophical aspects of deprivation and development. It eventually led to the acceptance of a multi-dimensional definition of development. A number of indices for human development are now used to describe a country's development. This was not just an intellectual achievement. It produced the practical result of donor organisations vetting these indices while committing loans and grants. This, in turn, induced the developing economy governments to initiate serious interventions in nutrition, health, literacy, and other living conditions that the indices were based on.

---

## 9.13 Industrialisation

It was generally accepted in the post-war period that poorer countries must industrialise to develop a decent standard of living. Standard of living depends on average income which is determined by average productivity. Agriculture along with other primary activities was the largest sphere of activity in poor countries and workers' productivity in those sectors was very low. That explained why those countries were poor in the first place. If they did not industrialise, countries would have to continue with primary sector activities. Of course, agricultural productivity could be raised with mechanised farming. But that would require an average worker to work on a larger land area. Because the amount of land was fixed, that would allow fewer people to work. So it was not possible to increase productivity per worker without displacing a sizeable number of farm workers from work.

Industrialisation was needed to escape this problem. Per worker productivity in manufacturing is higher. So when a worker leaves agriculture to take up an industrial job, productivity increases on balance. Hence, rapid industrialisation means rapid increase of per worker productivity and also average per capita income. Further, industrialisation draws workers from the countryside leaving fewer workers there. That creates an environment where farm mechanisation can be tried out to increase farm productivity.

## 9.14 Getting Money

Industrialisation would, however, require large investment. Early in Europe's industrialisation investment came from the wealth accumulated in the previous two centuries of overseas trade and plunder. But the modern developing countries did not have wealth for significant investment. Investment could come only from saving a part of their current income. But income was close to subsistence level and most of it was needed to just keep alive. Hence saving was negligible and could not be easily notched up. Developing countries were thus caught in a 'vicious cycle of poverty':

A country is poor because its productivity is low; productivity is low because it does not invest in machines and industry; it does not invest because it cannot raise adequate saving; it cannot save because people are very poor.

This is a circular chain saying in effect that a country is poor because it is poor! But this summed up the position of countries that gained independence after the Second World War.

Thus funding of industrialisation was an arduous task. You can get an idea of the difficulty by looking at examples from the developing countries of that time. India saved 8.6 of its GDP in 1951. This is called the gross saving rate. A part of this would make good the depreciation of the country's capital stock and infrastructure during the year, which was 5 per cent of GDP. So net saving was 3.6 per cent of GDP. In a modern economy, the entire saving goes to banks or financial institutions and is then lent out to investors. But in traditional societies banking habits were not developed. So, not all the saving would be available for formal investment. In the Indian example, supposing that 3 per cent could be mobilised for investment, how effective would that be?

We can calculate this with a rough-and-ready measure called the capital–output ratio. The ratio tells us how much capital is required to produce a unit of income. This ratio is obviously different in different industries. But an average value can be worked out for the economy as a whole. The average ratio was estimated to be around 4 in India at that time. This means that investment of Rs 4 billion would produce Rs 1 billion of income per year. So if the economy invested 3 per cent of GDP, it would produce extra income of only ¾ per cent of GDP next year. Therefore, all the saving that the country could gather and invest, would produce an annual growth rate of only 0.75 per cent. Noting that India's population was growing faster, at around 1.7 per cent per annum, per capita income would not rise, but fall by approximately 1 per cent in a year!

## 9.15 Public or Private?

This example gives an idea of the enormity of the problem of financing economic development in the early stages. However, funding was not the only problem. It was not clear if private investors would invest in the right things even when they had or were given the funds.

Private businesses in developing countries of the time, with a few rare exceptions, were small and did not have the organisation and experience required for large industries. Second, there was the issue of profit incentive. Industrialisation would require investment in infrastructure and core industries. Private business had little incentive for investing in infrastructure like roads, bridges, railways, electricity, canals, and so on. Some of these are public goods and so it is difficult to get users to pay (see Chapter 4). Other goods such as power or railways are private but they require enormous initial costs. They also have long gestation periods meaning that it takes a long time to get to the production and sale stage starting from investment. These industries are not attractive from the view point of profit. Private business would rather invest in goods with quick turnover, ideally consumer goods for the relatively better off consumers. If private business is either unable to invest or not interested in developmental investment, then of course the government could be a possible alternative.

So, who would be the agent of economic change, the government or private business? This issue came to the fore as an important question of development policy. There were both practical and ideological issues. Governments played no direct role in the industrialisation of Europe and USA. They, however, helped indirectly—and that was a very important contribution—by developing infrastructure, legal system, and the rule of law. On the other side there was the USSR which industrialised at a much faster pace through central planning and government investment. What Europe and the US had achieved over more than a century and a half was accomplished by the USSR in the few decades between 1917 and the 1950s. Japan's economic development too was not spontaneously initiated by private business. After the Meiji Restoration in 1868 (see Box 9.6), the Japanese Government sponsored a process of investment and technical upgrade. It was inspired by a sense of national humiliation in the Japanese expedition of US Commodore Perry with his fleet of steamships and advanced gadgets. Though private property was not nationalised as in the USSR, private initiative in industry, banking, and trade was closely guided by the State. Japan too industrialised faster than Europe and USA. Both USSR and Japan had risen to the status of world powers by the time of the Second World War.

---

### Box 9.6: The Meiji Restoration

The 265-year-old feudal rule of the *Tokugawa shogunate* in Japan ended with the *Meiji* Restoration (some call it the *Meiji* Revolution) of 1868. The event returned the country to imperial rule. Leaders of the restoration, mostly young *samurai*, were motivated by the growing disarray in domestic affairs and the threat of foreign encroachment, particularly by America. A rule of *Meiji*, meaning 'enlightened rule', was proclaimed. It started an era of revolutionary political, economic, and social change known as the Meiji period (1868–1912). The Restoration started the process of modernisation and westernisation.

Soon after the restoration, Japan employed over 3000 foreign experts in priority fields such as science, engineering, western army and naval organisation, English education etc.; and at the same time sent Japanese students to Europe and America to learn science and technology. The government remained intimately involved and worked with the *zaibatsu* firms—the Japanese business houses for example, *Mitsui* and *Mitsubishi*. In the process, the country developed a disciplined and astute bureaucracy and a modern efficient government. Government services resembled those of the West though the governance system was different in command and hierarchy structure. The *zaibatsu* and the government led the nation together using technology picked up from the West. Beginning with textiles, Japan proceeded step by step into the production of the full range of industrial products. Along with industrialisation, the country developed a modern school system and higher education, health care, infrastructure, and a countrywide network of roads and railways. It maintained a protectionist economy, importing only materials and exporting finished products. It became the first industrialised country in Asia with a modern infrastructure and system of governance.

---

The majority opinion among economists was that the government's involvement was necessary, though it is needless to say that many remained opposed or sceptical. A number of reasons led to this conclusion. The first was the incentive issue discussed above. To involve the private sector in development projects the government would have to provide extra incentive. That would be at public cost any way. Second, there was the important issue of *development externality*. We can get the idea of this phenomenon with an example. Suppose a poor country has a large mineral deposit in a forest. Even though mining is a profitable activity, it is not so in this case. The investor will have to clear the forest and develop the area. A settlement with minimal amenities has to be developed to put up the workers who would do the groundwork. Then as mining starts, the settlement would require other infrastructure, for example, banks, hospitals, and schools. A transport network connecting to bigger cities and other industrial areas would be needed to carry inputs and outputs. The cost of all this would be formidable. Therefore, though mining is a generally profitable investment, it is not so in this case. The same applies to transport, housing, banking, hospitals, etc. However, if a number of firms simultaneously invest in these, then all of them and the mining will be profitable. They will generate demand for one another and together all of them will be viable. This relation among projects in the early development stage is known as 'development externality'. To start the development process of a poor country, large investment is needed in a bunch of industries at the same time.

Obviously, the funds required for these projects would be enormous. It would require large-scale borrowing and raising equity capital. Developing economies did not have the infrastructure for financial intermediation on that scale. Second, a number of related projects had to be begun in co-ordination. The rudimentary private business in developing economies of the 1950s was not capable of such organised and concerted activity. Governments were in a better position both for finance and organisation. A government could co-ordinate projects using its bureaucratic institutions. Most of the developing economies had inherited well-developed bureaucracies from their ex-rulers. Also, governments could mobilise more of the country's savings by taxation than private business could do through financial intermediation. A government could even raise the saving rate by increasing taxes.

There was also a political reason to favour the government to take the lead. In the newly freed countries nationalist political parties were in power. They did not trust domestic business as it had grown by collaborating with the earlier rulers. Business had generally allied with the rulers in the pre-independence nationalist movements. This, of course, was not universally true, but was very often the case. Further, left parties believed that colonialism in open form had become unsustainable after the Second World War and this had led to a formal retreat of colonial rulers. But colonies were necessary for the survival of capitalist economies no less than before. Hence, the capitalist countries were building an exploitative nexus with ex-colonies through trade and investment. They called it 'neo-colonialism'. Though few governments explicitly talked about it, they were influenced by these ideas and were wary of their own business as much as of trade and investment relations with industrialised countries.

So it was generally agreed that governments had to guide the process of development. But there was no consensus on the nature or extent of government involvement. The role of the government took many forms across the developing world. Almost everywhere governments got involved in infrastructure, power, irrigation, and health. In most cases, they regulated private business and commerce in varying degrees using and extending the colonial apparatus. Some governments raised money to invest in primary industries such as mining, marine fishery, forestry etc. In a few countries, for example, India, Egypt, Tanzania, and Sri Lanka etc. the government was involved in almost every sphere of the economy. India, for example, instituted five yearly plans which were formulated, executed, and monitored by the Central Government. Each plan would focus on a number of sectors and tasks, set goals, and arrange the required funding. Further, the government prohibited private investment in certain core sectors and set up public sector companies in these areas.

## 9.16 Import Substitution

Distrust of foreign trade and investment led to *import substitution* as a strategy of development in many countries. Import substitution, as is obvious from the phrase, is to produce domestically as many things as possible rather than importing them. The idea was to minimise the strategic hold of foreign capital. It worked by making imports prohibitively costly with stiff custom duty or outright ban. An additional reason for import substitution was the idea of nurturing infant industries (see Chapter 8). Such an industry can be protected by high customs duty or a ban. This would allow it to increase production, pick up economies of scale, and become globally competitive eventually. Once it became competitive, the industry would not require protection any more.

Import substitution was widely adopted by countries that had some industrial base and infrastructure to start with. They included South Asian countries such as India, Pakistan, and Sri Lanka; South American countries like Mexico, Brazil, and Argentina; and a number of African economies like Egypt, Kenya, and Nigeria etc. Left-leaning and pro-Soviet governments had a marked preference for import substitution. Full-scale import substitution was not feasible for relatively smaller economies or those with little industrial infrastructure. But the idea was generally accepted. The policy was a curious mix of economic and political ideas and prejudices. It was reasoned that a developing economy should expose as little of itself as possible to the rich industrialised world. It should keep its import bill small so that it can be paid by its exports to a large extent. This would keep the trade balance manageable; and the economy would not be at the mercy of foreign banks or advanced country governments. It is needless to say that this period saw an increase in resistance to international trade and investment. Custom barriers were raised by most developing economies.

Relatively smaller countries established trade and investment relations with the more industrialised among the developing economies like India, Mexico, Brazil, Nigeria etc. Many opened their doors to trade and investment by the USSR. As part of the Cold War strategy, USSR spent significant resources to wean developing economies away from the West. Developing economies in the Soviet camp attracted Soviet investment in infrastructure and some domestic industries.

Import substitution, however, was not universal. Some countries stood out with their regimes of relatively free international trade and foreign investment. These include a few Asian countries like Singapore, South Korea, Taiwan, and the Philippines. There were also a few countries in South America and Africa among the group. Finally, there was a group of politically unstable countries. On occasions, their governments would change through civil wars or military coups ushering in a swing from the pro-US to the pro-Soviet camp or *vice versa*. The political swing would be accompanied by changes in economic and trade policy.

## 9.17 Government as a Drag

Import substitution and the extent of government participation became a matter of controversy fairly early. On the positive side, import substitution led to the development of sizeable industrial sectors in a number of countries. This helped increase domestic markets and jobs. It also led to the development of towns and agglomerations around which a nascent industrial culture started appearing. However, this development was not comparable to anything like an industrial revolution even in those countries where import substitution was pervasive. The policy failed to foster the threshold level of productivity increase required for sustained industrial growth. Protected industries had little incentive to improve productivity and quality. Hence they remained uncompetitive in cost and quality no matter whether they were run by the government or the private sector. Infant industries were expected to develop expertise and scale economy in a reasonable period and then compete in the world market. This never happened. Thus, the people of these countries paid more for the protected products than warranted and would pay more for ever. Further, because of production at higher cost, these countries produced, saved, and invested less than their potential. Overall, rather than being a help, import substitution worked as a drag on the economy.

Further, import substitution created balance of payments difficulties. That sounds surprising because the policy was intended to reduce imports. But imports cannot be entirely eliminated in the modern world. Necessary items have to be imported, for example, oil, plants and machinery, chemicals, material inputs, essential food items, and medicines. Necessary imports increase as an economy grows because production needs inputs and income leads to consumption. But it was not possible to increase exports at the same rate. The protected industries produced sub-standard products at higher than world prices; they could not export to the world market. They sold some products to other developing countries but this limited trade was not enough to pay for imports. Hence, the countries had to rely on the export of primary products. But the demand for these products does not increase much even when world income grows significantly as they have a low income elasticity of demand. Thus, in spite of protection, developing countries faced negative balance of trade year after year, which pushed them into debt.

Not just import substitution, but other government controls were also found to produce harmful effects. Controls typically work with a system of permission for certain activities. As a result 'permission' becomes an indispensable input for production and business. Just as steel cannot be produced without iron ore, so it cannot be produced without a government permit. This encourages the development of a 'market for permissions'. Public officials who issue permits are like monopoly suppliers of the permits, and can ask for a 'price' for issuing them. Quite ironically, countries that put up more regulations to help the course of development corrupted their economy and governments more.

Corruption introduces large-scale inefficiencies and distortions. It gets some people extra income because of their position in the government system. This is like asking for a higher rent on one's property because it is close to the rail station or market or the beach. Economists call this phenomenon *rent-seeking*. Rent-seeking is a common feature of economies with significant government control. In this situation, regulators and officials tend to favour those who pay a bribe rather than those with higher merit or productivity. Hence, income allocation loses its link with productivity and becomes arbitrary. It undermines both efficiency and fairness. When developing countries started their journey, their political, legal, and administrative machinery was not well developed. To build this was as much a required part of development as was the increase of income. It is fair to say that government control and regulation generally undermined this process.

## 9.18 Should Governments take their Hands off?

The discussion in the previous section should not be interpreted as argument for *laissez faire*. To deny the role of the government completely would be a reaction born of over-simplification of a complex problem. The government has a number of very important tasks to perform in the early stages of development. What is required is to accomplish them with good governance and least possible rent seeking. I will briefly describe these tasks.

First, it has to build the infrastructure: roads, railways, bridges, canals, post and telegraph, and the power system. You would recall that private investment in infrastructure is unlikely in the early years as start-up costs would be enormous compared with perceived demand. So the government has to plan and design infrastructure, arrange for funds, and either build it or oversee its building by private business. The government also has to create the legal infrastructure for contract and property laws and an executive for enforcement. Quite often, developing economies paid insufficient attention to them and relied on the laws and apparatus left behind by the colonial rulers. That resulted in administrative bottlenecks, political difficulties, and tardy development.

Second, developing country governments have to intervene in absolute poverty. Inability to afford the minimum of things required for living is called absolute poverty. The minimum income needed to escape absolute poverty is called the poverty line. For a given country, the poverty line is calculated by studying the living habits of the very poor people and the prices of the things that they need. Developing countries started with a vast proportion of people below the poverty line. Further, when some industrialisation took place, people from the rural areas were attracted to industrial towns. This migration was generally larger than employment requirements in industrial units. This built up urban poverty, which is a different sort of problem from rural poverty. Governments had to provide housing, income support, and counselling to the migrants and facilitate their absorption into the earning process. This task required not just funds, but vision, sympathy, and continuous improvisation on the job. While the growth and development of markets may make some inroads into poverty—known as the 'trickle down' effect—the effect is too slow to rely on. Governments needed programmes dedicated to the removal of absolute poverty, both rural and urban.

Third, governments need to actively engage in health and education. These sectors attract private investment only to cater to the needs of the relatively higher income households. The government has to develop health care and education infrastructure for the others. Development has to aim at a state where everyone has access to these two services as they are indispensable for shaping human capability. At the same time, education and health have instrumental value for the economy too. Healthier and literate people produce a better workforce and lead to better governments and institutions.

Finally, the government has to handle the problems of externality and public goods in all economies, developing or developed (as discussed in Chapter 4).

Thus, governments do have important tasks in a development process. The negative experiences of import substitution and control have revealed the areas where their role may be counter-productive. But there are other areas where they have important roles to play.

## 9.19 Newly Industrialising Countries

Four developing economies of East Asia—Singapore, South Korea, Taiwan, and Hong Kong—attracted the attention of policy makers and economists in the 1980s. They had eradicated absolute poverty in no more than three decades and during the period also built high quality infrastructure, health care, educational institutions, and adequate housing. Quite amazingly, they did not have any significant natural endowments. They started their journey from a grim situation and at the time of their formation were looked upon as mere additions to the cheerless list of countries with mass poverty.

Singapore emerged from the clutches of Japanese occupation when the Second World War ended. It was taken over by the British who did not seem terribly interested in its development. Its political status and degree of autonomy kept changing. The uncertainty ruined any organised attempt at development or political reform and any chance of foreign investment. It finally joined the Federation of

Malaya to form Malaysia in 1963. However, Singapore was not happy in the Federation as it discovered many limitations to the prospect of its own development. It remained a sulking and quarrelsome member and was finally expelled from Malaysia in 1965. That made Singapore an independent republic and its remarkable journey of development started.

South Korea was created at the end of the Second World War and it adopted a republican constitution in 1948. It was soon dragged into the Korean War with North Korea. Armistice was signed in 1953. That was when a devastated South Korea shakily started on its path of development.

The Republic of Taiwan came into existence in 1949. In that year, the Kuomintang Government of China lost to the Peoples' Liberation Army of the communists and its leaders and supporters retreated to Taiwan. They established the new state, though it would work as a fully sovereign country only from 1952 when Japan formally gave up its territorial rights. Taiwan, like Singapore and South Korea, also started building its economy from scratch.

Hong Kong was reclaimed from Japan by Great Britain after the fall of Japan in 1945. The country hosted a massive number of immigrants from China. Immigrants came in two big waves. The first was during the Japanese occupation of China. The second was when the Peoples' Republic of China was proclaimed in 1949. Hong Kong was a poor, crime-ridden, overpopulated tract at that time.

All four countries had very high population density, they did not inherit much infrastructure from the past, had overwhelming proportion of poor and uneducated people, and were burdened by disease, crime, and corruption. As I wrote earlier, they had solved most of the problems of development by the 1980s. They attracted attention both for their success and also for their development policy, which was different from the rest of the developing world. They moved away from the majority policy of import substitution very early. Thereafter, they completely liberalised exports and imports. Further, they allowed virtually unrestricted foreign investment in physical capital, land, and financial assets. Because they stood out from the rest of the developing countries, they were placed in a separate group and given the title 'Newly Industrialising Countries'

(NICs). The name NICs was also extended to Brazil, Mexico, and Argentina which had replaced import substitution with an export-oriented policy some time ago, and were rapidly industrialising at that time. Brazil, Mexico, and Argentina are large countries with significant natural resources and already had a fair amount of infrastructure and skills. But the four Asian economies were small and over-populated and did not have significant natural resources. Hence they received special attention.

Openness to trade and foreign investment clearly helped the NICs. We saw in Chapter 8 that trade helps because it lets in goods that are cheaper elsewhere and saves the importing country's resources. If machinery and inputs are imported at lower world prices, it enables the importer to produce its exportables at a lower cost. That helps in gaining competitiveness in the world market. These effects were exemplified by the NICs.

Interaction with industrialised countries through trade and investment yielded other positives. Developing countries are often unable to sell in the world market because their products do not attain international standards. However, for a range of products—consumption goods, light electrical goods, machine tools, and so on—quality improvement does not demand much advanced technology or skills. The basic bottleneck here is the lack of ideas relating to the international standards, designs, packaging etc. Imports expose domestic engineers and designers to the international standards and can help them to produce up to those standards. More substantial innovations can be acquired through licenses, franchises, joint ventures, or by partly or wholly owned foreign investment.

The policy of openness produced all these benefits for the Asian NICs. They developed a range of industries that did not require very large investment and were able to produce world class goods using foreign technology. Liberal trade and investment helped in other intangible ways too. It opened up interaction with organisation and management principles, practices, and ideas from the industrialised countries.

Though the NICs opened up, they did maintain an amount of control over the economy. Foreign investment negotiations were often initiated by their governments. Governments also monitored foreign business activities closely. Relations between foreign business and domestic labour were influenced by the governments to a large extent. Yet there was significant difference between supervision in the Asian NICs and government control in other developing economies. In the latter, governments encroached on the freedom of private business to take economic decisions. For example, the government would often regulate or set prices. In some cases, legislation would prevent entry of a firm into an industry that it chose to invest in, and exit from an industry it wanted to leave. Governments also interfered in banks' credit allocation in many countries. But the NICs left the private sector's space for economic decisions mostly un-encumbered. They supervised social aspects and labour relations of foreign companies and were extremely strict on any signs of corruption. In other words, the NICs maintained what are called 'market friendly' policies throughout. They were careful to see that regulations did not disturb the basic orientation to markets, foreign trade, and investment.

## 9.20 The Present Scene circa 2010

The success of the NICs showed that trade and foreign investment formed a promising alternative. The idea was widely discussed and there was a groundswell of academic opinion in its favour. But developing countries in general were not too keen to alter their strategy yet, that is, in the 1980s. Domestic business groups protected by import substitution and subsidies had grown powerful in those countries. They acted against any suggestion of reform. Developing country bureaucracy had also grown in power because of the controls. They opposed any proposal of reforms for obvious reasons. Leftist political parties supported them as a matter of ideology and opportunist politicians joined them for political gains. Rent seeking had become a source of second income for many government employees who were also against decontrol and market reform. Thus the incumbent development strategy had bred forces that would oppose any change of course.

This *status quo* received two serious jolts—one just before the start of the 1980s and the other at the end of it. The first was the opening up of the Peoples' Republic of China in 1979 to the outside world. The second was the collapse of the USSR a decade later. These events had a very important effect on subsequent thinking about economic development and the developing world has not been the same again.

Before China opened its doors to foreign investment and imports in 1979, it was completely inward-looking. Except with the Soviet Union till the middle of the 1960s, China did not have any significant international trade or investment. Within a few years of opening up, it applied for membership of the World Trade Organisation (WTO) to highlight its earnestness about foreign trade and investment.[9] As China opened up it attracted huge amount of foreign investment and technology. Foreign technology and cheap domestic labour led to a spectacularly rapid increase of industrial production that was competitive in the world market. China's exports boomed along with its GDP and government revenue. The government used the revenue to build world-class infrastructure and raced to become the second largest economy with this outward-looking strategy. The episode showed the transforming power of international economic involvement, particularly of trade and investment. Given the socialist credentials of the Chinese Government, this development carried an obvious message to left-oriented political parties and trade unions in the developing world.

The second event was the collapse of the socialist economies of the Soviet bloc and the break-up of the USSR into smaller states. After the break-up in the late 1980s, information about income and living standards in the Soviet bloc, not easily accessible before, became available. It became evident that the inward-looking and non-market economies had been performing very poorly. Contrary to the belief outside, they had not generated significant economic and social development. The economic collapse of the Soviet Union in spite of its vast natural resources and talented manpower was attributed to its non-market economic policy and government controls. The breakup of the USSR and the opening up of China convinced many that inward-looking policies and reliance on non-market decisions were bad strategies.

[9] China was a founding member of GATT that later morphed into the WTO. But the Taiwan-based government withdrew from GATT in 1950 after communists established power in the mainland. In 1986 China applied to 'resume' its membership.

Egged on by the experience of the NICs and disappointed by those of the Soviet bloc and pre-reform China, developing countries started pondering a change of course. In the 1990s many of them introduced a set of changes called 'market reforms' to remove the hurdles to the work of markets that they had set up over the years. Some examples of these hurdles are listed in Table 9.1.

These hurdles make resource use inefficient as prices become arbitrary and do not bear any systematic relation with cost. At the same time, they benefit some groups of producers, consumers, or workers at the cost of some others. As a result, income distribution becomes unrelated to contribution. Market reforms aimed to eliminate these distortions. They were also expected to weaken corruption to some extent by removing officials' powers to decide economic variables.

In import-substituting countries the liberalisation of export and import was an important part of market reforms. Reform of trade policy and the reduction of tariffs were the foremost measures in the package. Other measures included removing export subsidies, liberalising foreign direct investment (FDI), and setting the foreign exchange market free from controls.

Table 9.1: Methods of Government Intervention

| Measure | Stated purpose |
| --- | --- |
| Price control | Fix a product's price to influence: (i) consumption and industrial use; (ii) income of producers. |
| Consumption and production subsidies | (i) Make a product cheaper for consumers; (ii) increase the income of producers. |
| Wage setting | (i) Set minimum wages; (ii) fix the relative wage structure for different jobs and skills. |
| Rent control | Set rent ceilings to force down rents. |
| Regulation of interest rate | Fix the rates on loans for different purposes and sectors. |
| Variation in commodity tax rates | Change the price of goods in relation to one another arbitrarily. |
| Import duties | Restrict the import of specific items. |
| Export tax | To help domestic consumers by restricting exports. |

Note, however, that these reforms are not just a matter of legislation. They require institutions and incentive structure to ensure their success. Consider the opening up of the financial market to foreign funds. Foreign finance comes into developing economies to make quick profits from fleeting change of returns, exchange rate, and security prices. They generally do not have long-term plans to keep their funds invested there. Hence they flow out of the economy as soon as there is an expectation of fall in returns. As a result the financial market becomes quite volatile with its opening up. Volatility is magnified as domestic finance anticipates the moves of foreign funds. The instability affects economic activities and, particularly, real investment. Therefore, an economy must plan for appropriate restrictions on the speculative movement of funds and set up methods to insulate other economic activities from the goings on of the financial market. In the same way, reform in other areas also requires supervision. Market reform is, therefore, not an instantaneous process of introducing legislation. The government has to build institutions, prevent abuse, and win a political battle against the vested interests of the pre-reform era.

East Asian countries, for example, Thailand, Malaysia, Vietnam, the Philippines, and Indonesia reformed their economies in the 1980s. Thailand, Malaysia, and Vietnam have been particularly successful in terms of growth and poverty alleviation. Countries of the earlier Soviet bloc directly opted for market-based and export-oriented development strategies as they built their new governments. All in all, most of the developing countries started operating open and market-oriented economies by the 1990s.

## 9.21 Policy Change in India

The largest of the developing economies and one of the last to switch over, was India. India was the most controlled economy outside the group of communist-ruled countries. The government owned and operated all large-scale services such as banks, insurance, railways, post and telegraph, telecom, power, radio, TV, and the airlines. It owned and operated oil fields and refineries. It also owned public sector companies in core areas like mining, metals, heavy engineering, heavy electricals, major chemicals, and fertilisers. The government used to fix prices in these industries. Private businesses were not allowed to invest in all industries. Where they were allowed, they had to get licences for initial investment and subsequent expansion of capacity. Major industries were protected by stiff tariffs. Foreign investment was discouraged to the level of prohibition. For 1989–90, the year immediately before India opened up, a study found that nominal rate of protection was 104.8 per cent on average. For semi-finished consumer goods, intermediate goods and capital goods the rates were respectively 140, 120, and 93 per cent.[10] This level of protection kept India's import to GDP ratio the lowest in Asia and hence export to GDP was also among the lowest. India had developed a diversified, though very inefficient, production structure during this phase. So its imports were mostly confined to oil and crude, some minerals, and a number of intermediate goods. India used to procure a large part of these from the Soviet Bloc using bilateral settlements. The collapse of the USSR ended the bilateral trade avenue and pushed India into a difficult spot. Its inability to export to the world market built enormous pressure on the balance of trade. Finally, in 1990–91 India did not have foreign currency to support more than a few weeks of imports and was forced to ask for an IMF loan. While granting the loan, IMF insisted on the liberalisation of India's foreign trade regime and significant internal reforms.

Many in the Indian administration were convinced for a long time that foreign trade and internal markets needed reform. The view had grown since the mid-1980s. But the opinion was far from unanimous; there was equally strong support for dirigisme from the left-of-centre political parties, domestic business, trade unions, and part of the bureaucracy. Hence, it was known that reforms would face stiff opposition and would need strong leadership and political will. The foreign exchange crisis gave the pro-reform leaders in the government an excuse to introduce an initial set of reforms with little opposition. The reforms have continued since then, though very slowly.

[10]Mehta, Rajesh 'Trade Policy Reforms, 1991–92 to 1995–96: Their Impact on External Trade', *Economic and Political Weekly*, Vol. 32, No. 15, April 1997, pp. 12–18, 779–84.

## 9.22 Do we have any useful Theory of Economic Development?

There is an important difference between the understanding of economic development in the early days and that prevailing now. In the 1950s the understanding was that significant investment, amounting to a 'quantum jump', has to be put through. The amount has to be somehow raised from domestic and international sources and allocated to strategic sectors. Once the cycle of low productivity is broken by large investment, the economy would take off on a path of sustained growth. Thereafter, as the income and tax base increase, institutions of governance, health, and education etc., and various other public amenities can be funded from tax revenue. The actual experience of developing countries in the last sixty years has undermined this 'economistic' view of development.

It is now understood that a very important, if not the most important, aspect of development is building institutions. Countries that have been more successful have created a trusted and able police force, and competent legislature and judiciary. They have also built institutions to produce good quality public goods and provide them in fair and transparent manner.

We should, however, note that it will be simplistic to say that the early development theory was wrong and the current one is correct. The reason is that the world itself has changed enormously between 1950 and 2010. In practical terms, capital and investment were in utter short supply in the early post-war world. The war had destroyed capital and infrastructure on a large scale. All countries, including the rich European countries, were struggling to get funds for reconstruction and investment. By contrast, the world of the early twenty-first century has a surfeit of global funds looking for investment opportunities. So in today's world, a country that develops efficient government and market institutions has no difficulty in attracting investment and technology and in increasing the income of its people. It can then use the enhanced tax revenue to remove poverty with its clean and efficient administration. Contrary to this, in the late 1940s and early 1950s, funds were seen as the first priority, as they were in serious short supply.

Coming back to our time, we can emphasise that good governance is the most important requirement. Whether a developing economy gets a good government is ultimately determined by the course its political evolution takes. And so a one-line lesson could be that it is political evolution that determines the trajectory of economic development. The effect of politics on the growth of a developed economy is only marginal compared to its effect on a developing economy. However, though politics is important, yet we cannot identify any particular brand of politics as the right recipe. Generally, it appears that political evolution has to provide the space and incentive for the growth of private economic initiative. Beyond this, it does not matter what brand of politics it is.

Evidence also discourages any generalisation about the form of government helpful for development. The last sixty years suggest that democracy and dictatorship both have very similar records: they have as often failed as succeeded in delivering development. We have cases like Mauritius, a democratic country which is a good example of economic and human development, and also the instance of India where democracy has created huge obstacles to development for more than four decades. Similarly, we have the case of Taiwan which worked under a one-party rule for forty years and developed in an exemplary way then, as well as later when there was transition to multi-party democracy. On the other hand, there are so many examples of failed one-party governments and dictatorships. Democracy, of course, is valuable by itself. The point we are making here is that it is not clear if it plays an instrumental role in economic development.

So, do we have a worthwhile theory of development? It seems that we have a bit more understanding now to realise that there cannot be a strictly 'economic' theory of development. No doubt the economic side of it has to be managed with insights from economics. On the economic side, reliance on markets and openness to the global economy go hand in hand with taking the responsibility of merit goods and public goods. But there are a significant number of tasks that are not directly economic. They belong to politics and governance. Even the economic tasks of managing public goods, merit goods, and externality require a clean and firm government and the rule of law.

# 10 Conclusion

## 10.1 In Lieu of a Conclusion

We had set out to make a sort of journey through the subject matter of economics. We wanted to survey the intellectual development in response to economic events, get some idea of the times and personalities, and at the same time build familiarity with the basics of the subject. Though economics is characterised by multiple points of view, our purpose was not to build opinions or take sides. Hence I do not want to end with any pointed observations or position. I will wrap up by simply summarising the journey.

We surveyed three broad groups of ideas. The first, the classical group, developed the *Laissez Faire* view based on competitive markets. Economists of this group regard markets as an efficient allocation mechanism. They, of course, acknowledge that large companies often sabotage competition and this reduces the ability of markets to allocate resources properly. So they would support regulatory action if it were necessary to ward off any subversion of the market mechanism. More recent supporters of this position are the neoclassical economists. They have developed the basic classical themes in more refined models of the market. They realise that markets fail from several other reasons apart from monopoly and imperfect competition, for example, externalities and public goods. They agree that the government has to act to get the outcomes closer to optimality in these situations. This is also the view of contemporary supporters of market liberalisation. They suggest the following list of do's for the government: (i) markets should be kept competitive and contestable; (ii) anti-competitive and restrictive practices should be curbed; (iii) externalities should be tackled through setting up missing markets; and (iv) the government should provide for public goods, but contract out their production to private producers, operating in contestable markets. On the macroeconomic side, they prefer supply-side policy to demand management. In the recent world-wide crisis following the housing market collapse in the US in 2007, they however agreed to demand-enhancing government spending in many countries. But they have been quite clear that they support demand-based actions only as emergency measures in serious recessions.

The second group is that of the socialists. It includes Marxists who held a very special position in the events of the last century. They believe that capitalism is a contradictory mechanism and on top of it, is grossly unfair to the majority of population. To keep it going, capitalists have to seek higher profit all the time. But that reduces the relative buying power of those whose income comes from sources other than profit. To sell the growing output of a capitalist economy, therefore, becomes increasingly difficult. They believe that this will produce recurrent crises in the capitalist order and weaken it to a point where other forms of social organisation are possible. The fall of the Soviet Union and the opening up of China to international trade and investment have led many socialists to revise their theories of capitalism. Of course, the fall of the socialist economic system does not logically mean that capitalism is not fragile. Yet, in the 1990s after the Soviet Union and other socialist states failed there was a major change in how people look at industrial capitalism.

The third group of ideas—Keynes and his followers—agree that capitalism has a problem of selling its output. Like Marx before them, they observe that the demand coming from consumption cannot buy all the output of an economy. So the rest has to be absorbed by the demand arising in business. But there is no necessary reason for this to happen. Business demand is temperamental depending, as it does, on expectations and fears. When it is inadequate, it is not possible to increase it just by cutting down interest rates. Investment responds to interest rate, no doubt. But the response is rather feeble, and more so in bad times. But then having almost agreed with

Marxists in diagnosis, Keynesians differ in their prescription. They do not think that private property and the market system have to be abolished to cure the problem. Private initiative, they think, is of paramount importance as it provides the incentive for progress. Their prescription for the demand problem is that governments should make up the shortfall. In the decades after the Second World War, Keynesians participated in policy making and helped develop institutions and procedures for this intervention. This has changed the face of capitalism radically from what it used to be before the war.

None of these three strands of economics has become obsolete. Like in the past there are believers and followers who confront one another's position and often with intolerance. However, there seems to be a subtle difference compared with the days before the 1990s. An increasing number of people reveal—in opinion polls, interviews, and in their writings and blogs—that they do not think of these ideas as inviolable truths and think of them as all partly true. Those who act and decide, for example, business companies, workers, farmers, bureaucrats, and politicians, have become fairly eclectic, much more than they used to be a few decades ago. They tend to support policies depending on the issue and the situation. They might demand hands off in one situation and intervention in another. They appreciate the features of modern capitalism as often as they criticise them. The idea that only one view can be true seems to be surviving more among specialists and ideologues.

This subtle change of attitude has influenced governments and other institutions quite visibly in democratic countries. Policy regimes have lost the rigid left–right stance that used to characterise most of the post-Second World War period of the last century. Even though specialists continue to debate using polarised phrases coined in the last century, policy itself has become more flexible and eclectic.

## 10.2 Are we Wiser than our Predecessors?

An interesting question at this juncture is do we understand the economic world around us better than say a century ago? It is perhaps safe to answer 'yes' if only because we are intelligent beings and as a race are likely to have learnt more through time. Yet, there is a catch. As intelligent beings we do understand the physical world progressively more as we interact with it. The physical world has unchanging laws, at least unchanging as far as a few generations of people are concerned. It is expected that smart beings in constant touch with unchanging laws would discover more and more of them. But the situation is significantly different with economic and social reality. The economy is an evolving arrangement and its laws of functioning in different epochs can be quite different. We may learn more about the system around us, but the very process of applying this knowledge to our lives, the society and the government, produces new institutions. These changes accumulate and, almost unnoticed, alter the nature of working of the system. We are approaching our social and economic system right now with our understanding of the yester years. It might take a while before we perfect this understanding. But by then the economy may be in transition to a different structure with completely different laws.

## 10.3 The Issues Now

Economies of the world have changed hugely in the last one hundred years. The change is not just in quantities, but also in nature and structure. Not only have new institutions come up but older institutions that are still in existence have also changed significantly. Stupendous increases in the scale of production have led to a dramatic change in the way production is organised and managed. Life outside the factories has also been transformed thanks to the revolution in governance, public health, education, transport, communication, and technology. The three sets of ideas that I used as a background have surely lost some relevance. They will, of course, remain important as themes in the history of economics. But they may not throw as much light on the present economic system as they do on the last two and a half centuries.

The breakdown of the Soviet state, end of the Cold War, opening up of China, and the rise of the emerging economies have further transformed the world economy and global equations. The resulting environment and enhanced global trade, investment, and migration raise new issues that are now central. They relate to the effects of cross-border capital flow, production and investment by MNEs, and increased migration. Capital flow—as portfolio and direct investment—and MNEs' market domination raise a number of questions. Countries, particularly smaller ones, have complained that their economic sovereignty is undermined: tax system compromised, domestic industries side-stepped, and workers subjected to exploitation by large overseas employers. Enhanced migration also raises difficulties. Richer countries feel their national culture is under threat from immigration and that their welfare system is undermined if not abused. On the other side, poor countries despair at brain drain and complain of exploitation of their less skilled emigrants in overseas labour markets. It is obvious that the world has to sort out the frictions arising from market and non-market interactions due to the intense globalisation.

A second set of issues arises from the awesome scale of production and its demand for primary resources. The stress on the atmosphere, water, forests and the green cover, the fertility of land, in short on the entire environment, is many times more than ever. According to some experts, we may very well be operating close to a threshold of catastrophe. The challenge here is to promote sustainable production and growth. By this we mean a trajectory that can be maintained without reducing our stock of environmental assets. Note that there are natural cycles and processes that do restore ground water, cleanse the atmosphere, and regenerate forests and animal stock. The challenge is to hold the demand for resources within bounds so that natural replenishment can restore them. There are, of course, many non-renewable resources used in production. Petrol and natural gas, coal and mineral ores are the most important. Sustainable growth would require making their use more rational and developing incentives to use renewable substitutes as much as possible. Intense search is on for substitutes for petrol, gas, and coal. However, technical discovery alone does not solve the problem. Economic policies are required to provide incentive for commercialisation and use of renewable substitutes.

The third, and the most important of all, is the issue of poverty. A very large part of the global population lives in absolute poverty. The estimate for 2007–08 places the number of people in absolute poverty at more than 1.3 billion out of a total population of around 6 billion. A person in absolute poverty cannot afford the most elementary needs of food, clothing, and shelter. Most of them are also unable to get clean water, power, health care, and education for children. Absolute poverty also results in the loss of self-dignity and the inability to participate in the society.

Many believed that poverty could be eliminated by establishing socialist societies. A socialist society is expected to abolish private capital and property and establish more equality. Some believed that such societies would inevitably arise as a reaction to poverty and exploitation in capitalist economies. The experience of the former Soviet bloc, however, has introduced doubts about the viability of Soviet-type political systems even if they could be established. Because of the one party rule, socialist governments were insulated from public opinion. They came to be dominated by party cliques making the social base of the government even smaller. Lack of systemic checks and balances that characterise democracy meant that there was no corrective mechanism. The only course left to the people to correct the course was to rebel and bring the governments down. Thus these systems may not be viable in the long run, nor is there any simple constitutional process of establishing them. Also it is not clear if all countries of the Soviet bloc had indeed succeeded in eradicating absolute poverty. Given all this, many now emphasise that we have to find solutions within the political and economic structure in which we would live in the foreseeable future.

One useful development is that poverty has been recognised as a global problem. It is no longer thought to be an issue of only those countries where the poor people live. This has enabled a flow of resources from international agencies and rich countries for intervention in all countries. In the short run, action against poverty takes the form of transfer of purchasing power to those who are desperately poor. While this has to be done as an emergency intervention, in the long run the problem is to find ways of creating jobs and income earning assets. You must be familiar with the saying, 'Give me a fish and I eat for a day. Teach me to fish and I eat for a lifetime.' This longer term task is more difficult as its success depends on the situation within the poor and middle income countries.

Whether we will live in a better world in the future would depend on how we tackle the above sets of issues. To recount, the first is to settle the frictions due to global interactions by creating appropriate institutions. The second is to minimise the civilisation's footprint on the environment and natural resources by developing sustainable production and use. And finally, the most important is to banish absolute poverty. A better world must be populated with people all of whom have a home, enough to eat, access to water, power, health care and education, and live with dignity by earning all this with their own factor income.

# Index

[*n* after a number denotes a footnote on that page. *b* after a number denotes the text box starting on that page.]

*A Beautiful Mind;* the film, 79b; the book, 80*n*.

Adams, John, 216, 216*n*.

Aggregate consumption; effect of wealth, 126, 126*b*; and future outlook, 133; and Marginal Propensity to Consume, 137*b*; as virtue, 147.

Aggregate demand, defined 121; and interest rate, 188–90; and recessions, 132–5; and fiscal policy, 144; and monetary policy, 145.

Aggregate supply; defined, 156; and price increase, 156–7; function, 156–7; and the Phillips Curve, 157–8; and inflation expectation, 160–2, 164–5.

Anti-competitive practices, see Restrictive practices.

Antitrust Laws, 62–3; and Microsoft, 62*b*; Sherman Act, 62.

Arrow, Kenneth, 9, 9*n*.

Asymmetric Information, 102–3; and efficiency, 103; in insurance markets, 103–6; and moral hazard, 104; and adverse selection, 104–6; and screening, 105–6.

Attack on currency, 135*b*.

Automatic stabilisers, 140, 170.

Autonomous demand/spending, 20, 146, 228.

Balance of payment, 167; and central banks, 190; and Bretton Woods, 233; and import substitution, 303.

Bank failure, 17, 185–7; in the 20th century, 187*b*.

Bank of International Settlement/ Basel Committee, 186*b*, 187.

Barter, 175–6; in a POW camp, 177*b*; in Indian countryside, 189*b;* in hyperinflation, 216.

Bartholomeu Diaz, 2.

Bentham, Jeremy, 36*b*.

Bretton Woods System, 186*b*;

history, 231–2; IMF, 232–34; problems of the system, 233–5; and breakdown, 235–38; GATT and WTO, 238–40.

Buchanan, James, 107, 107*n*.

Buffet, Warren, 205–6.

Bulls and Bears, 210–13.

Bundling, 62*b*.

Business cycles, 17, 142*b*, 198, 277; and employment, 117–118; and economic policy, 143–6, 148, 168; and politics, 159–60; and long run equilibrium, 166; and Schumpeter, 286*b*, 287; Kuznets, 292.

Capital-output ratio, 297.

Cartels, 56, 59, 63*b*, 75*b*; instability of, 75–6.

Central banks; and the liquidity trap, 134*b*; and money creation, 142; relation with treasury, 145–6, 192–3; tasks of, 183–7; conduct of monetary policy, 188–90; inflation control as the sole task, 190–1; disinflation and autonomy, 192–3; reform of New Zealand central bank, 194*b*; and fixed exchange rate, 234.

Clark, J.B, 287*b*.

Classical theory, 12, 17, 146–7, 316; and Keynes, 18, 20–21, 120–21; and unemployment, 118–9; and sticky prices, 122–6; and interest rate adjustment, 128–31; and Quantity Theory, 152–6; and neutrality of money, 214–5; on demand management, 173; and aggregate demand, 275; and stagnation, 262–7, 276.

Classification of countries, 290–1.

Cold War, 51*n*, 261, 277, 291, 302, 319.

Columbus, Christopher, 2, 2*n*.

Commercial banks, 134*b*, 180, 197; deposit creation and fractional reserve system, 182–83; history of, 184*b*; and working capital loans, 197, 203; failure, see Bank failure.

Competitive markets—overview, 52; features of, 54; in the real world, 57; and socialists, 50–1; subversion of, 53, 54, 55*b*; and number of firms, 83; Schumpeter on, 284–5.

Consequentialism, 36*b*.

Contestable markets, 56.

Corn Laws, 222, 224*b*; and Ricardo, 223; repeal of, 224; Anti-Corn Law League, 224*b*.

Counter-cyclical policy, 143–45, 146; problems with, 168–9.

Cournot, Augustin, 53, 73, 73*n*; equilibrium, 74.

Credit and debit cards, 180*b*.

*Das Kapital*, 15, 270*b*.

De Beers, 59–60.

Deadweight loss, 40; from sales taxes, 41; from subsidies, 41*b*.

Debreu, G, 9, 9*n*.

Deficit financing, 139*b*, 142; after Second World War, 152–3; and European inflation, 164–5, 192.

Demand function, 49.

Deposit insurance, 187*b*.

Depreciation, 297; definition of, 280; and the Solow model, 281.

Devaluation, 229, 235; competitive, 229, 233.

Developing economies, 47, 89, 142*b*, 293*n*; and trade deficit, 234–5; and the Uruguay round, 240; and baby industries, 247; and FDI, 257; and intellectual property rights, 260; and related terminology, 290–1; development strategy, 291–2, 300–5; and NICs, 306–9; and market reform, 309–12; and politics, 315.

Development economics; the need for, 290–2; difference from growth theory, 293–5.

Diamond-Water paradox, 23–4.

Dickens, Charles, 4.

Disguised unemployment, 34.

Domar, Evsey, 277–80.

du Pont, 32*b*.

Dual economy, 88–9, 290,

Dumping, 244–5.

Duopoly, 73, 75; Cournot equilibrium, 74.

Economic goods, 24.

Economy of scale, 27*b*; and baby industries, 247–8, 248*b*.

Effective demand, 44.

Efficiency wage, 119*b*; and Henry Ford, 119*b*.

Efficiency; explained, 24–5, 34b; and marginal product, 25–6; of competitive markets, 30–2, 52; and fairness, 43–5.

Entry barriers, 52, 55–7, 83, 83*b*, 309; in monopoly, 57, 59, 62, 63*b*; and monopolistic competition, 71.

Environment and the economy, 92, 100, 260, 320, 322.

Equity, 195, 199, 199*n*, 300; risk of, 199–200; for venture capital, 203.

Exchange rates, 51, 126, 135*b*, 136*n*, 229–30, 229*n*, 273*b*, 312; effect of interest rate on, 189; in the Bretton Woods system, 233–5; and after the Bretton Woods, 238.

Exogenous demand/spending, see Autonomous demand.

Externality, 90; explained, 90–2; positive, 92–3; corrective tax (subsidy), 92–4; and missing markets, 94–5; merger, 95; and bargaining solution, 96–7; and tradable pollution permits, 97–8; development externality, 299–300.

Finance Companies, 202.

Financial assets, 195, 217, 256, 307.

Financial institutions, 125, 142, 189*b*, 198, 208*b*, 210, 297; explained, 195; importance of, 196.

Financial intermediaries, see Financial institutions.

Financial markets, 129, 134*b*, 208–10, 208*b*; efficiency of, 203–7; and bubbles and crashes, 208–14; Keynes on, 212; and herd behaviour, 212, 214.

Financial wealth, 126*b*.

Foreign Direct Investment (FDI), 256–7; effects of, 256; in developing economies, 257.

Foreign investment, 135, 167–8, 302, 306–8, 309, 310, 313; portfolio investment, 256.

Free Market Tradition, 8–12, 34*b*, 52, 54; central proposition of, 30; the logic of, 31–2; and fairness, 44–5.

Free Riding, 100–1; and community ties, 101–2; and *Seva* Café, 102*b*.

French Revolution, 27*b*, 28*b*, 32*b*, 34*b*, 130*b*, 262, 262*n*.

Friedman, Milton, 148, 152–4, 152*n*, 162–63, 165–66, 166*n*, 174*b*; and monetary policy rules, 171–72.

Fund Management companies, 201, 205.

Game Theory, 73, 77–8, 79, 79*b*, 81–2.

GATT and WTO, 232, 310*n*; purpose, 238; modality of functioning, 239; Doha agenda, 239–40.

GDP and GNP, explained, 20*n*, 129*n*, 133*b*.

Globalisation, 135, 186*b*, 260–1, 320; and migration, 253–5; and need for short term income support, 261.

Gold Standard, 229, 231, 233; and balance of trade, 229–30; difficulties of, 230–1.

Gorbachev, Mikhail, 51, 51*n*.

Government and economic development, 303–306; reform of import substituting countries, 309–12; market reform in China, 310; market reform in India, 312–3.

Government failure, 106–7.

Government spending; in UK, 139*b*; Europe, US and Japan, 141–2; views on, 136–42.

Great Depression, 15–19, 19*b*, 120–1, 123, 131, 132–3, 140–1,

146, 149*b*, 187*b*, 188, 208; and protection, 227–8, 231, 276; how it started, 212–3.

Harrod, Roy, 277–8, 278*n*.

Harrod-Domar model, 278–79; and problems of inflexible assumptions, 279–80.

Harsanyi, John, 79*b*.

Hayek, Friedrich, 50*b*.

Health care system; Soviet bloc countries, 111; middle income and developing countries, 112; dual system 112; financial support for, 112–3.

Hicks, John, R., 154.

Human capital, 167, 254*b*, 289.

Hume, David, 34*b*, 217; on inflation, 153; on trade and mercantilism, 218.

Hyperinflation, 176; defined, 215; in Germany, 215–6; other instances, 216.

Income distribution, 5, 7, 41*b*; and markets, 44–5; and socialist countries, 51; and globalisation, 261; and non-market intervention, 311.

Index fund, 205.

India; MRTP Act, 63*b*; Competition Act, 63*b*; industrial licensing, 63*b*; Reserve bank of India, 189*b*.

Industrial Organisation Theory, 88.

Industrial Revolution, 3, 3*n*, 4, 4–8, 12, 53, 184*b*, 291, 303.

Industrialisation, 13, 217, 224*b*, 226*b*, 293; rationale, 295–6; financing problem, 296–7; public or private initiative, 297–301; and import substitution, 301–4; and government control, 304; and corruption, 304.

Inflation, 21, 115, 116, 139, 139b, 149; definition and measurement, 150; in Europe, 150–1; and Quantity Theory, 152–4; and labour market, 157–60; and inflation expectation, 163, 164–65, 193.

Input demand, 27–8.

Intellectual Property, 239, 259, 289; and MNEs, 260.

Invention and innovation, 70, 111, 259–60, 308; 16th century, 5b; 17th century, 9b; of money, 176; role of, 273, 283, 284–285, 288–9.

Investment banks, 197; separation from commercial banking, 187b; and venture capital, 203.

Investment companies, 199; products and clientele, 199–200.

Investment; equality with saving, 129; effect of interest rate, 131, 131b; and bad news, 132.

Invisible hand, 11, 32, 34b, 40, 55b, 78.

ISP markets in the US, 83b.

Japaneses economic development, 298; Meiji restoration, 298, 299b.

Kalecki, Michal, 142b.

Keynes, J.M, 15–19, 19b, 93b, 146–7, 147n, 188; and socialism, 21; economic policy of, 20–21, 136–42, 228; on capitalism, 30; on classical theory, 18, 120–122; on long run equilibrium, 147; sticky price interpretation, 122–6; on interest rate mechanism, 131; and Roosevelt, 148; and Lenin, 175; on financial markets, 212; on Malthus, 262n; biography of, 278, 278n.

Keynesian multiplier, 137b, 164; and price rise, 156, 164.

Keynesians and Keynesian policy, 23, 93b, 121–2, 136, 140–2, 146–7, 154–5, 172; and counter-cyclical policy, 143–44, 146; and the New Deal, 148, 149b; and Hitler's Germany, 149b; and aggregate supply, 156; and price increase, 158; policy making, 317–8; New Keynesians, 122n.

Kuznets, Simon, 292; and statistical data, 292; and pattern of development, 293.

Labour market; equilibrium, 17, 27–8, 45–7, 118–19; adjustment mechanism, 118–9; and capitalism, 12–3; and inflation, 151, 157–8; effect of exports on, 251; and migration, 252–5, 320.

Labour-intensive production, 33, 245b, 251n; effects of export, 250–1.

Laissez Faire, 20–1, 136, 166, 305, 316.

Lange, Oskar, 49, 50b, 51.

Law of Diminishing returns, 26–7, 27b, 28b; and stationary state, 266, 275, 281–2; and technical progress, 273, 287.

Leading indicators, 169–70.

Liquidity, 182, 237, 134$b$; explained, 182$n$, Keynes on the demand for, 212.

Lucas, Robert, Jr, 273$b$.

Macro equilibrium: short and long run, 160–3, 166.

Macroeconomic Policy; expansion and contraction, 138–9; fiscal and monetary, 144–5; cheap and dear money, 145, 181–2; conduct of monetary policy, 188–90.

Macroeconomics, 21, 28$b$, 115, 155, 174, 188, 275–6; and statistical data, 292–3.

Malthus, Thomas, Robert., 262–5, 262$n$, 263$n$; the population problem, 263–4; Malthusian checks, 264; and sustainable growth, 264, 265, 266; judging Malthus, 274–5.

Marco Polo, 178.

Marginal product; explained, 25; diminishing, 26; and input demand, 27–8.

Marginal cost; explained, 38; and competitive equilibrium, 38–9; and price in non-competitive markets, 39.

Market equilibrium, 11$n$, 16–7, 18; and opportunity costs, 36; and supply, 38–9; in the long run, 83; the Swedish view, 287$b$.

Market fundamentals, 209–10; $vs.$ market opinion, 211–214; Keynes on, 212.

Market mechanism, 16–17, 119, 123; and Keynes, 20; and socialists, 50–1; and long run growth, 262–70; and market failure, 90–2, 98–100; and asymmetric information, 102–6.

Marshall, Alfred, 19$b$, 93$b$, 287$b$.

Marx, Karl, 13$b$, 14–15, 270$b$, 271–72, 284, 285; and J.B. Say, 130$b$; on Malthus 264–5; judging Marx, 275–6; and the mechanics of capitalist crisis, 267–70; and socialism, 267; and under-consumption, 267–9, 275; disproportionality, 269–70.

Marxism and Marxists, 15, 23, 50$b$, 142$b$, 175, 317; on monopoly, 53; position on Keynesian economics, 173.

Mercantilism, 28$b$, 34$b$, 218.

Merit goods, 111, 115, 315; government production of, 110–4.

Microeconomics, 32, 36$b$, 115.

Migration, 217, 252–5, remittance from, 252–3; change of pattern, 255; and globalisation, 253–5; and migrants' rights, 255; and brain drain, 254$b$.

Mill, James, 36$b$, 130$b$, 265.

Missing markets, 94–5; and merger, 95; bargaining solution, 96–7; permits market, 97–8.

Money-definition and measurement, 178–80; and open market operations, 134$b$; commodity money, 176–7; in POW camps, 177$b$; paper money, 177–8; creation by central banks, 142; in post-War Europe, 152; in hyperinflation, 176, 215–6.

Money market assets, 199, 199$n$, 202.

Monopolistic competition (also see Product differentiation), 58; characteristics of, 70–1; and advertisement, 71–2; and brand names, 72.

Monopoly, 31; in history, 53, 60; defined, 58; in public sector, 57, 60; and substitutes, 59–60; pricing, 61–2.

Monopsony and oligopsony, 58.

Mortgages, 189, 200–1; subprime mortgages, 213; securitisation of, 214.

Multinational enterprises (MNEs), 119*b*; characteristics and types, 257; why firms become MNEs, 258–60; effect on host and source countries, 260.

Nash, John, 79, 79*b*, 80*n*; Nash equilibrium, 79*b*.

National accounting, 28*b*, 143–4, 292.

Natural monopoly, 64–5; pricing for, 65–6; operated by governments, 66–8; reform of, 68–9; privatisation of, 69*b*.

Natural output, 160–63; as long run equilibrium, 166; and supply side policy, 167–8.

Natural rate of unemployment, 153, 158, 162–3, 165; and supply side policy, 167–8.

Neo-classical theory, 12, 19*b*, 126, 275, 285, 286*b*, 287*b*, 316; on short run demand management, 173.

Neo-colonialism, 301.

Newly Industrialising Countries, 306; history, 306–8; and economic policy, 307–9.

Newton, Isaac, 27*b*, 27*n*, 287*b*.

Non-cooperative equilibrium, 74; games 79*b*.

Normal rate of profit, 83, 105.

Oil Shock, 75*b*, 186*b*.

Oligopoly, 31, 57, 64; and strategic decisions, 73–4; equilibrium, 74–6; and business ethics, 82.

OPEC, 41, 75*b*.

Open market operations, 134*b*, 181.

Opportunity Cost; explained, 33; of unemployed labour, 33; and prices, 36, 54; of labour, 45; and monopoly, 58; of time, 88; and comparative advantage, 220–1, 222*b*.

Outsourcing, 67.

Pareto, Vilfredo, 12, 12*n*, 17.

Pension Funds, 200, 201, 202.

Phillips, A. W., 151, 157–8; Phillips Curve, 151, 157–8, 158*n*; and inflation-unemployment trade-off, 159–60, 164; in the long run, 165–6.

Physiocrats, 27*b*, 27*n*, 28*b*, 32*b*.

Pigou, Arthur, Cecil., 92, 93*b*, 126; Pigou Effect, 126, 126*b*.

Policy rules, 171–2.

Poverty; and industrial revolution, 6–7, 13; and redistribution, 44–5, 52; vicious cycle of, 296–7; absolute, 305–6; and trickle down, 306; removal of, 314, 320–2; in NICs, 306–12.

Prediction in economics, 272–6, 273*b*.

Price Discrimination, 84–6; price setting in, 86–8.

Price elasticity of demand, 61; and substitutes, 61–2, 87; in price discrimination, 87–8.

Prices; competitive, 38–9; and information, 47–9; in socialist countries, 47–9, 51; and monopoly, 61–2.

Prisoners' Dilemma, 77–8; and oligopoly, 78–9; and co-operation, 81–2; and social norms, 82.

Product composition, see product mix.

Product differentiation (also see Monopolistic competition), 58, 71; and advertisement, 71–2.

Product mix, 43–4.

Production by government; of private goods, 108–9; of public goods, 109–10; of merit goods, 110–4.

Progressive income tax, 170,

Protection; effective rate of, 245b; import restrictions, 34b, 132–3, 259; early history of, 221–8; and colonial America, 226b; and the Civil War, 226b; and Smoot-Hawley Act, 132, 227, 259; forms of, 240–5; reasons for, 245–50; baby industries, 247–8, 302, 303; and computer industry of Brazil, 248b; and import substitution, 302.

Public goods, 90; characteristics of, 98–9; under-production of, 99–100; production by government, 100.

Public-Choice View, 106–7, 107n; and policy rules, 170–1.

Quantity Theory of Money, 152–3, 152n, 215, 230; Hume's exposition of, 218.

Queuing; in socialist economies, 47–9, 51; in health care systems, 112.

Ramsey, Frank, 41n; and Ramsey Rule, 41b.

Recession, 17, 18, 20, 115, 120–1; how they start, 132–5; of 2007, 213–4.

Regression analysis, 126b.

Restrictive practices, 62–3, 62b, 63b.

Ricardo, David, 219b, 265–6; on comparative advantage, 219–21, 222b, 250; and Corn Laws, 222–4; and the stationary state, 266, 282; judging Ricardo's stagnation theory, 272–5.

Risk; measurement of, 197, 197n; and return, 198; diversification of, 198; and insurance, 103–6; attitude towards, 198–9; and finance companies, 202.

Safety net, 69b.

Samuelson, Paul, 174b, 276, 286b; on Friedman, 174b; on comparative advantage, 222b.

Saving; of households, 201–2; of governments, 202; of pension funds, 202–3.

Say, J,B., 130b; Say's Law, 130b.

Schumpeter, Joseph, 11n; short biography, 286b; view of capitalism, 284–7; on entrepreneurs, 284–7; as an Austrian economist, 287b.

Selten, Reinhard, 79b.

Sen, Amartya, 37n, 294–5, 295b.

Share markets; efficient market hypothesis, 203–6; cognitive biases in, 206; and socially optimum investment, 207–8.

Shares, see Equity.

Shaw, George Bernard, 22.

Smith, Adam, 10–1, 11*n*, 12, 13, 15, 17, 23, 31, 34*b*, 40, 55*b*, 217; on mercantilism, 218–19.

Socialist societies and economies, 1, 44, 47–49, 75*b*, 111, 228, 239, 252, 261, 291, 298, 302–3, 310–2, 313, 317, 319, 321.

Socialists, 12–15, 13*b*, 50*b*, 142*b*, 317; and markets, 50–1, 51*n*; and the Corn Laws, 224*b*; and Schumpeter, 285.

Stocks, see Equity.

Solow, Robert, M; early life, 280; growth model, 280–3; and stationary state, 281–2; and diminishing returns, 281–2; and technical progress, 282–3; and statistical verification, 283–4; and endogenous growth, 288–9.

Soros, George, 135*b*.

Sovereign funds, 202.

Specialisation, 34*b*, 219, 250.

Stagflation, 151, 165.

Steinbeck, John, 18.

Stock market, 17, 57, 96, 108, 202, 208, 212.

Subsidy, 41, 41*b*, 106, 240, 242–3, 245; and poverty, 44–5; and externality, 92–3; for farming, 240; for export, 242–3.

Substitutes and complements, 48, 59–60, 70, 87, 98, 161, 320; factor substitution in production, 279, 280, 281.

Supply side view, 129–30, 130*b*; policy, 118, 166–68, 173, 317.

Sustainable growth, 262, 264, 265, 320, 322.

Tariff and quota, 240–2.

Tata, 258.

Technical progress; and the Solow model, 282; and Schumpeter, 284–7; and endogenous growth, 288–9.

*The General Theory*, 18, 19*b*, 121–2, 122*n*, 124, 134*b*, 141, 142*b*, 149*b*, 212, 212*n*.

The Liquidity Trap, 134*b*.

The New Deal, 148, 149*b*, 150*b*.

Time Series data, 126*b*, 283, 289.

Trading equilibrium, 220–1; good and bad equilibria, 249.

Transfer payments, 144; as policy, 147.

Trusts, see Cartels.

Tulip Mania, 208*b*.

Turgot, Anne Robert Jacques, 27*b*.

Unemployment; during Great Depression, 16–7, 20, 33–4; measurement of, 116; by choice, 117, 119; frictional, 117; structural, 117; seasonal, 117; long run trend, 118; cyclical, 118.

Unit Trusts, 200, 201.

Unskilled labour, 46–7, 250, 253.

Utilitarianism, 34*b*, 36*b*, 37*n*.

Utility, 36*b*, 287.

Vasco da Gama, 2.

Wage rate; competitive markets, 45–46; and fairness, 45; efficiency wage, 119*b*.

Walras, Leon, 11–12, 11*n*, 17.

Wealth effect, 126, 126*b*.

Wilde, Oscar, 23.

Workforce; definition, 116; and participation ratio, 116.

World Wars, 1, 188, 261; First, 19*b*, 186*b*, 215, 226–7, 229, 231, 286; Second, 16, 18, 33, 50b, 136, 146, 147, 148, 164, 168, 177*b*, 186*b*, 187, 192, 194*b*, 216, 231, 239, 276, 290, 297, 298, 301, 306, 307, 318; and US trade, 228–229; and inflation, 150–1, 154, 157.

zero interest rate, 131, 131*b*.

For Product Safety Concerns and Information please contact our EU
representative GPSR@taylorandfrancis.com Taylor & Francis Verlag GmbH,
Kaufingerstraße 24, 80331 München, Germany

Printed and bound by CPI Group (UK) Ltd, Croydon, CR0 4YY
08/05/2025
01864358-0002